The Book of Becoming:

Why is there something, rather than nothing?
A Metaphysics of Esoteric Consciousness

The Book of Becoming:

Why is there something, rather than nothing?
A Metaphysics of Esoteric Consciousness

Ronald Alan Meakin

BOOKS

Winchester, UK
Washington, USA

First published by O-Books, 2015
O-Books is an imprint of John Hunt Publishing Ltd., Laurel House, Station Approach,
Alresford, Hants, SO24 9JH, UK
office1@jhpbooks.net
www.johnhuntpublishing.com

For distributor details and how to order please visit the 'Ordering' section on our website.

Text copyright: Ronald Alan Meakin 2014

ISBN: 978 1 78535 157 0
Library of Congress Control Number: 2015941050

A CIP catalogue record for this book is available from the British Library.

Design: Stuart Davies

Printed in the USA by Edwards Brothers Malloy

We operate a distinctive and ethical publishing philosophy in all
areas of our business, from our global network of authors to
production and worldwide distribution.

CONTENTS

Introduction   1

Part I. Cosmos   **5**

Chapter One. The Nature of the Cosmos   7
1.00. Introduction   8
1.01. The Emerald Tablet   10
1.02. The Cosmogony of the One Dimension and the
     Two Realms   25
1.03. Perfection   28
1.04. The Theory of Ideas   31
1.05. The Constituency of the Subtle Realm   35
1.06. The Interaction between the Subtle and Material
     Realms   45
1.07. The Law of Attraction   49
1.08. The Subtle Particle   50
1.09. The Story So Far   50

Chapter Two. The Structure of the Cosmos   51
2.00. Introduction   52
2.01. The Star Maker   54
2.02. Particle Matter   63
2.03. The Archaeus Particle and Its Field   67
2.04. The Vis Formatrix   73
2.05. Enter the Soul   77
2.06. Gaia   87
2.07. The Story So Far   89

Chapter Three. Consciousness   91
3.00. Introduction   92
3.01. The Process of Consciousness   92

3.02. Consciousness – One Possible Model   97
3.03. Layers and Levels of Consciousness   109
3.03.01. The Potential Conscious Layer (P-Consciousness) 110
3.03.02. The Normal Layer of Consciousness
        (N-Consciousness)   112
3.03.03. Neo-Consciousness (H-Consciousness)   116
3.04. Thought   118
3.05. Altered and Higher States of Consciousness   133
3.06. The Mundus Imaginalis   139
3.07. The Law of Attraction   142
3.08. An Emergent Gestalt   146
3.09. The Story So Far   147

Chapter Four. Evolution, Destiny, Fate, Good and Evil,
        and then Inevitably, Death   149
4.00. Introduction   149
4.01. Evolution   150
4.02. Destiny   162
4.03. Fate   171
4.04. Good and Evil   176
4.05. Death   181
4.06. The Encounter with Previous Life Experiences   185
4.07. The Story So Far   190

Part II. Cosmic Interaction   195

Chapter Five. The Interactive Cosmos   197
5.00. Introduction   197
5.01. Three Principles: The One, the Subtle and
        the Material   198
5.01.01. The First Principle: The One Source of All Things 198
5.01.02. The Second Principle: The Subtle Realm   201
5.01.03. The Third Principle: The Material Realm   202
5.02. Perfection   204

5.03. The Immaterial Reality of the Subtle Realm   210
5.03.01. Free Will   212
5.03.02. Time   224
5.03.03. Justice and the Virtues   233
5.03.04. Science and Technology   239
5.03.05. The Genus of All Lifeforms   241
5.04. The Subtle Realm Re-Conceived   243
5.05. The Material Realm Realised   245
5.06. The Soul Complex   249
5.07. The Cosmic Interaction   256

Chapter Six. The Interactive Universe   259
6.00. Introduction   259
6.01. Consciousness   260
6.02. Consciousness and Co-creation   268
6.03. Consciousness and Evolution   275
6.04. Consciousness with Destiny and Fate   278
6.05. Consciousness with Good and Evil   280
6.06. Consciousness and Death   282
6.07. Consciousness and Gaia   284
6.08. Consciousness with Dark Matter and Dark Energy   289
6.09. The Interactive Universe   290

Chapter Seven. The Nature of Belief: Religion, Spirituality
    and Mysticism   291
7.00. Introduction   292
7.01. Belief   293
7.02. Religion   296
7.03. Religion with Atheism and Science   316
7.04. Spirituality   320
7.05. Mysticism   324

Part III. Becoming   **331**

Chapter Eight. Becoming   333
8.00. Introduction   334
8.01. Cosmos   334
8.02. A Field for All Disciplines   338
8.03. Beyond Reason?   344
8.04. The Act of Becoming   346
8.05. Evolution as an Act of Becoming   347
8.06. Choice and Free Will as Acts of Becoming   358
8.07. Time and Change as Acts of Becoming   361
8.08. The Act of Becoming Gaian and the Importance
    of Death   366
8.09. The Mystical Act of Becoming and the
    Mundus Imaginalis   368
8.10. The Act of Becoming More Thoughtful   371
8.11. The Act of Becoming a New Reality   372
8.12. Becoming   373

The Narrative   381

References, Sources and Further Reading   390

This book is dedicated to my dear friend Debra Dussman, 'The barefoot Chesnut' of Alaska, USA, whose life and work in the spiritual arena was a shining example, that benefited all of humanity. May she rest in peace on whatever plane of existence her spirit now resides.

My grateful thanks go to Alan Brown of Göttingen, Germany, for his steadfast work in reading my drafts and in advising on the use and presentation of the English language.

My special thanks go to my wife Annie for her continued support during the five-year period when this book was researched and written and for keeping me anchored in our earthly reality. Her love of life shines brightly as a beacon of hope for us all.

Introduction

Why is there something, rather than nothing?
Are you searching for answers? How do you determine the reason for our being here? Can you recognise any purpose or direction to our own existence and that of our ancestors and descendants?

The 'Why' question asked above was one that kept arising during a recent study of theology, philosophy and esotericism at university, where it became apparent that there was little or no consensus towards an answer that was able to take account of the various aspects of life as we experience it today. During discussion periods, usually in the local pub, friends and fellow students would venture their opinions and this confirmed that most of us appeared to be searching for some sort of understanding as to how and why we are here, and what the future may hold.

As one might have expected, opinions ranged across the entire spectrum of human experience, with views that were passionately held and expressed, but which arose mostly from the self-interest of the individual, or from conditioning applied throughout childhood and sometimes beyond. There were very few that were willing to truly open their minds to all possible answers; very few who were prepared to think freely, possibly on a different level, to take account not only of the experience of others, but also of all of the possibilities that were opened up before them.

Do you have an open mind? Are you able keep it open to any or all of the possibilities that exist in a reality that might not be as certain as it appears upon first consideration? These are also the questions that have driven the context of this book and are the questions that will challenge your freedom of thought throughout. The benefits, for readers who achieve the open state of mind that this book encourages, are immense with a possible outlook that enables the freethinker to look at the scale and depth of the problems that face the human race from a fresh and ultimately optimistic point of view. This book is not meant to be academic and readers will recognise that there is little or nothing that is new within it, but existing views have been challenged and some are approached from a different direction, in an attempt to provide a clearer and more complete view of our reality.

Some of the concepts described herein are difficult to accept at first (or even second) glance. This is intentional; they are designed to challenge your reason and logic, to extend your perception; to take to task the scope and the influence of the body of science and technology, of the workings of politics and philosophy, of the nature of the arts and of creativity, and the success and failure of religion and religious practices.

These difficult conceptions are then placed within the scope of our social and communal reality and our cultural and traditional heritage in such a way as to meld each aspect of reality to each of the others, in an attempt to present a holistic view of the current human condition. From this vantage point we then proceed to sketch a means whereby it might be possible for the human race to continue to prevail, to maintain dominion, to survive and to flourish on planet Earth.

This book was written because the need was felt to attempt to answer the 'Why' question stated at the head of this page and to bring together the various strands of reality in an attempt to weave them into a single thread. The current trend towards keeping each aspect of reality in a discrete, separate compartment, or sub-compartment, with often jealously guarded boundaries, can only lead to the growth of a disparate and fragmented, factional reality in the future. The world stage has a theatre of reality that is much larger, by far, than the sum of its constituent parts and we must, through our own perspective, learn to grant to each act its just and virtuous worth, no matter how small. The absence of even the smallest act on the world stage renders the theatre of our reality incomplete.

Part I describes those characteristics of the Cosmos that go to make up our current reality. Each aspect derives from the foundations that modern science and technology are laying down in their quest to define the existing patterns upon which our reality rests. At each point, those non-scientific aspects of reality that we believe are a part of our existence are overlaid on the scientific foundation, in order to bring into focus an expanded world or Cosmic view; a view that requires each of us to consider and, if possible, accept the possibility that there exists a reality beyond that which we encounter through our natural senses. Part II develops the ideas presented in Part I to the point where we are able to consider one possible future that is available to humanity. Part III seeks to describe that possible future.

Help along the way is taken from a wide range of sources commencing with a translation of The Emerald Tablet by Sir Isaac Newton and culminating in modern conceptions of neuroscience and genetics, with the Gaia theory of James Lovelock and Lynne Margulis playing a prominent role. Robert de Ropp's *The Master Game* will also feature as the only game worth playing in the topic of consciousness discussed throughout. Topics such as 'The Law of Attraction', the laws of nature demonstrated in 'The Golden Ratio', the part played by Jaynes' concept of 'The Bicameral Brain' form part of our considerations as to how we have arrived at our present state of development.

If you believe that your mind is truly open, to even the tiniest extent, then this book may serve to focus your thinking upon constructs of reality and future development, in order to determine, for yourself, if life on Earth stands any chance of survival. Whether or not you agree or disagree with the nature and structure of the Cosmos described herein, or the possible

3

future of what we, as a race, are capable of becoming, is not relevant. You are challenged to come up with your own scenario of how we have arrived at the point where we are, and what the future holds for our development.

The process of undergoing such a challenge with an open mind and the ability freely to think any possible thought is one that is not only fulfilling but is exhilarating in the recognition that the next level of consciousness, available to us all, becomes a probability, with access thereto recognised as a possibility. However, be warned, keeping your mind genuinely open with the capacity for freethinking requires a great deal of effort and persistence.

So now, are you prepared? Do you consider yourself to be in a position to tackle one of the most difficult questions you will ever be asked? If so let us ask you directly:

Why is there something, rather than nothing?

RA Meakin
Devon
United Kingdom
November 2014

Part I

Cosmos

Chapter One

The Nature of the Cosmos

Alone!

Suddenly conscious,
but from whence or where?
For whence and where had no existence
in the un-located, emptiness that was also of my essence,
and of my consciousness.

Alone!

Suddenly aware,
in the empty, spaceless, formless, timeless zone
into which I came.

I was the totality of all that existed,
there was nothing else but me.

I was in everything,
and everything was in me.

I enclosed everything,
and everything in me was at my centre.

I was Full of Ideas,
I was bursting with energy.

But had no 'where' to go,
no 'space' to fill,
no 'time' for change.

I was One.

I was Alone!

∞

1.00. Introduction

The term 'Cosmos' is used throughout this book to encompass the existence of all known and unknown realities. This includes all realms and dimensions which are accessible through our natural senses, together with those that exist beyond our ability to encounter sensually. The term 'Universe' is reserved for that realm that is the experience of our daily lives through its encounter with our natural senses. We have called this reality 'the material realm'.

About 6 million years ago the genus of the lifeform 'Homo' emerged, over a period of time, from the general family of Hominoidea, hominids or apes, to become prominent members of the subdivision of hominins, which includes Homo sapiens together with the range of our immediate ancestors.

The fossil record provides sparse evidence of the evolutionary development of this branch of Homo-classified beings, but the information in the field is being supplemented by corroboration from modern scientific techniques such as DNA profiling. Over this period there have been identified at least twenty-five different species of the Hominin family, of which Homo sapiens are the last remaining, most successful, example.

According to the Natural History Museum in London, around 4 million years ago a hominin species of the *Homo Australopithecus afarensis* is recognised as possibly the oldest of our human relatives to consistently walk on two legs. After a long gap in the fossil record, we find *Homo erectus*, who lived from about 1.8 million to as late as 200,000 years ago, making them the longest surviving species of hominins to date. It is believed that they were most likely the first to spread out from the African continent and were the first who were known to use tools.

Other species of hominins, such as *Homo heidelbergensis*, *Homo neanderthalensis* (Neanderthals) and *Homo floresiensis* evolved, usually possessing characteristics that became ever closer to those found in the emergence of modern humanity. DNA evidence tells us that an element of crossbreeding took place and may be seen in the genetic constitution of humanity today. This evidence also confirms that Homo sapiens coexisted alongside some other, now extinct, species of the Hominin family.

Modern humans are said to have emerged some 200,000 years or so ago, but there is no evidence that they developed the cultural and behavioural aspects of life that is represented by music, art and religion etc. It was not until about 50,000 years ago that behavioural and cultural patterns developed sufficiently for the then human race to become associated with modern human culture, as it appears today, albeit then in an embryonic form.

However, it was the change from a nomadic lifestyle to one of a more settled and agricultural nature, that took place about 12,000 years ago, which had the greatest effect upon our development. We may say that an acceleration in environmental change was precipitated following the advent of living in community, in groups that slowly increased in numbers, with consequent growth in the numbers of the worldwide human population.

Following our change from a nomadic way of life, to one of sedentism in a settled form of community, an increased capacity for introspection arose. This became a significant factor in the development of humanity by encouraging the initiation of questions concerning the origins, purpose and nature of human existence, which then became important to address and which ultimately lead to the growth of great civilisations.

We therefore commence our discussions with an important,

early version of a text that possibly arises from this latter period of sedentariness, which seeks to provide a means whereby we might begin to understand why and how anything came to exist, in the first place.

The text concerned is that found on records deriving from The Emerald Tablet.

1.01. The Emerald Tablet

It is not the intention here to repeat a history of the thinking that has already been recorded about the nature of the Cosmos even though such thinking is so deeply rooted within the human psyche that it has remained in the forefront of human thought from the beginning of our conscious racial reality and especially following the change to sedentism as a lifestyle. Nevertheless, a historic or ancient record that is very relevant to the nature of the Cosmos proposed herein proves to be a good starting point for discussion. That body of thought is to be found on The Emerald Tablet.

A tremendous amount of commentary has been written concerning this record, resulting in numerous interpretations, all of which give rise to many diverse forms of practice. These include psychology and alchemy, with Hermetic principles being incorporated to form the foundation for The Law of Attraction, and which support orders that include the Rosicrucians and the Freemasons. This short list is by no means exclusive, but gives a flavour of the powerful influence that The Emerald Tablet has been seen to generate throughout its history.

The source of the writings and the Tablet itself are the subject of much speculative mythological origin. Some say the Tablet originates from Egypt or Greece, others say China, whilst yet others claim Arabia or even India as the most likely source. Some claim that the writings are about 2,500 years old; with allusions, supported by Egyptian hieroglyphs, that place it between 5 to

10,000 years old; others will only allow them to be from the ninth or tenth centuries of the Common Era. The present location of the Tablet is unknown and shrouded in mystery, but it was reputedly placed on display in 330 BCE by Alexandrian scholars. Said to be carved from a single piece of green crystal, scholars now generally agree that its origins arise from a mysterious character named Hermes Trismegistus, although considerable mystery still surrounds this mythical figure.

Trismegistus means 'thrice greatest' and this term appears on the Tablet alluding to the author's wisdom and knowledge of the 'whole world' or Cosmos. But some thought should also be given to the idea that it may arise from a complex of mythological and historical characters. These involve firstly an Egyptian God named Thoth, believed to be the vehicle of knowledge, the source of 'The Word' that grants enlightenment and which shows the pathway to inner knowledge summed up as the 'Soul of Becoming'.

The Second Hermes, Amenhotep IV who, prior his accession as Egyptian Pharaoh, changed his name to Akhenaten, arrived on the scene, according to the Ebers Papyrus, sometime after the Great Flood. Subsequently, he deposed the prevailing view that supported the distinction between energy and matter into a belief that all matter had a subtle immanent character that not only displayed its essence, but demonstrated a tenet of The Emerald Tablet, that of living in truth within the 'Operation of the Sun', seen as the original will of The One Mind, or The Absolute Truth.

Balinas who also changed his name, this time to Apollonius of Tyana, is regarded by some as the Third Hermes, principally due to his role in preserving the text of The Emerald Tablet and in teaching its principles throughout Egypt and Arabia during his lifetime as a contemporary of Jesus of Nazareth.

Hermes may thus be seen as a person of thrice-fold wisdom, originally thought to refer to alchemy, astrology and theurgy, but which also may be interpreted to incorporate the psychology, philosophy and spirituality of the Cosmos. As we have seen, a further interpretation of Thrice-Great may be perceived in Hermes as a God, as a man-God in the sense of an Egyptian Pharaoh, and as a common man.

Such Hermetic interpretations and incarnations serve to form a trinity that has endured in many similar forms throughout modern human history. Whatever view is taken of Hermes/Thoth, the basic thrust of the teaching recorded on The Emerald Tablet manifests itself as a revelation of ultimate hidden knowledge or absolute truth, which forms a spiritual pathway to enlightenment and knowledge of one's inner being, and of the nature of the Cosmos.

According to BJ Dobbs' commentary[1] Sir Isaac Newton's translation of the text on *The Emerald Tablet* of Hermes Trismegistus reads as follows:

The Emerald Tablet.

Tis true without lying, certain & most true.

That wch is below is like that wch is above & that wch is above is like yt wch is below to do ye miracles of one only thing.

And as all things have been & arose from one by ye mediation of one

so all things have their birth from this one thing by adaptation.

The Sun is its father, the moon its mother, the wind hath carried it in its belly, the earth its nourse.

The father of all perfection in ye whole world is here.

Its force or power is entire if it be converted into earth.

Seperate thou ye earth from ye fire, ye subtile from the gross sweetly wth great indoustry.

It ascends from ye earth to ye heaven & again it desends to ye earth and receives ye force of things superior & inferior.

By this means you shall have ye glory of ye whole world & thereby all obscurity shall fly from you.

Its force is above all force. ffor it vanquishes every subtile thing & penetrates every solid thing.

So was ye world created.

From this are & do come admirable adaptaions whereof ye means (Or process) is here in this.

Hence I am called Hermes Trismegist, having the three parts of ye philosophy of ye whole world.

That wch I have said of ye operation of ye Sun is accomplished & ended.

Note on Translations:

Alternative translations exist aplenty, ranging from sources found in twelfth century Latin, to that of Roger Bacon in the thirteenth century. Jabir ibn Hayyan and other Arabic translations may also be found together with a hypothetical Chinese original translation from Aurelium Occultae Philosophorum by Georgio Beato, and Kriegsmann's translation from the Phoenician (allegedly); whilst Sigismund Bacstrom translated from Chaldean. Madame Blavatsky's translation and that of Fulcanelli from the French (by Sieveking) may be found, as can that from Idries Shah.

(The list of translations shown is not meant to be exclusive but indicates the extent of international interest in the teaching found on The Emerald Tablet over a period of millennia.)

Although very interesting in themselves, the mythological origins of Hermes and The Emerald Tablet are not of principle concern to us here, beyond the need to provide a foundation for a background to our considerations. It is in the content of the writings that we will look to commence our proposals. We have seen that many translations have been made of the alleged original text, all expressing the same direction of meaning but, for our purposes, we have used the translation cited above, made by Sir Isaac Newton from the seventeenth century, which was not published until after his death. However, the language used in Newton's translation is naturally somewhat archaic for our purposes and, consequently, we have updated his translation into more modern English, for ease of reference. It is to this updated version of the text, shown below, that we shall refer to in our deliberations.

The Emerald Tablet

All that follows is the absolute truth.

That which is below is like that which is above & that which is above is like that which is below, to accomplish miracles for one purpose only.

As all things arise from one and are mediated by one:
so all things are born and adapted from this one.

Its father is the sun, its mother is the moon,
The wind carries it within it, and the earth nurses it.

The father is all of perfection here in the world,
if it is converted into earth truly,
whereupon its power and force is complete.

You should separate the spiritual from the gross,
the subtle from the material,
truly and with great industry,
as it ascends from the earth to the subtle, and back again,
and in so doing receives the force of all things subtle and material.

By these means you shall have dominion of the whole world
and all things will become clear.

Its force is above all other forces,
because it can convert every subtle thing to penetrate every material
thing.

This was how the world was created.

From this basis everything may be adapted
because the means are contained within this process.

This is the word of Hermes Trismegist,
possessed of the three parts of the philosophy that sustain the whole
world.

The process I have described from the father is complete.

The Hermetic postulate, 'As Above, So Below', is perhaps the most common, popular adaptive mantra that has arisen from the text of The Emerald Tablet, but what this meant to the Hermetic scholars of their time throughout at least the past two millennia and, indeed, what it may mean to today's Hermeticist, is the subject of much speculation and interpretation. To give some foundation to our proposals relating to the nature of the Cosmos, we will consider the following interpretation of the Hermetic postulate and its supporting text.

All that follows is the absolute truth.

Initially Hermes is attempting to convince readers that the wisdom he is about to impart is true, beyond any doubt. This is very easy to proclaim and we might well claim that, 'Well he would say that wouldn't he?' We must therefore assume that this very brief opening sentence was meant to convey something of a deeper understanding of the nature of truth itself and to gain such a greater understanding; we must look at the text that follows.

all things arise from one and are mediated by one:

It is clear from this statement that, in this text as a whole, we are dealing with a single monolithic power or force that is capable of giving birth to creation, indeed the creation of 'all things'. No small claim but one that sets the pattern for what is to come.

The father is all of perfection here in the world,

The means by which the creation of all things is stated here as being 'The father', the male aspect of the force or power of creation.

separate the spiritual from the gross, the subtle from the material,

The introduction of two realms of reality is presented: the subtle, or that reality which does not engage with the five senses possessed of humanity, and the gross – that which is formed from the material content of the natural Universe.

Its force is above all other forces, because it can convert every subtle thing to penetrate every material thing.

A recombining of the subtle and the material is expressed now to form a unity in the creation of all things.

the means are contained within this process.

This is the process through which creation exists, the means to which we owe our very existence.

The process I have described from the father is complete.

This is the way it was, is and will be.
The nature of the truth involved now takes on a more defined state.

The point that arises from the consideration of the selected text elements is that the truth we are being asked to consider is a truth that arises from the power or force that created the Cosmos and is one that affects our existence and being. Not a small, insignificant truth, but rather a great, complete or absolute truth, one that contains all knowledge, all wisdom and one that commands full belief.

So we are asked to view the truth proclaimed in the first sentence of the text, in referral to the remainder of the text, as the ultimate truth and as such incapable of deceit, and of containing no lies or untruths.

Because it is dangerous to select extracts from the whole text, lest context is lost, it becomes important to give some consideration to the remaining passages on the Tablet as they appear in full.

That which is below is like that which is above & that which is above is like that which is below,

It is perhaps significant that Hermes commences the disclosure of the great, absolute truth with the statement that has become popularised as The Hermetic Postulate: 'As above, so below'. Popularity yes, but which maybe has robbed the original of some of its poetry and completeness and has introduced into the concept axes of construction that are not necessarily relevant, in that they may set conditions upon its interpretation.

Yes the form is postulated 'as above, so below' but it is preceded by its counterpart 'as below, so above'. Therefore we can see an immediate two-way traffic, a form of correspondence that is proposed between that which is 'above' and that which is 'below', and that which is 'below' and that which is 'above', a correspondence that is not immediately apparent in the popularised postulate.

The flow of creativity, knowledge, wisdom, being, experience etc., i.e. whatever your mind sees as being associated with the 'above and below', is transferrable, in its essence, between one realm and the other in each direction. We will come to enlarge upon this statement later in our discussion of the interaction between these realms.

However, it is critically important when approaching these considerations that we genuinely adopt an open mind and that whatever form of belief arises for you, from these concepts, it is your own and no one else's, albeit that you may personally arrive at beliefs similar to those expressed by others. Considering 'the above' to be some etheric, nebulous realm of the fantasy imagi-nation or as a cosy sort of 'heaven' may not help us in our understanding the nature of the Cosmos to be modelled here. In fact any label attached to 'the above' will inevitably result in the attachment of associated conditions, and thus will introduce limitations that will not serve us well in our considerations.

But it may well be that the opposite applies to our consideration of 'the below', in that our interpretations and understanding need to be founded upon as firm a base as possible. Even though there will be many uncertainties and anomalies associated with that base, 'the below' must relate to the natural reality within the material realm of the Universe, and in particular to our own reality lived here on planet Earth, as experienced by each of us.

'As above, so below' has also been expressed as having a vertical axis of structure. It is also important to disabuse our minds of such restrictions and limitations. The open, freethinking mind may well interpret this mantra thus: 'as within so without' or 'as no-where, so some-where'. The significance of giving one's own mind the freedom to visualise and determine these terms cannot be overstressed, but it is also very important to do so without introducing alternative restrictions and limitations that are simply different labels.

To alter the way we think takes great effort and is extremely difficult to accomplish but, in so doing, if it becomes possible for us to interpret 'above and below' without attaching alternative labels of any sort, then this may be the closest we may come to an understanding of the terms in an unconditional, uncompromised way.

The postulate phrasing continues:

to accomplish miracles for one purpose only.

thus advising that it is the interactive flow, or correspondence, between the below and the above and the above and the below that enables something to occur.

The miracles referred to are then described as:

> As all things arise from one and are mediated by one:
> so all things are born and adapted from this one.

This description states its belief in one thing, a monolithic force or power not only capable of giving birth to everything that exists, by direct or indirect means, but also of having done so.

So we have the establishment of a realm 'above' and a realm 'below', a clear two-way correspondent interaction between these realms, that enables the miracle of all things becoming eventually created.

The beginning of the third element of the Tablet text translates as:

> Its father is the sun, its mother is the moon,

and here we need to remember the context in which the Sun and the Moon were regarded, possibly millennia ago, at the time when the Tablet text was written. The Earth was the centre of the Universe around which the Sun continuously revolved. As the largest body in the sky, it was the most important factor in any consideration of nature and life as a whole. The Sun was, and indeed is, the giver of life on planet Earth.

The Moon was that visible heavenly body that affected life on Earth in many ways, particularly in the female reproductive cycle.

Therefore it is not surprising that the Sun should be regarded as 'the father' or creator of all life and the Moon be regarded as 'the mother' that governs the cycles of life. So that when the text continues:

The wind carries it within it, and the earth nurses it.

we are able to recognise a transmission emanating from The One Source of All Things, directed towards the Earth. Life from 'the father', carried by the wind of the father, which is then affected by 'the mother' and is nurtured within the Earth.

Differing belief systems have and will continue to attribute various spiritual names to 'the winds of the father' and in today's scientific world the process of solar winds and the distribution of particle matter from super novae may provide further different meanings. However, the process of the Sun transmitting life to the Earth, whereupon it is nourished and then affected by the Moon, seems as good a starting point as a description of nature and natural law as there can be.

In concluding the third element of the text:

The father is all of perfection here in the world, if it is converted into earth truly, whereupon its power and force is complete.

We are reminded of the tenets expressed in the second element of the text in that the miracle of all things, including life, arises from a process involving a flow between two realms of reality, above and below, subtle and material; that they arise from one thing. Such a flow commences from a state of perfection, but may not remain so in the gross, material realm, unless its nourishment, or treatment, here on Earth, matches the principles to be found in the character of the subtle realm.

The source of much alchemical practice is founded in The Emerald Tablet, particularly the third and fourth parts. In order to elevate the imperfect back to the perfect, the search for elements of the perfect life that emanated from the father/Sun became the principal spiritual 'great quest' of alchemy.

Which leads us directly into the fourth part of the text:

You should separate the spiritual from the gross, the subtle from the material, truly and with great industry,

whereby some instruction is given as to how to nourish the miracle of life thus transmitted. Separate the known elements into their discrete parts, refine the parts until they are as pure as is possible, then separate the subtle from the material, i.e. recognise the energy of The One Source within the created element and which remains within the material gross.

Here the object is to seek purity of matter by continual refinement and then to contemplate and, if possible, illuminate the subtle, hidden aspect of its existence. In other words, seek to understand all that is within your purview both materially and spiritually. It is easy to see not only how and why alchemical roots sprang from such a text as this, but also how the foundation for scientific development was initiated.

Then:

as it ascends from the earth to the subtle, and back again, and in so doing receives the force of all things subtle and material.

Once refined, contemplated and understood, the power or force imbued within will recombine the subtle and the gross into a form that corresponds to the extent of the purity of the intention and industrial endeavour applied and achieved. The aim was, and still is, always to have a higher resultant ratio of subtle to material. The epitome of the alchemical great quest and modern scientific methodology encapsulated in a process and a reaction.

That a multitude of alchemical practices arose from such a concept as this was perhaps inevitable. The search for perfection and a closer association with the mystical nature of creation has always been a strong driving force in human nature.

So strong was the effect of these 'instructions' upon the practitioners of alchemy that, far from its common representation as an inferior ambition, fuelled by greed, embodied in the search to be able to convert base metals into gold, most genuine alchemists should be applauded. In attempting to understand and refine the nature of matter, the aim was the understanding and hastening of the process of regaining perfection. Alchemical practices, over hundreds, or even thousands, of years resulted in a 'Golden Chain' of alchemical endeavour, with an ever-closer ambition to target and achieve perfection, that was only supplanted when modern science might be said to have taken over from the point where alchemy left off.

Before looking at the fifth part of the text, it is interesting to point out that several new ideas arise from the practice inherent in the processes outlined in section four of the text. These areas will be developed later in this book, but include the imaginal (not the imagination) that can be used as a key tool in the process of adaptation and transformation which, together the resultant co-creation arising therefrom, allows the creation of one's own reality and the effective use of the laws of attraction.

The fifth part of the text goes on:

By these means you shall have dominion of the whole world and all things will become clear.

Having described how the Cosmos was created and by whom, we are advised that, if we follow the principles laid down so far, our reward will be a clarity of understanding and knowledge and that we will be in alignment, synchronised with the force of creation.

For:

Its force is above all other forces,

because it can convert every subtle thing to penetrate every material thing. By achieving such a level of clarity, alignment and synchronisation the subtle and the material become melded, indivisible, as one: part of the perfection that was originally created. This is a form of gestalt whereby the total whole becomes far greater than the sum of its parts and where the parts are not discernible or divisible from the whole. The nature of gestalt will become a common theme when we come to consider the Gaia theory and the nature of the evolution of the higher levels of consciousness that are now to be found in humanity.

Simply put, the sixth part confirms:

This was how the world was created. From this basis everything may be adapted because the means are contained within this process.

This is how it was and this is how we come to be as we are. A reaffirmation of the process of creation and co-creation.

The seventh part not only provides an elaborate signature to the text and the process described therein but also tells us that the process described is complete and contains everything requisite for an understanding of the reality of the Cosmos:

This is the word of Hermes Trismegist, possessed of the three parts of the philosophy that sustain the whole world. The process I have described from the father is complete.

It may readily be seen that our simplified précis of The Emerald

Tablet provides the basis for many religious constructs, many of which are prevalent to this day. Indeed it is difficult to identify any serious religion that does not owe something of its doctrine to this text. Everything that manifests within the material realm of reality arises through the Hermetic philosophy expressed in this text, including all that arises from a base of reason and logic and also everything that results from the spiritual and mystical ethos of the motion described thereon.

Our purpose here is not to investigate a history of religious constructions – we will touch on this area in Chapter Seven – but rather is an attempt to understand the nature of the Cosmos that we all inhabit and interact with, both sensibly and spiritually, and how our reality is derived therefrom.

The Emerald Tablet forms a suitable foundation from which to launch our attempt at such an understanding.

1.02. The Cosmogony of the One Dimension and the Two Realms

The Emerald Tablet describes the existence of two realms of reality, the above and the below, but also predicates the notion that both of these realms arise through the mediation of The One. As we have said, this labelling is not helpful in our considerations because restrictions and limitations are bound to arise.

Nevertheless, we do need to clarify our thinking in relation to the cosmogony of one dimension and two realms of reality, as defined on The Emerald Tablet, in order to avoid confusion. The labels we have chosen to use involve an entirely separate dimension; one that, paradoxically, can have no label because it is not available to our consciousness and because there can be no limits or restriction associated with its existence. It is the dimension from whence The One Source of All Things originated and which continues to house that consciousness. Our labels for the two mediated realms of reality that arise from this source dimension are 'the material realm' (substituted for 'below') and 'the subtle realm' (substituted for 'above').

The material realm is the easiest one for us to understand because it is represented by the experiences that our five senses encounter in our everyday existence. We are, to some extent, able to see, hear, touch, taste and smell all that is around us and we take for granted, and accept the existence of the material that provides the encounter with those senses. Even that which we cannot necessarily see or hear etc. is often explained, by science, as being the product of processes involving materials and/or the five senses.

For those who do not wish to acknowledge that there is anything beyond that which our senses can encounter, which includes many scientists, atheists and humanists, the material of our universal reality is all that there is and generally speaking, for them, nothing else exists. This is usually because any need for anything else to exist is not perceived.

This point of view has gained much ground since scientific endeavour has succeeded so spectacularly well in partly uncovering the patterns of reality that govern our material existence, resulting in a strengthening movement towards a form of scientific modern atheism and/or materialism.

But for many others this view does not fulfil a human need to acknowledge the many, so far unexplained, phenomena that are experienced through means that appear to be beyond the reach of our senses. The existence of a subtle realm of reality seeks to validate these unexplained phenomena and also attempts to provide a vehicle by which the material realm could come into being.

The word 'subtle' is used to label the realm of a 'transcendent otherness' in the sense that it alludes to something that not only is delicate, precise and difficult to describe, but is a mystical mystery. Mystical because it seeks to describe something that is symbolical, allegorical and is beyond normal human comprehension.

The existence of the subtle realm is not subject to a methodology involving the standards of empirical proof, so beloved of scientists, yet its existence is necessary to provide answers to those questions that science may not be prepared to consider as being within its scope.

Questions such as 'Why is there something, rather than nothing?' – the answer to which has been the ultimate quest of human intellectual endeavour. Other questions arise from this quest such as 'What is intuition and how does it work?' and 'When encountered, how can we explain the unexplainable?'

The cosmology proposed herein will seek to provide a format that allows everything possible to become a reality, but before we proceed to delve into what we can describe as a transcendent form of mysticism, we must recognise that the subtle realm exists everywhere. It is not in any place as we understand place to mean, it is every-where and every-when, simultaneously, and is contiguous with everything that exists in our material reality. The subtle realm may be said to have no boundaries other than those which arise from its expression within the material realm.

This is why labels such as 'alongside', 'without', 'above' etc. do not help us to understand the nature of its existence. Labels such as these suggest that there is a physical place where we might find the subtle realm. There is not!

This is not an easy concept to understand. We shall come to see that everything in our material realm automatically contains a mystical element of the subtle realm and that there is a very close, symbiotic relationship between the two realms brought about through various layers of consciousness.

Perhaps the easiest way to envisage the subtle realm might be as an analogy with a normal radio, where, simply by turning a knob or dial, we can change the frequency to obtain a different programme, from the exact same equipment in the same space. That is not to say that the subtle and material realms operate at different frequencies whilst occupying the same space/time facilities, but this analogy is one that will serve us in trying to understand the relationship between the two realms. This relationship is one of mutual dependence for its means of expression, as we will see as we progress through our proposals.

So to be clear, our model proposes three realms of reality. A dimension that encompasses all other realities, the character of which is unknowable to everything outside of its existence and which is the Source of all other realms and dimensions and everything within them. The Cosmos, as we currently perceive it, is made up of this Source dimension and two other realms, the subtle realm of Ideas and the material realm of our Universe.

1.03. Perfection

One of the most important ideas arising from The Emerald Tablet, and one that became a very significant driving force for its followers and for philosophers, is the notion of the 'perfect condition'. That perfection exists within our material Universe may not be a provable fact, because conscious life on Earth is itself imperfect and flawed, and relies, at least in part, on our five senses, which also are variable in their efficiency and could always be improved. Accordingly, we cannot be capable of recognising perfection, even if something were represented to us as being so.

As simple examples, a line drawn between two points perceived to be 'straight' or one representing a 'perfect circle' is not perfect when examined at very close quarters. A surface, thought to be perfectly smooth, is no such thing when examined under a microscope. Furthermore, everything in our material reality always, always decays.

However, the need to believe that perfection not only exists, but is also achievable, is one that humans cannot ignore. Alchemists, religious adherents and subsequently scientists of every discipline have, throughout our history, sought to achieve perfection in whatever direction their endeavours have led. Alchemists in their attempt to understand and refine the purity of material exemplified, or maligned in the drive to change base metals into gold, or to enhance spiritual consciousness in a great quest to raise it to a level as near perfect as can be. Religious adherents in their belief that closer association with their deity results inevitably in their becoming closer to a perfect ideal; and scientists in their search for knowledge of how and why things work, by uncovering the perfect patterns of life and reality that have existed from the start and which have served to sustain the Cosmos and our race to date.

The question arises, 'Does perfection exist at all?' Is it reasonable for us to determine that perfection does not exist in the material realm of our Universe? The fact of the matter (literally) is that we do not know. It has already been said that we, being imperfect, are not in a condition to recognise perfection, even were we shown it. But does that mean that perfection does not exist? A flower at the pinnacle of its bloom may appear to represent perfection, yet that same perfect flower will inevitably decay and lose its perfection.

Can we then say that perfection does exist, even if only fleetingly? Surely the nature of perfection requires that once perfect, always perfect, otherwise the seeds of decay being inherent in the perfect condition must render it imperfect. That a state of change in our universal reality exists universally must render perfection as an impossible state for us to achieve.

Is a changing state then a condition that denies the existence of perfection? Must perfection be unchanging or immutable? We have seen that the third part of the text on The Emerald Tablet tells us:

The father is all of perfection here in the world, if it is converted into earth truly, whereupon its power and force is complete.

Thus introducing us to the notion that perfection does exist, but not in our material reality, unless its force or power is exactly transformed and reproduced in its transmission from the subtle to the material realm, a condition which to date has not been evident.

Perfection may thus exist, but only in the subtle realm:

As all things arise from one and are mediated by one

by way of an Idea that is unchanging in its form, and which is the perfect model, the ideal for everything that exists in the material Universe.

Such a notion – that the subtle realm is one of perfect Ideas that, when transmitted to the material realm, become subject to adaptation and transformation which then render them imperfect in the material existence – does not invalidate the Hermetic Postulate. It is not essential that the form of something has an identical counterpart that exists in each realm, but only that the existence of everything in the material realm is formed from the essence of that which is its original Idea in the subtle realm.

It is important to recognise and understand that everything in our experience originates from an idea.

We can recognise that some ideas arise from within the human organism, resulting from the development and/or combination of ideas that have previously impinged upon our consciousness. But some ideas seem to originate from a source that appears to be outside our experience, as though appearing, perhaps by chance, from nowhere, or from 'out there' somewhere. The coming into existence of an original idea, within our consciousness, raises the question of its origin. It is clear that consciousness plays a large and very significant role in the origin and development of ideas.

We have now ventured into territory remarkably similar to that of Plato's theory of Ideas and Forms.

1.04. The Theory of Ideas

Plato proposed that a realm, or world, exists beyond the capacity of our five senses to encounter. This realm is populated by Ideas or forms that give to all things in our material Universe their nature, or being. However, throughout the time since Plato, many problems and contradictions that are inherent within Plato's realm of Ideas have become apparent and have caused scholars to discuss in an attempt to reconcile.

Initially, our material reality either participated in, shared in, or imitated the Idea from whence its origin sprang from within the subtle realm. But participation and sharing by multitudinous, differing entities in a single Idea gave rise to that Idea becoming apparently divided into many parts. The notion of imitating an Idea is similar to the notion of our reality being a reflection of the realm of Ideas, one that we often hear expressed when considering the incomplete Hermetic Postulate quoted only as 'As above, So below'. Yet, if we consider the complete Postulate, by adding in 'As below, So above' we can see that the notion of participation or sharing in the world of Ideas grants more credence to our thinking.

A number of principles arise from Plato's dialogues that seem to impose limitations upon the constituents within the realm of Ideas and, whilst it is not necessary to undertake an in-depth analysis of these principles, a brief look will lead us to a better understanding of the relationship between the realms under consideration.

According to Sir Anthony Kenny, in *A New History of Western Philosophy, Vol 1.*,[2] these principles are:

Commonality: which is where several things have identical characteristics because they all share or imitate the single Idea which is that characteristic.

Separation: which requires that the Idea is distinct from all things that share the identical character.

Self-Predication: which requires that the Idea of something is itself that something. (The object that is the subject of the Idea exhibits or demonstrates its own definition, without further explanation.)

Purity: which ensures that the idea of something contains nothing other than that something.

Uniqueness: states that nothing but the Idea of something truly is complete in being that something.

Sublimity: means that Ideas last forever, cannot be perceived by the senses and cannot change and can have no parts.

Plato was to abandon the principles of *Purity* and *Uniqueness* and was to adapt *Self-Predication* in order to overcome problems that arose for Ideas to become compliant with all principles simultaneously.

Such abandonment and adaptation may be due to the literal inclusion of all things into the realm of ideas. That the Idea of Man (Humanity), Justice and Virtue etc. were formed from an Idea, in a realm other than that of our material reality, seems to be one that has merit, but to assert that 'bed' or the concept of 'large' also exist as Ideas seems to be unnecessary and even irrelevant.

If we start to consider those Ideas that give form to our material existence then those Ideas should only be composed of the essence of things required to convey its form in such a way that, once transmitted to the material realm, transformation or adaptation in the Hermetic sense depicted on The Emerald Tablet may then take place.

Plato's six principles may not be compromised if we consider that the realm of subtle reality contains only 'the true essence' of the Idea involved.

Commonality, Separation, and *Sublimity* are generally accepted as conditions for Ideas to exist in the subtle realm, although the condition of *Sublimity* will need further examination. *Commonality* is unexceptional because it is apparent that several things may share in the essence of one Idea without distorting the character of that Idea.

Separation as a principle requires us to understand that Ideas each exist as an individual entity themselves in another realm, independent of our own ideas, and containing only the true essence of that Idea. When we consider the true essence of something existing in the subtle realm, then that essence must, by definition, contain no trace of other essences, **until** following transmission, transformation or adaptation within the material realm, whereupon it may result in more than one essence becoming combined.

The greater the number of Ideas that exist in the subtle realm that define the more mundane, lower things that exist in the material realm, the greater will be the difficulty in maintaining *Purity*. If indeed it is necessary for 'bed' to exist as an Idea then other Ideas such as 'large' or 'small' or 'soft' or 'hard' can indeed become part of that Idea, and thus the Ideas themselves will lose their pure essence and become mixed or diluted. However, one condition may prevail in the material realm that does not apply to the subtle realm, and that is that the mixing or dilution of subtle Ideas may only occur here (below) and not there (above), so that *Purity* may not be compromised in the subtle realm of Ideas.

Alternatively, if it is not necessary or relevant for Ideas of mundane or lower order things to exist at all in the Ideas realm, then another umbrella Idea might need to exist from whence all lower order things originate. The essence of such an Idea might be the abstract Idea of 'Technology', in the same way as the abstract Idea of 'Justice' or 'Virtue' relates to and includes many facets of the original Idea.

The latter of these two alternatives provides greater scope for adaptation and transformation following transmission to the material realm, and gives significant weight to understanding why our reality is as it appears: imperfect and containing both good and evil. It is this alternative that we will accept as being more relevant and complete.

Given that an Idea in the subtle realm maintains its *Purity* through its essence, we can see that its *Uniqueness* would also remain intact, by excluding other essences, for the same reason. Similarly, any problem arising with the condition of *Self-Predication* does so because the Idea itself is taken to be more than the abstract essence of the thing it was intended to represent. It is man's consciousness, in its relationship and interaction with the Ideas in the subtle realm, that causes the problem.

The tendency exists for us to look at something in the material realm, and then transfer subconsciously our thoughts about what that something is, to the subtle realm, thereby imbuing the Idea with more than its pure essence. Once viewed as an abstract form of its essence only, then the Idea itself becomes the essence, the essential core of that which it is meant to be, thus fulfilling its condition for existence in the realm of Ideas.

We can therefore see that an essential part of the theory of Ideas is the notion that Ideas in the subtle realm must be abstract Ideas, and must be only the essence of that which they are intended to become.

The principle of *Sublimity* generally remains unchallenged as a condition for it to assume a role in the realm of Ideas. That Ideas can last forever, that they are not perceived by the senses and have no parts are unexceptional elements of the Idea itself, but does the need to change remain part of the principle? Change assumes that the Idea in question must have been incomplete and thus imperfect, or different from its original form. So, if an Idea changes, it becomes a different Idea, and this cannot be so.

Yet Ideas do appear to change. The Idea of mankind (genus Homo) has evolved through many phases of existence, some changes being very significant. Concepts of justice or virtue have changed in the material Universe, but this may be by adaptation within this material realm.

So two ideas arise that might explain such apparent change. Firstly, that such change takes place only in the material realm, by adaptation, leaving the subtle Idea unchanged. Secondly, that the scope of the Idea in the subtle realm is much larger than anything that can be seen to exist in the material realm, but has not yet been perceived, creating the notion that, to date, we have not accessed the subtle Ideas to their full extent. This does not mean that only part of an Idea exists because the Idea itself cannot have parts, but it does mean that mankind is not yet capable of perceiving the Ideas of the subtle realm to their full extent.

The latter of these two ideas will become more important when we come to discuss the relationship of consciousness to the constituents of the subtle realm and the relationship that the complex of evolution, destiny and fate has with consciousness.

1.05. The Constituency of the Subtle Realm
Having looked at the notion that the Ideas within the subtle realm form the pure and abstract essence of all that is formed in the material realm, we need to consider what Ideas form the content of the subtle realm. In addition we will look at whether all Ideas have the same weight of importance both in the subtle realm and once transmission to the material realm has occurred.

But before considering this we will look at the words from The Emerald Tablet:

As all things arise from one and are mediated by one: so all things are born and adapted from this one.

words that indicate that everything that is within the subtle realm arises from The One Source of All Things, but which itself is not contained within that realm.

The Source of All Things has been called by many names, 'The Good' in Plato, 'The One' by Plotinus, YHWH (Yahweh) by the Jewish nation, Allah, the Muslims, God for the Christian followers of Jesus of Nazareth, Krishna for Hindu followers etc., etc. We will refer to The Source of All Things within the subtle realm, and following any subsequent transmission, within the material realm, as 'The One Source' because, unlike 'The One' as is the expression used on The Emerald Tablet, 'The One Source' does not imply the involvement of any sort of being or entity.

Notwithstanding this, we should bear in mind that Plotinus, the third century CE philosopher who developed many of the principles of Neo-Platonism, offers us a deep insight into the nature of 'The One', or what we have determined as The One Source. According to his pupil follower Porphyry, Plotinus proposed that there was no way by which The One could be described. Instead a negative or apophatic language needed to be used to describe what The One was not.[3]

In doing so a paradox is immediately set up. This is because, although The One Source is to be thought of as a single source of all that is, such an entity, necessarily being a unified whole, without composition or plurality, is at one with, and part of, all the things of its creation. Perhaps an easier way to understand this paradox is to think of The One Source as a simple single force or energy, or consciousness, of an origin before all things came into being. Whilst being essentially simple in its nature, it is simultaneously of an extensive, multitudinous complexity that has become part of everything that is. The One Source becomes a part of all things, in all of existence, whilst remaining singular and in separation from that same existence.

As we have said, we should not think of The One Source as a being or an entity at all, because to do so immediately places limits or restrictions on its very existence, and no limits or restrictions can apply to The One Source, in any way. This again may be a very difficult concept genuinely to understand. How can something that has no form, no limitations or restrictions, something that is totally nebulous and etheric be, at the same time, The One Source of all that exists, including our material realm of apparently solid reality, with its multitude of forms? To even approach an understanding of such a paradox requires of us to empty our minds and thoughts of preconceived ideas of what God or The Source etc. is and enter a zone existing beyond standard reason and logic, to one of natural freethinking in order to then enter a state where limits and restrictions cease to exist.

This is what The Emerald Tablet is seeking to unlock within us.

Following the Tablet text, there is stated to be The One Source from whence 'all things are born and adapted from this one' and, if we accept this statement, a hierarchy within the Tablet text begins to emerge. There is 'The One Source' before, above or outside of all things, and then there is all that the subtle realm contains. Naturally The One Source from whom all things arise takes the highest place in such a hierarchy, even whilst being separate from its creation of the subtle realm.

But that is all that the Tablet text has to say about the subject.

About the constituents that make up the subtle realm, bearing in mind that such a realm must be capable of containing the Ideas of everything that could possibly come into existence in our material realm, we are left to our own devices to arrive at the constituency contained therein, and whether they form a hierarchy within themselves.

In seeking to establish such constituents and any hierarchy, there arises an inevitable diversity of approach and this diversity has resulted in the formation of many religions and cults, some of which have survived for millennia.

If we are to consider the nature of the subtle realm, and subsequently our own reality, then we must be prepared, once again, to set aside, even if only temporarily, the conditioning that has resulted from religious, philosophical and political dogma, together with scientific and technological methodology, all of which has been, and still is, restricting and limiting our outlook.

Many will seek to say or will earnestly believe that their particular belief system is the one that frees us to consider the nature of the Cosmos; but in truth, it is only by completely freethinking, unencumbered by dogma, methodology or labelling, that each of us is able to come to an independent view of reality. This is not to say that religion, philosophy, politics, science or technology etc. have no value in themselves. On the contrary, each discipline may be seen as a vehicle that preserves tradition, culture and data, which increases, or develops our knowledge that will contribute to the whole, once each of us has determined an absolute truth for ourselves, as required by The Emerald Tablet.

Consequently, the constituents of the subtle realm proposed in this model are not meant to be complete, exclusive or fully defined. Others will add or subtract constituents or approach the constituency from a different angle. This is of no matter, so long as the content of the subtle realm is arrived at individually, by a process of independent and free thought. It is an element of free consciousness that is capable of producing the flow of thought which, not only results in everything that has existed or currently exists, but also can produce everything that can exist.

So what are the constituents of the subtle realm?

If we accept that there is One Source of All Things, from which everything arises, we can see that that is the supreme force or power in the entire Cosmos, which needs little further description. Everything arising from The One Source does so from mediation by The One Source itself and, as such, has given rise to the notion of such a consciousness as that continuously holding the entire Cosmos in being. The Ideas, arising from the mediation of The One Source, form all of the constituents of the subtle realm and, rather than the Ideas occurring in a haphazard or unstructured manner, a hierarchy seems to be not only acceptable, but inevitable.

So the first rank of Ideas in this realm would be concerned with the highest ideals that come to form, and perhaps to govern, our material reality. Bearing in mind that such Ideas are each perfect within themselves and represent the true abstract essence of that Idea, then we can make a reasonable guess at those Ideas most likely to be included in the first tier of importance.

Such an ideal condition as Free Will may well form the highest tier of subtle Ideas. Free will grants to us the facility of putting into action the desire of our consciousness and consequently becomes the agent by which we are able to do or be anything at all within the material Universe. Free will is the means that enables creation and co-creation, and the way that free will interacts with consciousness, and vice versa, will determine the course of everything that follows.

The failure by beings of higher consciousness to act with positive free will, often because of the influence of external considerations, restricts, limits or hinders development not only within the individual, but also of the race as a whole. It is not always easy to act with free will because the choices expressed by our consciousness are often difficult to determine, and may offer to us tough alternatives that sometimes leave us exposed, vulnerable or uneasy.

Furthermore the benefits that living in society or community grants to us may lead to the restriction or limitation of the choices we are prepared to make and, on these occasions, free will may also be regarded as suffering restriction and limitation. Finally and most importantly, conditioning, especially over many generations, only serves to confuse, or restrict, our approach to the choices made by our consciousness and their subsequent execution by our free will.

Nevertheless, free will is clearly that which enforces human endeavour, through its expression of the conscious choice, and as such must be regarded as the most important element of the human constituency and the constituency of the subtle realm. We will expand on the nature of free will in Chapter Five.

Notwithstanding all of this, it is our interaction with the next (second) tier of Ideas, which is that of Time, that enables us to become a part of a co-creative act that introduces the possibility of change, ensuring that evolution and development can take place. Time as an Idea arising from the mediation of The One Source of All Things and held as an abstract essence in the subtle realm must exist if time is to be considered as an element that can affect that which is contained in the material realm.

Thus, Time in the subtle realm exists, but in a form that is entirely different from time here in our material reality. All of Time in the subtle realm exists within a single instant, or in a period that has no time lapse at all, and is in a form that contains everything that can affect us here in the material realm. Such effects include evolution, development, ageing, decay, deterioration and change to and in material elements, and also provide for the passage of energy, heat, sound and light etc. The measurement of time is a human device that exists for our convenience and does not form part of the subtle Idea.

An analogy for this model of time is that it is similar to the nature of light, which can be observed as both a waveform and a particle stream, simultaneously. In this analogy, Time in the subtle realm might be seen as the waveform, containing all time in one instant. Whereupon transformation is caused by inter-action with consciousness so that it manifests, in the material realm, as a stream that is characterised by its ability to flow or pass. All of Time exists analogically as a waveform, in one instant, contiguous with all of time as a stream, simultaneously, but in different, separate realms of reality. This model will be discussed further in Chapter Five and will give us an insight into the means whereby clairvoyance and precognition might be able to work.

Our free will, acting through time, now empowers our consciousness to approach the (third) tier of Ideas, which enable our existence to become sustainable, communal and less encumbered by conditioning. These are the Ideas of Justice and Virtue, including ethics.

Justice and the Virtues are those abstract forms that are the essence of the very highest Ideals by which those lifeforms that have consciousness of self aspire to become the closest they can to a state of perfection. These ideals will influence everything in our daily lives and, subject to the extent of our interaction with subtle Free Will and Time, will come to determine the nature of our interaction with the Ideas of Justice and Virtue, which then become the guiding principles that govern our actions.

The greater our efforts are to attain justice by virtue, the closer we will be able to approach the ideal of perfection, and the more clear and defined will become the choices available to our consciousness, over time, activated by the free will we bring to bear. In being some of the highest ideals in the subtle realm, Free Will, Justice and Virtue not only establish a model by which we are able to approach perfection, but will become crucially important in determining the nature of our afterlife, as later discussion will seek to show.

The next (fourth) tier contains desirable elements or traits that, once engaged, offer its recipient a pathway towards the ever-higher tiers of aspiration. Such Ideas might be related to the abstract characteristics of Science and Technology. The Idea of Science as an abstract form is a difficult one that might appear to have many parts, such as chemistry, physics, biology, palaeontology etc., etc. But you should bear in mind that we are considering an abstract concept of Science, one that contains the essence of all Science, in one Idea.

We might prefer to think of this Idea as containing the pattern of Science, as a whole, that comes to govern the physical aspect of the material realm and which should be regarded as being a pattern of such complexity, integration and interaction that it can be seen as being similar, in its complex, integrated, interactive scope, to that prescribed for the planet Earth by James Lovelock in the Gaia theory.

Thus every single aspect of science is dependant on every other aspect for its continued existence. All of Science forms a single, self-regulatory pattern contained in one Idea, that human consciousness is in the process of uncovering, through its interaction with the Idea itself.

It is only here in the material realm that we might separate Science into many disciplines or parts and, in so doing, most probably restrict those engaged only in an aspect or part of science from seeing the whole pattern contained in the one Idea.

Technology goes hand in hand with Science and should be considered to arise from it. Plato's Idea of 'bed' or other Ideas such as, say, 'car', 'table', 'chair', 'television', 'computer' and 'microscope' etc., etc. form a kaleidoscope of myriads of things arising from one Idea, one pattern of technology, that should be seen in a similar light to the pattern of Science described above. Such a pattern would include engineering, manufacturing, applications etc. that are complex, integrated and interact with each other and also with the pattern of Science.

Science and Technology, taken together, enable all material things to come into existence in our reality, making it unnecessary for individual Ideas of individual things to exist in the subtle realm. Humanity has not yet uncovered the whole pattern of Science and Technology and this is due in part, not only to our own limitations, but also to our ongoing evolving development. Not because Ideas of Science and Technology exist in parts in the subtle realm.

A fifth tier might contain the essence of each genus of life: humanity (Homo), all other animal forms, canine, equestrian, feline, bovine, reptile, rodent, insect form etc. together with all vegetable and flora genres, and all minerals etc. This Idea must be considered under a heading of 'lifeforms' because, as we shall see when we come to discuss evolution in Chapter Four, millions of different species have come into existence and millions have become extinct.

This does not represent a change within the essence of an Idea because the passage of time does not take place in the subtle realm. Rather it exists there, in its entirely, in one instant. Furthermore, as we shall see in Chapter Three, it is the nature of the consciousness that inhabits all lifeforms which results in an unchanging foundation for their existence.

You should note that, in this model, all constituents are contained within a single realm of reality. All are fully interactive and, notwithstanding any hierarchy, are dependent on each other yet retain a discrete existence. Furthermore, there are no direct replicas of anything to be found existing in our own material reality. We are not reflections of something that exists in the subtle realm; everything here in the material realm contains the essence of the Idea found in the subtle realm, originating from The One Source.

We begin to see a model emerging that proposes that the entire Cosmos is not only a manifestation of the mediation of The One Source of All Things, but also a Universe that demonstrates a direct relationship with such a mediation, through the subtle realm. Note also that, so far, this model of the subtle realm does not contain anything of the material structure of our reality. This is a consideration that will be included when discussing the structure of the Cosmos in Chapter Two.

The constituents listed above must only be regarded as indicative and are not intended to be exclusive. Any arrangement of constituents is possible or even probable as is their place within any hierarchy. You should come to your own conclusion concerning this.

A summary of this model of the constituency of the subtle realm may be expressed in the form of a hierarchy, as shown below. This is a model that relies on an understanding that only the abstract essence of an Idea is present in a form that is capable of interaction, at all points, with any consciousness that exists in the material realm; that is to say, anywhere within the Universe.

The One Source of All Things

Free Will
Time
Justice and the Virtues
Science and Technology
Genres of lifeform principles
Humanity. Animals. Vegetable. Mineral etc.

It is to that interaction that we will turn next.

1.06. The Interaction between the Subtle and Material Realms

If we are to consider The Emerald Tablet in its entirety, particularly the complete Hermetic postulate, then we must address the interaction between the subtle and material realms, an interaction that takes place in both directions. Because we are conditioned to look up towards the subtle realm of perfect Ideas, it may be easy to envisage what it is that those Ideas grant or give to us in the material realm, and which become the very nature of our being and all that is around us. But what is it that we, as the material aspect of the Cosmos, can give back to subtle realm by way of this joint interaction?

In considering this aspect of the postulate we again look at the text on the tablet that says:

As all things arise from one and are mediated by one: so all things are born and adapted from this one.

and

The father is all of perfection here in the world, if it is converted into earth truly, whereupon its power and force is complete.

To approach an answer to this major question, we have to set aside those considerations that have tended to inhibit or even disable the mind of humanity in its relationship with that which might be considered to be 'perfect'. That we are imperfect is accepted and apparent, but we strive for perfection and should have no inhibitions in considering ourselves capable of approaching and interacting with perfection.

This is because the perfect, unchanging, unique, pure Ideas that are the constituents of the subtle realm have no form of expression within that realm. Their only means of expression is realised in the material realm, through the interaction described on The Emerald Tablet. Our interaction with the realm of perfect Ideas is not avoidable.

Furthermore, in considering: *'The father is all of perfection here in the world'* it also becomes apparent that the Father of all perfection also finds His/Her/Its means of expression in our material reality, by way of the same interaction.

Thus The One Source and all of the Ideas within the subtle realm rely on the material realm for their means of expression so that the relationship between all three aspects of the Cosmos is symbiotic, indivisible and fully integrated, whilst each aspect retains its discrete existence.

Furthermore, the interaction with the subtle Idea of Time enables change to take place in the material realm. Such change includes the process of evolution and sets up the need for destiny and fate to exist alongside time, a subject we will discuss in Chapter Four. The passage of time in our material reality results in change here, but not in the subtle realm, where all time exists within one instant. Once change ascends from material to subtle, then the subtle Idea is not changed but only becomes more greatly realised, exposed, uncovered or fulfilled, and the vitality integral with such realisation, uncovering and fulfilment etc. then becomes inherent in the material change in our reality, and so the process rolls on and on.

Such concepts as these grant to the material realm an extremely important role indeed to play in the nature of the Cosmos. The idea that everything in the material realm is that which allows the subtle realm its very means of expression and realisation may come as anathema to those that believe that humanity is unworthy to even approach the state of perfection that exists in mediations arising from 'The One Source'.

In religious terms, it may be personified in Thomas Cranmer's prayer of humble access: 'We are unworthy of approaching the state of 'Godliness' perhaps because we are all sinners.' But the notion that arises, from our model under discussion, is that The

One Source of All Things gains its mode of expression through the subtle realm of its mediation and from the interaction of consciousness from within the material realm.

We will look at the presence of good and evil when we consider consciousness, but for now we need to understand that, at its core, the very nature of the Cosmos can only be realised by the expression of the subtle realm from within its material counterpart.

Whether that which is in the material realm is worthy of such expression, or not, is irrelevant when considering the interaction between the two. The realisation of the subtle Idea, its uncovering towards a fulfilment of its purpose, can only occur through the expression of the material realm realised through the interaction between the subtle and the material.

So how does such an important interaction occur? The answer is simple: through the means of consciousness. Because humanity is conscious of itself, because it believes that it exists, because it is aware of its surroundings and is capable of intelligent thought and introspection, it is easy to propose that an interaction between human consciousness and the Ideas in the subtle realm is possible. The Emerald Tablet describes the process thus:

> *You should separate the spiritual from the gross, the subtle from the material, truly and with great industry, as it ascends from the earth to the subtle, and back again, and in so doing receives the force of all things subtle and material.*

Upon its initial interaction, consciousness encounters the subtle Idea that is without any form of material application, adapts it to a material form and offers it back to the subtle realm, whereupon it is imbued with additional vitality and transmitted back to the material realm where the process repeats itself continuously.

Such a process causes questions to arise as to what happens to our thoughts and whether they survive somewhere, in some form, in perpetuity. We will look at this aspect of consciousness, and the possibility of a 'Noosphere', a receptacle of all thought, later.

An interactive process such as that between consciousness and the subtle realm of perfect Ideas may be proposed as possible, but three further questions immediately arise. How does consciousness come into being before material form is involved? How does consciousness interact with the subtle realm, and does the same interaction apply to those animal forms that may not exhibit thought or self-awareness processes, or to the flora, vegetable or mineral components of our material reality?

To answer these questions we have to consider that consciousness exists at a subatomic level and that not only are there different levels of consciousness, but there are also different layers of consciousness. We will go into these aspects of consciousness in more detail in Chapter Three, but for now it is sufficient to recognise that everything within our material realm has a direct relationship to its essence in the subtle realm, and that the nature of this relationship involves a vehicle for transmission that we term 'consciousness'.

This will necessarily involve a different form of consciousness that falls outside our normal definition and understanding of the word. An example of such a different type of consciousness may be found in the Gaia theory, viewed as a macro organism with self-regulating properties that do not exhibit a thinking form, yet operate as a unity, to allow stable conditions for life on planet Earth to exist and, most importantly, to continue to exist.

The very nature of consciousness is impossible to define. It relies on the material realm as a vehicle whereby it is able to function, but we cannot point to any particle of material and say, 'That is consciousness.' Attempts have been made to reduce consciousness to a biological electrochemical process within the brain and yet we are all aware that the process itself cannot determine what we think, or how we interpret the input of data that our brain subsequently processes. Consciousness remains a mystery – one of great beauty and enormous, possibly unlimited potential and vitality, and we shall see how this mystery of beauty, potential and vitality come together to form our consciousness later in Chapter Three.

1.07. The Law of Attraction

The Emerald Tablet has provided the means for the foundation of many movements throughout its long period of history. One significant testimony to its power of survival lies in the modern day concept known as 'The Law of Attraction'. The principles involved are very simple in their essence.

Having described the nature of the interaction between the subtle and the material realms, we shall see later in our discussions that, in compliance with the thrust of The Emerald Tablet, reality is something that is relevant to each individual and is to a great extent created by each of us to suit our condition and circumstances. It is the interaction between the subtle and the material realms, as suggested on The Emerald Tablet, that defines the means whereby our consciousness establishes our reality.

We will expand on the process involved that enables the law of attraction to work, later in Chapter Three, once we have discussed the structure of the material realm in Chapter Two, and the nature of consciousness early in Chapter Three. Sufficient to say at this early stage that consciousness holds the key by which the law of attraction is enabled, and the particulate structure of the material realm and its relationship to the Ideas found in the subtle realm form the foundations from which this law becomes possible and is able to work.

1.08. The Subtle Particle

Before we turn to look at the structure of the Cosmos in Chapter Two, we will introduce one further, important element of the subtle realm, the idea of a subtle particle. Such a particle not only exists within the originating dimension that houses The One Source, but also exists in the subtle realm and the material realm, simultaneously.

The importance of the existence of this particle cannot be overstated, partly because, as we shall see, it forms a 'bridge' between the subtle and material realms under discussion, and allows a pathway to exist that will also permit us to traverse from one realm to the other.

1.09. The Story So Far

The Emerald Tablet has provided a suitable starting point towards an understanding that the Cosmos is formed of one dimension and two realms of reality, the material and subtle realms. The nature of the material realm is experienced through our five senses and explains the reality in which we spend our daily lives. The subtle realm is that which exists beyond our senses and contains the essence of perfect Ideas arising from the mediation of The One Source of All Things. These become translated into the means by which both the material and subtle realms find their expression, and which are the principles and ideals by which we seek to govern society. The interaction between the two realms takes place through the medium of consciousness and forms an ongoing, continuous process that results in evolution and development of life in the material reality.

Chapter Two

The Structure of the Cosmos

I was alone!

No form of my own,
no way to express anything,
no means to know myself.

Nothing mattered.

But then:

Bang!

Suddenly it did!

Consciousness mattered.

In a singular burst of energy,
'Space' came to exist,
the 'Where' was located,
One at a 'Time'.

The Cosmos inflated.

My consciousness had caused it to be,
had freely willed it to be so,
had cast the seed of myself into the motion of growth,
in the place I had formed.

I had made all of my Ideas and my energy available

in the seed of myself.

I had set the pattern of existence,
into form and being.

I had become The One Source of All Things!

Now I would be able to see,
to hear, to smell, to feel and to touch
all of it.

And so much more,

as the expression goes.

2.00. Introduction

Having looked at the nature of the Cosmos – the way in which it might be layered into realms of subtle Ideas and of material reality – we now turn to look at how such a model might be structured to enable the interaction described so far to operate.

Science has done a great deal in modern times to uncover the patterns that govern the existence of all material reality. The twentieth century came to show us the nature of the atomic structure of all things that had hitherto only been conjecture, hypotheses or theory. Now we began to understand how matter itself was constructed and we quickly learned how we could deconstruct matter and release the immense quantities of energy that hold it together; energy which had been imbued within its particle structure, at its creation.

Neither science nor religion, however, has achieved any significant degree of success in their conclusions concerning how, say, the big bang event came to happen, what caused it and what if anything existed before. Similarly, the brane clatter hypothesis, where multiple, expanding universes 'flatten out' to form 'curtains' or 'branes' that eventually come to interact with each other to form further universes, is meaningless, until a believable description is provided as to how the curtains or branes first came into being.

Equally, in the case of religion the existence of a God or deity is taken for granted as the starting point for the existence of everything, whilst any explanation of why anything exists, or how the deity itself came into existence in the first place, is sidestepped at best or, at worst, ignored completely.

Any truly freethinking individual will acknowledge from the outset of their thinking that an answer to these fundamental questions is not possible with any certainty and it is necessary to recognise not only that this is the case, but that it should continue to be so. If it were possible for science or religion to provide the answer to these questions with an acceptable degree of 'proof' then the essential thrust of life's enquiry would be satisfied with the inevitable result that life would cease to evolve or develop, because there would be nothing left to discover. Perhaps this will be the nature of the end game at some time in a distant future, yet to be encountered, but for now we will have to accept that the answer to this question is beyond our ability to solve.

Nevertheless, we take the view that it is incumbent upon us, as a race of enquiring individuals, to at least try to understand the nature and the structure of the Cosmos that is unfolding in front of our senses, and beyond their scope. This despite the fact that we will remain unable to explain either what caused the Big Bang, how the curtain branes come into being or how God came to exist.

Our explanations, hypotheses and theories proposed in this discourse seek to take into account elements of science and religion, philosophy, physics and metaphysics in combinations that satisfy the conditions so far thought to be prevailing in the

Cosmos, as seen today. We start with the formation of the stars.

2.01. The Star Maker

Let us consider a hypothetical premise that a single form of consciousness may have existed in a separate dimension and that this consciousness wished to experience knowledge of itself, but being alone and separate had no means by which it could do so. In order to achieve this experience, such consciousness would need to separate a part of itself from its whole in such a manner that the nature of the separation would result in a form that would be able to recognise and experience the difference of being separate.

Enabling such a separation would necessarily mean that the part which was separated would have to be 'free' in order to be able to recognise the nature of its own experience. The lack of such a freedom would signify and entail a control by the original conscious entity, and this would defeat the object of the separation, which was to satisfy the desire for the experience of self-knowledge. Essentially this is why consciousness in our physical Universe has free will available to it.

So a means was brought into existence whereby a rupture occurred in the veil that separates the dimension housing the original consciousness from everything else. This rupture allowed a separate element of the consciousness to become 'free'. Part of this process entailed allowing light-bearing particles from the original conscious essence to be emitted and transferred from that dimension into other 'places'. The means by which this transfer was enabled involved transfer by a particle energy field, also emitted by the same conscious essence, and this energy remains in the Cosmos and is indestructible. The energy field carries the minutest of subatomic particles that are able to exist simultaneously in all dimensions and realms of reality.

Thus, that part of the consciousness originating from the Source dimension, by becoming 'free', allowed the foundation of the material realm to come into existence and, as we shall see, subsequently allowed our Universe to form.

This same consciousness, which initially had no form or means of expression, also founded the existence of a hidden, subtle realm of reality, which became an intrinsic but separate element of the Cosmos. This Cosmic realm was linked to the, as yet, unformed material Universe realm by the energy field that carried the particles mutually to the two realms of reality, initially to the subtle realm and from there to the material realm. Those particles that came to inhabit the subtle realm moulded the consciousness imbued within each particle so as to be able to represent the pure essence of Ideas that emanated from the original Source. This subtle realm of Ideas awaited its mode of expression through an interaction with the consciousness found in the material realm.

So far as the material realm is concerned, such a transfer of particles as the one proposed took the initial form of the minutest volume of mass that it is possible to envisage, which comes to exist at the highest temperature that it is possible to achieve. This ultra high temperature mass continued to exist in that form for the shortest amount of time that it is possible for such a mass to exist. The existence of this short-lived, ultra high temperature minute mass has been labelled as a 'singularity'.

Almost immediately, and well short of the shortest period of time that we can perceive, this mass started to expand very, very quickly indeed and became the foundation of the Universe, of which we are a part. Such expansion has been labelled as 'inflation'.

The space into which the singularity could inflate did not exist prior to the transfer of energy from another dimension to the two separate realms of reality, and the change evidenced by inflation means that time also came into existence simultaneous and contiguous with the singularity. So, along with matter, heat and energy, space and time also came into existence with the arrival of the singularity.

For the sake of giving such a transfer a name, science may call this event the 'Big Bang' whilst the religious community may believe it to be 'the beginning'. Essentially, both names refer to the same event.

We can now recognise that the light-bearing particles and the energy transfer field, both being of the essence of the original entity of consciousness, erupt into both realms of reality but culminate in the reality of our material Universe. These particles are now known to arrive in twinned pairs, which are, to all intents and purposes, identical, or at the least possess identical potentiality, each to the other.

Once in the material realm light-bearing particles each go their own way, as is the nature of light, which is to travel in all directions simultaneously. Each particle has its own twin-related counterpart, but there is no purpose or form to the existence of each pair of particles because the nature of their duality has not yet been determined. Thus, the physical material Universe was, at its inception, in a state of unformed matter in chaos.

Immediately following the initial transfer of particles, our material Universe was so very small and dense that, even though expansive inflation was occurring, the particles that were emitted into it started to collide and to combine with each other until, very shortly thereafter, a build-up of groups of particles begin to exhibit an ever-greater intensity of mass, heat energy and light.

Whilst some particles remained free and unassociated, others were drawn or gathered together through the means of a developing field of energy that arose from the mass of the particles as they conglomerated. This is the field of gravity. Eventually enough particles grouped together to form huge masses that we know as stars. Once a star has formed, a chain reaction commences that produces increasing pressure and heat that then transforms groups of subatomic particles into other materials or elements within the envelope of the star. We have come to define these other materials in the periodic table, which is organised on the basis of their atomic numbers, their electron configuration and recurring chemical properties.

The process of star making has been continuous from very shortly after the big bang event, and continues to today. Our material Universe has been formed in this manner.

Free and unassociated particles remain at large within our Universe and operate to affect the development and adaptation of lifeforms that arise on the satellites of those star systems that become sympathetic to the continuing existence of life thereon.

Remembering that a subtle realm of Ideas also came into being at the same instant as the unformed material Universe, the Cosmos may thus be said to be structured in three realms, the material realm of our immediate experience, the subtle realm where the essence of all Ideas reside and the original dimension of existence where The One Source remains. The subtle and material realms are the ones available to our consciousness, whereas the original dimension is not.

Two things arise from the emission of twinned particles into our material Universe. The first, as we have said, was that a creative furnace was brought into being, in the form of the stars, and it is this formation that comes to form the basis for life. This process is ongoing even today after what we believe to be 13.8 billion Earth years of star creation, where untold billions of stars have been formed by this process.

This star formation allows particles to be transformed or transmuted from one state into another, with each particle and each grouping retaining the essence of its emission and its emitter. Perhaps the manner of transmutation developed in a similar way to that of superatoms where elements can be made to exhibit characteristics of other elements by the introduction of an additional atom within a cluster.

Eventually stars either overheat or their core collapses, and this produces explosions called novae or super novae that broadcast vast amounts of energy, together with much of the material elements that the star has produced during its lifetime. Through this process, matter becomes free and recognisable in a form that we have come to know, and is distributed throughout the entire Universe. This enables the conditions for life to develop on planets where the right conditions pertain. We are thus said to be 'the dust of the stars'.

The second point arising is that some transmuted particle pairs combined, which enabled the potentiality for the development of an evolutionary lifeform. Such lifeforms attracted similar combined particle pairs which accumulated to the point where they were able to evolve into a complex entity. In common with the rest of the still undefined Universe, such a complex had no particular form or shape, but was one that still had the derived particular characteristics of its originator. These lifeforms were able, as their accumulation grew, to become aware of the surrounding, undetermined energy and light-bearing particles, and were able to observe these phenomena through a growing conscious awareness. In so doing, the observing awareness automatically determined their function or condition.

So the originator of the emitted particles, The Source, had thus created a lifeform from the essence of its own consciousness, a lifeform which then observed the state of the then Universe, which subsequently collapsed and in so doing eliminated alternative forms of the Universe and consequently determined our Universe, from its state of chaos, into its form and function of being as we know it. In quantum terms, consciousness, as the observer, enabled the Universe, in its dual nature, to take physical form.

Every pair of particles, once emitted, having originated through the original big bang/creation event, forms the centre of its Universe.

This is a paradox that forms an enigma, in that each particle might be said to occupy a place which is at the centre of the

Universe whilst, at the same time, occupying all other places where the Universe might exist. This principle has mystical overtones that we will discuss in Chapter Seven and forms the basis where all spaces and locations are said to be at the centre of existence, whilst each of these spaces or locations may be said to enclose all others!

This is extremely difficult to comprehend or envision because it defies normal or standard models of logic and reason. It relies on an ability in anyone attempting to understand the concept to suspend, or to set aside, or better still to see through and beyond normal reason and logic, without losing their value and importance. However difficult this may prove to be, it is necessary to attempt to understand that the nature of any particular place in the Universe is not singular, nor is it confined to one location.

Necessary, because the nature of the subtle realm follows similar principles in that it exists every-where and no-where at the same time, whilst remaining as the central focus of our existence. It is also evident in the way in which life was to develop, which followed the same principles where, ultimately, there is no singular reality allocated to humanity. Rather there are a large number of realities that each form the centre of consciousness of an individual organism, each of which displays features that are capable of comprehending and perhaps becoming part of, or encapsulating, all other realities.

We must come to understand that the Universe, by coming into existence via the big bang event, which also brought space into being and commenced the passage of time, holds within it the answer to the paradoxical nature we have described concerning spaces and locations. Arising from a single Source and from a singularity, the Universe occupies all of the space that is an intrinsic part of itself. It contains all of the energy and matter within that intrinsic space available to it, and is in motion through the intrinsic energy within it that forms part of its gestaltic matrix.

Thus, we need to rethink our understanding of the nature of volumes, spaces, places, locations, energy flows and the passage of time, from a three-dimensional concept to one of multiple further dimensions that allows everything in the entire Cosmos to be in all places at all times, whilst simultaneously enclosing all places and times within it.

The Universe, and our consciousness, may then be understood to have no boundaries or edge to them and may be said to occupy an infinity of places, all of which are its centre.

Mind bending and mystical stuff this. Stuff that flies in the face of rationale and which requires us to set aside the normal interpretations of reality that are based solely on reason and logic. How can the centre of the Universe be every-where and no-where at the same time? How can there be no boundaries to the extent of the Universe? Logic forbids both aspects. But if we can begin to perceive a situation that exists beyond the standard model of reason and logic, there opens before us a multitude of alternative realities that also exist beyond our logical interpretation.

The importance of seeking to comprehend attributes of the Cosmos that appear to defy reason will become apparent in Chapter Eight.

To further complicate the matter, we should understand that what we call our Universe, within the Cosmos as a whole, is a gestalt, one formed of matter, energy, space and time, unified by consciousness in one single creation, arising from one event. Each is critical to the existence of the Cosmos and the Universe as separate elements of something that go to make up the unified gestalt that is the whole.

Such a gestalt as this will be seen as a model that repeats through the pattern of nature as found in the complex which is discussed in Chapter Three, in respect of the formation of the soul. The gestalt that we call the Cosmos is constituted of the elements described above that are inseparable and insoluble in that each relies upon the other for its existence, the whole of which then becomes significantly greater than the sum of its parts.

Once emitted from the Source dimension, the energy transfer field continues to exist forever, perhaps as a form of energy, perhaps as a physical substance, perhaps as an Idea. Each is inextricably linked to and is indissoluble from its counterpart wherever it is located within the Cosmos as a whole. Some pairs of particles combine within the same grouping so that, once the observer had determined the form and function of the Universe, the physical result may be one of dual particles existing in the same star grouping.

In the process of combination, the aggregation from microscopic into macroscopic physical bodies causes a change to occur to the character of the physics involved. This is evident as a stabilization of the micro particular substance from a non-determined nature to one capable of recognisable determination. This becomes very important because the dual nature of the existence of the Universe now comes into being as a relational form.

Perhaps this is because a dominant quantity of negative or positive particles was present from either its light-bearing or energy transfer field nature, at its point of combination. The outcome then becomes dependent upon the exquisitely minutest variation in conditions that can occur in or at combination.

Each star system will thus live and die according to conditions occurring at its initial combination of dual particles – some will die by super novae and some will die from the death of heat. Some will live long and some will die young. The death of stars by super novae allows smaller planetary bodies to form, bodies that are constituted from the transformed elements of the star itself.

This process includes some of the opposite twinned pairs of particles that become contained within the planetary formation, which allows for a relational planetary world to develop – one which contains the potential for male and female, positive and negative, good and evil, black and white etc., etc. within its constituent being. This is why the natural world exhibits balanced characteristics within its constitution and is why it is important to try to maintain that balance within our, or any, environment.

We might say that when some dual particles combine into a star system, and become large enough to be recognised as classically physical substances, they possess an intrinsic capability of the expression of their own life and death. We will see this characteristic necessarily repeated wherever lifeforms come to exist on planets orbiting suns that are expressive of an evolutionary process of adaptation.

The physical Universe is therefore made up in this manner and takes the form of birth and death cycles of physical star systems as a means by which new life is propagated from the death of something else. This principle is applied at all levels of existence where science can demonstrate that, in the organic world, new life springs from the death and decay of the old.

Whilst the emission of particles continues, then so will the Universe continue, but should it stop then the beginning of the end will start – the end times will be upon the Universe. The energy that keeps bodies apart will diminish and the Universe will cease through lack of energy.

Bearing in mind our understanding that the Universe has no boundaries, or edge to its existence, and consequently fills the entire space and time continuum that is available for it to occupy, if the rate of emission is increased then the expansion of the Universe is quickened and the space and time available to it also expands. This may be the reason for the apparent acceleration of the expansion of the Universe evidenced in 1998 through the Hubble Telescope. Conversely, if the rate of emission decreases then the expansion of the Universe will initially stabilize and then reverse into contraction, with the amount of space and time available for its occupation also contracting.

Not all of the emitted pairs of particles become combined into star groups or go to form the subtle realm. Some light-bearing particles remain in isolation, free and unassociated. One particle of these remaining twinned, isolated light-bearing pairs, once their duality has been determined, may collide with star-formed groupings and may either be absorbed into sustaining its life, or promoting its death. Alternatively, it may go to form gravitational fields which keep physical objects in an attracting relationship. The counterpart particle may congregate into energy wells, which may initially go to form 'dark matter'. The energy transfer field particles may operate in the same manner, but with the counterpart of the pair going to form 'dark energy' rather than matter.

In Chapter One we described the nature of the Cosmos based upon a subtle and material realm being available to us through our consciousness, and having considered how the Cosmos including our Universe came into being we will now go on to explore and develop the structure of the Universe from the model outlined above.

2.02. Particle Matter

As we have said, it is now known that particles are emitted into our material Universe in twinned pairs probably by means of a particle energy transfer field. Each particle carries an element of the energy of its emission that is the imprint of its emitter, the signature of all things, of its creator, a sort of hallmark, that enables the transfer of mass and allows or even encourages subatomic particles to group together to form whole atoms and molecules. In this way the singular monadic nature of particulate matter takes on a dual role, that of matter, plus an element of creative energy that is capable of 'creative union' with other matter. Without both, matter would be devoid of motion at subatomic levels and would remain unchanging and undeveloped.

We do not intend to embark upon a detailed study of the atomic structure of matter, but it is important to understand that all matter is composed of particles and that all particles comprise sub-particles. Differing molecules of matter may arise due to the number and assembly of the various, electrically charged subatomic particles that exist and that go to form the structure of matter. Each element of matter will comprise a different collection of atomic and subatomic particles, and the number of combinations available in the process of forming different substances is large enough to produce a very large number of different material elements. A very brief history of the recent development of the particulate structure of matter will help in understanding not only the diverse nature of matter but also the simple elegance of its systematic structure.

Until the early part of the twentieth century, the atom was thought to be the smallest component part of matter. Then in 1911 Ernest Rutherford discovered that each atom comprises a nucleus and some electrons. As research science during the twentieth century developed it was discovered, in 1932, that each nucleus was formed of smaller particles called protons and neutrons and then, in 1947, that these particles were themselves held together by further particles called mesons. In 1964 it was discovered that each proton or neutron was composed of even smaller particles called quarks, of which there are at least six different sorts. Furthermore, quarks were held together by yet smaller particles that have been labelled gluons.

It has been surmised for some considerable time that the very smallest of these subatomic particles would be considered as the foundational building block of all matter.

As we can see, a scientific search has been going on, throughout the twentieth century, to study subatomic particles in order to identify the smallest sub-particle building block of matter, a sub-particle that was increasingly difficult to find and observe due, not only to its extremely microscopic size, but also, as it transpires, to its very brief discrete existence.

In 1964 it was proposed by Peter Higgs that there existed a field, similar to, but different from, a gravitational field or an electromagnetic field, that when excited yielded particles that allowed other particles to gain their mass. In order to prove that such a field existed it was proposed that if a particle which interacted with this field could be detected then this would provide effective proof that both the field and the particle did indeed exist.

The field was labelled by science as the Higgs field and the particle was labelled a 'boson' known usually as 'the Higgs boson'.

Such a great scientific insight and the subsequent endeavour by a large group of scientists, culminating in the construction of the Large Hadron Collider at CERN laboratory on the Franco/Swiss border, have been successful to the point where, in July 2012, scientists were able to confirm the existence of the Higgs field and thus the Higgs boson particle. This immense achievement is to be congratulated because it confirms important ideas concerning not only the nature of the Cosmos, but also the structure of the Universe.

In 1993 Leon Lederman had labelled the boson particle, at that time only the subject of speculation, as 'the God particle', because of the fundamental part it was thought to play in the foundation of all other particles and subsequent matter. This epithet was not considered to be helpful because science regarded the term as inappropriate, by imbuing the boson with mystical qualities that did not relate to the principles of the scientific methodology involved.

However, whilst it is necessary for scientists to remain focussed in order to bring their methodology to fruition, it may be that something is lost by this less than holistic approach to our everyday total existence. James Lovelock[4] describes the problem as one arising due to:

> *the malign effects of twentieth century separation of science into neat compartments where specialists and experts can ply their professions in complacency*

and goes on to give a typical example that attributes ignorance on the part of physicists to the 'soft sciences'.

This principle applies to the entire bank of knowledge where specialisation and absolute focus yield good or excellent results whilst, on occasion, failing to relate or allow those results to be associated with some other areas of study or discipline that lie beyond their immediate remit.

Such a particle as the boson is extraordinarily elusive, partly because of its incredibly small size and also because it decays into other particles almost immediately upon its release from its carrier field within the material realm. Whilst not labelling the boson the 'God particle', we must consider it to be the prime candidate for becoming the fundamental building block of all material existence by enabling matter to gain its mass and then become larger subatomic and atomic particles. Such a particle also carries an element of the energy of its emission that is the source of the motion characteristic of all matter.

It is perhaps no wonder that the particle and its associated field of energy have been so difficult to find; so scientifically elusive.

Because of this, and in order to differentiate it from the more mundane value that science has attributed to it, we shall in future reference call this particle the 'Archaeus Particle'. Furthermore the field that interacts with the archaeus particle is a field of energy that we shall separate from something that is within the exclusive remit of science to rename as the 'Archaeus Field'.

Our renaming of this particle and its carrier field of energy is not done to take anything away from the scientific methodology and attributes that have established their existence in the first place. Rather it is done simply because our concept of this field and particle goes so far beyond the current scientific inception and because many esoteric thinkers will endow this particle and field with properties yet to be established, including some of a mystical nature.

Consequently, this may lead to a wish by many scientists to disassociate our thinking from the remit of their research and development, a process that will be assisted by our thus renaming.

2.03. The Archaeus Particle and Its Field

The Archaeus particle may be likened to what science calls the Higgs boson particle that has proven to be so elusive that, until very recently, its existence was not certain. Even now its existence cannot be demonstrated as sustainable because, upon its observation, it immediately decays into other particles and itself becomes nothing that we can yet define.

The term archaeus that we are attaching to the Higgs boson particle is named after its medieval philosophical meaning, being alluded to by the likes of Paracelsus (1493–1541) as 'the glue that binds heaven to the material reality of our Universe'. Setting aside such emotive reference to heaven, these particles come to exist in the subtle realm through their emission there, carried on a field of energy, the archaeus field.

They are impressed with a mark of the original consciousness that is The One Source and they also come to exist in the material realm, with the purpose of transferring mass to other, larger subatomic particles, and thus eventually to all matter. This, in itself, gives this particle a materialistic epithet as the 'material of the creation of all matter', as without the archaeus particle all other particles and thus matter itself would have no mass.

It follows that, whilst embedded in the archaeus field, within the subtle realm, the particle itself would have no detectable mass and that, once released from the archaeus field of energy, as may come to happen within the material realm, it imparts its energy to give mass to the subatomic particles encountered there. It then almost immediately ceases to exist, by decaying into those other subatomic particles.

Thus it is apparent that science has been searching for something that itself has no mass and, consequently, its mass cannot be measured simply because there is nothing to measure. However, it is important to acknowledge that there exist within our material Universe phenomena that have no mass but which are capable of being measured. Simple examples would be concerned with radio waves or X-rays or radiant heat waves.

It appears that the archaeus particle does not fit neatly into any of these sorts of phenomenal categories. Its existence may only be detected through its reaction or release from the archaeuic field of energy that then grants it mass, prior to which it might be said not to exist because it has no measurable characteristics. Yet it must exist, or pre-exist, in order to be able to take on mass, which it is able subsequently to transfer to other subatomic particles.

This is yet another paradox that challenges our notions of logic and that, once again, requires us to modify or even abandon our previous notions concerning the nature and creation of matter.

Having no measurable characteristics in the material realm, until its release from the archaeus field of potential mass, the archaeus particles do not simply come into being once subatomic and atomic particles with mass are required. They already exist, in abundance, through their emission into the subtle realm of Ideas, from the dimension that houses The One Source, where they also continue to exist simultaneously. They, and their field of energy, may be thought of as a background that supports all Ideas, one that is formative because they enable fulfilment of those Ideas that require material in order for them to become expressed.

The archaeus particles never actually leave the Source dimension or the subtle realm but, having been impressed at their emission with an element of the consciousness that has been separated from the whole, they extend their massless self from within the Source dimension into the subtle realm and from there to our material reality. They then become subtle plus material, in combination which, upon their release from the archaeus field, come to exist in all three realms simultaneously, as The Source in one, as a massless background in the next and as the fundamental building block of material in the other.

We are now able to see how The One Source may actually experience the knowledge and awareness of self that was the object of its creation of two further realms of reality.

Furthermore, the likelihood exists that the archaeus field and particle will prove to be the common factor if the existence of alternate Universes to our own becomes proven. There can only be One True Source of All Things and its signature will pervade all existences and all realities, in whatever dimension or at whatever frequency they occupy. Such a possibility as this imbues the archaeus particle with mystical characteristics that open many doors to the possibility of experiencing other dimensions, realms or vibrational frequencies. By being the common factor, this also allows for the possibility that any separation between dimensions, realms or vibrational frequencies may be bridged to permit common experiences, at a non-ordinary conscious level.

We begin to glimpse the means whereby it may just be possible that a 'feeling of otherness' may be experienced by some individuals who are susceptible to receiving information from non-ordinary sources.

Be that as it may, so far as our own Cosmic reality is concerned we should ask the question: 'Is the archaeus particle of itself an actual Idea that forms an additional constituent of the subtle realm?' According to the text on The Emerald Tablet, every thing comes into being through the mediation of The One Source, and in this respect it may be said that the subtle element of the archaeus particle is a constituent of the subtle realm and thus could be regarded as an Idea in itself.

However, it may not be said that the existence of the material aspect of this particle within the material realm arises from an Idea within the subtle realm. This is because the archaeus particle, being the fundamental building block of all other particles, forms an intrinsic part of all of the various subtle Ideas that are translated to the material realm. Consequently, considerations of perfection involving separation, purity and uniqueness, as discussed in Chapter One, would be compromised.

We must therefore look for an alternative means by which the archaeus particle and its associated field can exist in both realms simultaneously, whilst enabling or facilitating the transmission of Ideas from one realm to become a reality in the other. The answer to this we will call 'the Dark Wave-Particle duality form hypothesis'. This label takes its name, as an allegory, from a fundamental property of the elementary particles within the material Universe where, paradoxically, they can express their existence as both a particle and a waveform simultaneously. This is shown in the nature of light, which can be scientifically demonstrated to behave as having simultaneous dual characteristics, that of a waveform and a particle stream, depending upon the method used for its observation and measurement.

Science has, for some considerable time, proposed that there exists between the solid elements of our material Universe (which constitute about 5% of the universal volume) both dark matter (about 25% universal volume) and dark energy (about 70% universal volume). The word 'dark' is used to describe something secret or hidden, a mystery that, to date, remains esoteric by its definition and in its nature.

The nature of dark matter is a mystery that is currently the subject of much scientific research and experiment. Consequently, at the current state of development we may only conjecture as to the nature of its existence. Perhaps it is in some way the opposite of normal matter, some form of antimatter; perhaps it is the vast number of neutrinos, those virtually massless non-electrically charged particles that travel about the Universe at the speed of light, through all solid matter, changing only when encountering positively electrically charged particles; perhaps it may possibly be the unfulfilled mass of matter awaiting its reception of mass, following the translation of the archaeus particle from subtle to material realms.

All of these conjectures are possible, but one that appears to us as being most likely is that dark matter is formed from the residue left over when the archaeus particle has decayed, having once imparted its mass to the material particles inhabiting the material realm. Such residue would have little or no mass left to it and might appear as a 'ghost particle' that has little by way of characteristics to represent it.

The dark energy element of the universal constituency also remains a mystery, but is one that is held by some to be responsible for the fact that the Universe is expanding at an accelerating rate, rather than contracting, as might be expected, if only the gravitational field that permeates the entire Universe is taken into account.

Our hypothesis proposes that another field, essentially the archaeus field, also permeates all realms of the entire Cosmos; and within this field, whilst inhabiting the subtle realm, there is embedded the subtle element of the archaeus particle. This subtle element comes to inhabit both the subtle and material realms simultaneously following its extension from the subtle to the material realm.

As we will see in Chapter Three, it is a form of universal consciousness, even in its lowest layer of being, that excites the Ideas within the subtle realm, and in so doing translates those

Ideas to form our universal material reality. As a direct consequence, the energy within the archaeus field, that forms the background to the Ideas in the subtle realm, is released to fuel the acceleration of matter in our Universe.

Thus the energy within the archaeus field is the means whereby the archaeus particle is emitted into the subtle realm and then extended into the material realm, which then becomes dark energy, that 70% of the volume, which is the energy that keeps all heavenly bodies apart accelerating away from each other.

Whilst residing in the subtle realm the archaeus field of energy, and its subtle particle, takes a form similar to a 'waveform' of existence, which is then observed as a 'particle stream' following its translation to our material realm, caused by its encounter with a form of universal consciousness that can essentially be regarded as an observing apparatus. Hence our naming of our proposal as 'the Dark Wave-Particle duality form hypothesis'.

Having, so to speak, a foot in each camp of the subtle and material realms, we are now able to see not only how the archaeus particle functions primarily as the means to enable material to gain its mass, but also becomes the form of a bridge between the two realms, by having a simultaneous presence in all realms of reality, together with a means of transport from one to the other, using consciousness as the key that unlocks and motivates the mode of transport.

When we come to discuss consciousness and its various layers and levels we will see that it is across this bridge, between the realms, that consciousness is able to traverse, in both directions, and it is also the means whereby the Ideas in the subtle realm are able to transpose and interchange their essence into the material realm, and back. It is in this process that we are able to envisage the motion that is described on The Emerald Tablet.

The driving force that enables and promotes these interchanges is one that pervades the entire material reality, giving vitality to the Universe that we inhabit. We will call this force of vitality the 'Vis Formatrix'.

2.04. The Vis Formatrix

Physicists today are generally keen to point out that all that exists within the whole Universe which is our home is governed by the laws of physics. It is physics, and only physics, that determine the phenomena, construction and outcome of all that our senses can experience. This is a statement that hardly needs making because its truth is self-evident. Of course the Universe is constructed and maintained in accordance with a set of laws determined within a discipline that we have labelled 'physics'. The question that arises naturally from this scientific given is: *'How did such a set of laws come into being in the first place?'*

The answer to this question has proved over several millennia to be both elusive and divisive. We suggest that the inclusion of a form of energy deriving from the creation of all matter is a proposal that combines or unites the divisions that have prevailed for so long.

The origins of the term 'vis formatrix' need not concern us in any great detail; suffice it to say that it was Emanuel Swedenborg (1688–1772) who, following Paracelsus and van Helmont, saw it as the force that enabled creation to occur, it being the first element in his doctrine of series and degrees. This doctrine sought to establish a systematic means whereby the power of the infinite might be transposed into the finite through a series of steps or degrees, being *purpose, cause* and *effect*. Purpose in the Swedenborg doctrine is thus related to the transmission of the source of infinite power, by stages, to the finite realm of material endeavour.

For ease of use and simplicity we will abbreviate this term to *'formatrix'*, and we will use this idea in a development so that it may become regarded as the primal force of all nature, giving rise to the entire pattern of cosmological construction and evolution and which provides the foundation for the Neo-Platonic idea of a Universal Soul.

Now we see introduced a force that energises, animates and gives vitality to particulate matter, a force so great that it permeates the entire structure of the Universe without any diminution whatsoever, even as the Universe accelerates and expands. In so doing the formatrix is not only seen as the creative force behind the structure of the Universe but also becomes that which sustains its repetitive pattern throughout nature.

We have proposed that every archaeus particle that exists bears the hallmark or signature of the consciousness of its emitter and we can now imbue to this particle, through its hallmark, an energy or force that grants the vitality of life to its otherwise inert existence. The signature or hallmark of its emission forms a part of every archaeus particle and becomes the receptor that enables the creative force of the life principle to enter that subatomic particle, and subsequently all of matter, to vitalise the entire material realm, in whatever form. Such vitality is expressed in many forms, that of motion particularly at the atomic and subatomic levels and in the life force that inhabits all lifeforms on planet Earth.

As the archaeus particle may be regarded as the foundational building block of all matter so formatrix energy may be regarded as that which brings motion to matter and animates life within it. In so doing it enables the establishment of its pattern of existence to be sustained, a pattern that may be seen to be repeated throughout nature.

An example of such a repetitive pattern may be found in 'The Golden Ratio' exemplified in the Fibonacci number sequence, which is to be found throughout nature and that may be seen used in the aesthetics of design, architecture, music, art, finance and even the human body. The ratio of 1:1.618 is expressed in the form of a spiral, seen when observing both mega objects such as spiral galaxies and micro objects such as snail shells, and is held stable by means of the formatrix energy giving vitality as a constant form throughout nature and its derivations.

It is this primal force entering through the archaeus particle that grants to matter its stability and enables it to become established.

Furthermore, this force regulates the interaction between different systems of materiality so that they become a system that is ecologically sustainable and balanced. The Gaian self-regulatory theory may be a prime example of the effect of the formatrix energy pervading all of matter. We will discuss Gaia later in this chapter.

Another example of the formatrix primal force in action is seen as 'The World or Universal Soul' proposed by Plotinus.[5] In *The Enneads* his pupil Porphyry (c234–c305 CE) writes:

First then let every Soul consider that it is the World Soul which created all things, breathing into them the breath of life, into all living things which are on earth. The World Soul sets them in their order and directs their motions, keeping itself apart from the things, which it orders and moves and causes to live.

For Plotinus the formatrix energy would be represented as the breath of life which gives to all that exists its animation and vitality, whilst at the same time endowing that life with a constancy that is seen universally.

The relationship between the archaeus particle and the formatrix can be seen as one of critical importance to our very being and to that of the existence of all that is. That which is The Source has established the means by which matter may come into existence and thereupon has imbued such matter with mass and the means of maintaining its form and becoming alive in terms that we understand. Thus it is this relationship that is crucial to the development of life and consciousness throughout the material Universe and within the subtle realm. In the first instance it becomes the formative means of establishing life, then subsequently it forms the crucible of evolution, and then becomes the engine of development of consciousness and life.

We are able to identify this relationship as a means of purpose, cause and effect similar in its concept to a series of degrees as proposed by Emanuel Swedenborg.

Although the amount of formatix energy, like the amount of mass, in each particle is constant, once converted from its subtle to its material existence the strength and the power of the formatrix energy present does not remain constant. As particulate matter increases its complexity, then the energy of the formatrix naturally gains strength also; but in its case, the increase is an exponential one. The extent of the vitality granted by the formatrix energy increases by the sum of the parts contained within each particle of matter at any one time. The Emerald Tablet once again gives us the clue to this exponential increase:

as it ascends from the earth to the subtle, and back again,

and in so doing receives the force of all things subtle and material where it can be seen that, by its transmission between the subtle and material realms, the form under transmission gains greater force which, in the case of the vitality that the formatrix energy provides, becomes ever greater and superior within its particulate structure.

Essentially this is why the more complex and higher level a lifeform comes to evolve, the greater is its vitality; its enlivened life principle.

Yet by itself the archaeus particle and the formatrix energy cannot give to those higher level conscious beings their sense of being, of identity, the necessary depth of ego or the ability to access the subtle Idea of Free Will. For these attributes we will need to look deeper into the archaeuic/formatrix relationship.

2.05. Enter the Soul

The text of The Emerald Tablet once again gives us the clue to the means by which we may consider that which grants to us our sense of being:

> You should separate the spiritual from the gross, the subtle from the material, truly and with great industry, as it ascends from the earth to the subtle, and back again, and in so doing receives the force of all things subtle and material.
>
> By these means you shall have dominion of the whole world and all things will become clear.
>
> Its force is above all other forces, because it can convert every subtle thing to penetrate every material thing.

Hermes thus recognised that the relationship between the subtle and material realms was one of motion where each becomes dependant upon the other not only for its expression, but also for its development.

Such motion is confirmed by Plotinus who has said:

> The Creative World Soul sets them in their order and directs their motions, keeping itself apart from the things, which it orders and moves and causes to live.

A picture has emerged that sets all of life in motion, one that may be regarded as perpetual so far as life can be said to continue to exist. The question that then arises from such a feature is 'What is the purpose of such motion?' and the answer to that must be something to do with the evolution and the development of life.

It is implicit in the fact of the existence of such motion as this that life did not simply appear in the material Universe fully developed with nothing left to evolve. Science has now grown to the point where this should be regarded as a given. This being the case, then life itself must play a part in its own development, its own evolution, and this part is played through the interaction of consciousness with the Ideas of the subtle realm – an aspect of the motion described by Hermes and Plotinus.

As consciousness gathers itself, to itself, through the means of a more and more complex union of particles, as proposed by Pierre Teilhard de Chardin and described in Chapter Three, so the capacity, or amount, or volume, of consciousness available to such a union also grows. If we regard humanity as the most complex grouping of particulate matter currently in existence on planet Earth then we are also saying that humanity possesses and exhibits the highest structure of consciousness currently available and in existence here.

The particulate matter that forms the vehicle for the human lifeform is energised by the formatrix energy that permeates the entire Cosmos and it is this combination of the structure of complex matter resulting in higher consciousness, activated by the energy, of the formatrix that gives rise to the development of that which we call 'The Soul'.

An agreed description as to what comprises the soul has, historically, been very elusive and, indeed, many in the scientific field, particularly those involved in neuroscience and biology, do not even admit to the existence of, or the need for, a Soul. After all there is nowhere in the physiology of the human being to where we can point and say, 'Look, there is the soul.'

However, it is our view that the absence of a soul would leave a void within us, resulting in a lack of substance relating to the purpose of life and to that of identity and ego. For ourselves, and perhaps for millions of others, there is a natural assumption that a soul exists as an intrinsic part of the nature of humanity and so, given our development arising from the nature and the structure of the Cosmos described so far, it is incumbent on us to attempt to define the nature and constituency of the Soul.

Beyond the particle structure that forms all elements of matter in our realm of reality and its enlivenment by a form of energy that inhabits every particle in existence, which grows exponentially and which then allows creative union and development to occur, there must be an additional form that is capable of raising the individual to a level beyond that of mere enlivenment. After all, the minerals of our material reality together with its flora and fauna all exhibit particulate structures and are alive in the sense that they are capable of developmental change say from solid to liquid form, from liquid to gaseous form, from dust to rock or from seed to plant growth and fruition. Furthermore all of these aspects of our material reality share with everything else in existence the motion that is inherent in the nuclear structure of all things.

But there is something beyond all of that, which grants to life an ability that allows consciousness of self, a sense of identity, an egotistical form that, if all held in true balance, will encourage personal development and use of free will. These elements, which come into play beyond the basic formatrix energy of life, will form the basis of our constitution of what we call 'The Soul'.

Consider, the archaeuic, particulate form of life, set in motion, endowed and enlivened by the formatrix energy, as a matrix that enables everything in existence to have the potential to possess a soul. However, it is the higher forms of consciousness, those that have gained the most vitality from the formatrix energy, that are able to elevate such a matrix as this, once sufficient complexity of particulate structure has taken place. This enables us to become conscious of ourselves and forms the basis upon which the individual can co-create its soul. Higher layers of consciousness, and then higher levels within that layer produce an intelligent thinking process, self-awareness and an egotistical element that, taken together, form the basis of The Soul.

Then, just as the material conception of life evolves and develops, so do the constituents of the soul. Self-awareness, intelligence and the ego, all founded in consciousness, evolve to give a sense of individual identity and, once this is established, then the soul takes on the ability to assimilate within itself the essence of the Universal Soul, which might be said to originate from within the constituency of the subtle realm.

Through higher or altered levels of consciousness we are able to learn how to understand the nature of free will; how to accept the effect of adaptive change, enabled by time; we can absorb the rigours that come with revelation and initiation into esoteric knowledge, through a deepening understanding of the pure essence of justice and virtue. As we become able to enter the higher levels of consciousness, the balance between self/identity and the ego changes to allow it to correspond to an ever-increasing extent with the Universal soul.

The soul therefore may be described as the formative energy that enlivens life, as a form of consciousness, that comes to demonstrate increasingly higher levels of self-awareness and, with it, intelligent thought and an ego that complements and fulfils identity. Once formed thus the soul becomes capable of elevating itself to higher levels of co-creation involving altered states of consciousness and a meaningful relationship with the subtle Ideas of free will, time, justice and virtue.

We do not therefore envisage the soul as a separate single entity that enters the body of a person at say birth or conception, but rather as a complex of elements and abilities that meld together to form a gestalt, an enhanced conscious unit of identity and self-awareness.

That is not to say, however, that, in the higher forms of animal in our material reality, such a unit may well begin to build its association of form in the womb, soon after conception has occurred.

Such a concept as the soul, herein described, marches alongside the evolution and development of life in our reality and will continue to evolve with humanity and other forms of animals so long as time continues to be created and passes into what we call the past. In addition, an important question arises from this soul complex and that is: 'What happens to the individual soul once the death of the material vehicle that houses it occurs?'

Ironically, the answer to this question arises, allegorically, from the field of science and involves the postulate that the amount of energy existing in the Universe always remains constant in that it increases through its emission from the Source dimension, and none of it ceases to exist. Rather it is transformed or converted into other forms of energy. This even after allowing for a certain amount of disorder to occur through the process of transformation, where some of the energy involved will not be available for conversion through wastage or inefficiency. The extent of such disorder to an arrangement like this has been labelled by science as 'entropy', arising from the Greek *entropia*, meaning to 'turn aside'.

Life in its entirety is enlivened by the energy we have called 'formatrix' and it is upon the matrix, formed in part by this energy, that the soul is co-created by elevating the energy into a conscious ability of self-awareness. This being the case, the energy of life cannot be destroyed but must continue to exist in its developed form or must become converted into another alternative form of energy.

The extent of the formatrix energy present and which energises all material life is in part transmitted, to the product arising from the reproductive system, to give life to the next generation. The remainder stays with the lifeform until its death, whereupon most of it is converted into alternate forms of energy.

But the soul, having no material content of its own and relying upon the matter/formatrix of the vehicle housing it for its expression, 'turns aside', continuing to exist, vitalised by the remaining formatrix energy that is subject to entropy, without any material support, where it is then able to find its means of expression in, or on, another, different plane of existence.

Where and how this other plane of existence exists is a subject for further study that may be influenced by personal belief systems. Some may even deny the existence of such a plane of existence, in which case their Soul will not inhabit such a plane that, for them, does not exist. For those that do believe in the existence of such a plane of existence, then this will indeed exist, in conformity with the co-creation of their genuine soul desire.

The word genuine is used here to differentiate the soul's true desire from that which is only wished for, or from that which we are not prepared to make any effort to achieve. The soul's true desire and intent is supported by our actions and deeds, expressed through the choices we make. Thus the way we live our lives out, through our choices, according to our soul's desire during our whole lifetime will be reflected in the nature of any afterlife available to us, and this will be based on the deeds undertaken, even if not always fulfilled.

Choice is that which is founded in our consciousness, supported by the free will available to us through the interaction of our consciousness with the subtle Idea of Free Will, discussed in Chapter One. Those souls that do not believe in a further plane of existence, who do not will it into being during their lifetimes, will lie dormant in a place that is nowhere and has no characteristics of any description. We might say that it is a zone of non-place, un-located and differentiated by the absence of anything. This zone should not be thought of as a place of punishment or as a sort of hell, because it is a non-place of nothing at all, where some individual souls might prefer to lie. However, a problem may arise for any souls that mistakenly find their ongoing existence lying within this zone, a point we will discuss later in Chapter Five.

We are reluctant to place a label on this plane of existence or to suggest that it forms a third realm of reality. It may well form another such realm but alternatively we might regard it as an extension of the subtle and material realms in combination, a sort of extension of both. This latter view might arise essentially due to the notion that such a plane of existence comes into being only through the activity and interaction between the subtle and the material realms. It is through this interaction that the energy of elevated consciousness co-creates and develops the soul, and its continued existence beyond death does not rely on the pre-existence of an alternative or different reality.

Many people have expressed their curiosity as to what the purpose of life could be and we might look towards this model of the Soul to find the glimmer of a possible answer. Having suggested that the two-realm cosmology, which is available to consciousness, came into existence in order that the original Source of consciousness, as a whole, might experience and find knowledge of itself, then perhaps the purpose of our existence lies in the development and elevation of the formatrix energy, to form a co-created soul that continues to exist, beyond the death of our material component.

Perhaps we are a production line for the co-creation of souls that soak up all experiences encountered during our material existence and then, upon our death, deposit these experiences as memories within the Universal Soul, which may then be taken forward on to another plane of existence, or dimension.

However, a word must be said concerning the death of the very young, that is to say wherever a soul complex has come to exist, sometimes even before birth, but which has not had the opportunity to gather any experience and memory. Difficult questions arise concerning why such souls should come into being if, upon the premature death of the hosting individual, there is no experiential memory that can be taken forward on to another plane of existence. There appears on the surface to be no purpose to the brief existence of these innocent souls.

Any answer to this question can only be speculative, but is likely to do with the need for some form of totality, a form of completeness, to be established within the Universal Soul. The Universal Soul by its very nature must be representative of all aspects of soul experience, including that of the innocents as well as the long-lived souls that have fully experienced all aspects of living, including the full range of good and evil.

This is not to say that the death of embryonic or immature souls has any 'built-in' inevitability or purpose, or is part of some 'master plan', but arises simply from the evolution and development of life in all its wider forms. We shall see in Chapter Three that evolution is a process driven by natural selection which encourages or perpetuates the beneficial traits of any species.

The corollary to such a process of the refinement of such beneficial traits is that weaknesses may also be transmitted through the genetic reproductive system. The evolutionary process filters out most weaknesses over many generations of adaptation, but until that process is complete the experience of premature death will continue. Premature death due to disease and war etc. also forms a part of our evolutionary heritage in this respect, and the imperfect nature and ability of humanity at its current stage of development can also contribute to untimely, unnatural death.

The death at the embryonic stage of life or soon after, the demise in infancy and the entire range of premature deaths are an intrinsic part of life and its evolutionary development. Whilst this offers little or no comfort to those left grieving by their passing, such deaths form part of the totality of the life cycles that by these means are maintained in a broad balanced relationship. We must remember that the souls of all live on, entropically, in a form of indestructible energy that maintains, amongst its other constituents, its consciousness.

The nature of death and its inevitability will be discussed in Chapter Four.

On some occasions an interesting effect arises from the development of the soul complex described, one that, for some, is of prime importance. This concerns the nature of the relationship between one soul and another.

Having seen how archaeus particles are emitted in twinned pairs, most of which separate and go their own way, the situation may come to exist where some such pairs come together again, although being in different bodies, and are reunited through the constituents of the soul complexes described.

Such reunifications are very rare, but when they do occur the effect upon those individuals concerned is extremely pronounced. They become (re)united as 'twinned souls' that connect as though enmeshed as one entity, as though the vibrations of their motion and being are fully synchronous, each with the other.

Some few individuals have experienced a meeting of what they call a 'soul mates' with whom they share a very close relationship. Whilst the depth of the relationship of soul mates is very close, it bears little resemblance to the total depth of a twin soul relationship. Soul mates is where two souls of sympathetic outlook come into relationship and work to co-create a harmony of existence and understanding between themselves.

Whereas, twin souls instantly recognise each other from the outset of their initial meeting and become reunited. Being one half of a twin soul grants to both of the persons involved an absolute unity of being, that is totally natural, requiring no effort to produce a complete and total harmony, each with the other, and with their environment.

Once reintroduced, both halves of the twin soul relationship join together in an unstoppable bond that creates a rapport of truth and understanding between the two that can only be described as complete and authentic in the manner portrayed by WH Vanstone in his book *Love's Endeavour, Love's Expense.*[6] Here the total accord between the twin soul participants will not even consider the expression or imposition of any limitations of any sort, will not seek to introduce any form of control between them and will freely exhibit complete giving of the self, with natural engagement at all points.

It is as though both halves of the twin soul operate at the same vibration or frequency, which manifests as a complete understanding and knowing of each other through a form of communication that does not rely only on the physical attributes of our being, but also uses the immaterial, mystical aspects of human reality to produce a transcendent form of relationship that goes far beyond anything previously experienced.

Twinned souls then naturally exhibit a totality of peace and harmony between themselves, their fellow human beings and, most importantly, towards their environment. The aura of peace and harmony that is associated with those individuals fortunate enough to experience the fusion that is twinned souls is often recognised and desired by the onlooker, without any understanding of its cause or origin. The melding of the two souls concerned results in a level of joy, harmony and understanding that for them goes way beyond that of any other relationship.

Most of humanity is unable recognise a twin soul relationship, unless they have directly experienced it; whereupon the conscious view of their connection to the Cosmos will have expanded beyond all previous recognition, to create within them landscapes and vistas of potentially unlimited cosmic horizons, without boundaries.

Examples of twinned souls are extremely rare indeed.

In the event that twinned particles come together in one human being, then the effect is also very profound. The person involved appears to possess significantly greater powers of observation, co-creative capacity and understanding. They often appear to be masters within their environment with abilities that go well beyond that which is considered normal for their time. The existence of such people is even more rare than twinned souls and has had a marked effect upon the history and development of the human race. Perhaps this is the foundational nature for those who appear to achieve cosmic consciousness, as will be discussed in Chapter Three.

2.06. Gaia

Having considered the Cosmos in terms of the particulate structure of our Universe, the energy of its enlivenment and the resultant evolutionary adaptation that has resulted in the higher forms of consciousness and the soul, we will take a brief look at the development that has taken place in the adaptation of our planet Earth which has enabled life to persist and prosper.

The Gaia theory was initially proposed by British scientist Dr James Lovelock and later embraced by Professor Lynn Margulis the microbiologist. Margulis' work on the symbiotic relationship between differing bacteriological organisms, that subsequently evolved to form cells with nuclei, including all of the cells within the human body, introduced a new view of evolution that incorporated a cooperative rather than a competitive adaptive relationship. Organisms that cooperated with other organisms, symbiotically, prospered to a greater degree than those subject only to the survival of the fittest.

Her work complemented that of Lovelock who theorized that all living organisms, together with their surrounding environment, have evolved to form a single living ecosystem. This system is an adaptive one that is self-regulatory in so far as it appears to keep conditions on the planet just right for life as we know it to continue to exist.

The principle involved here is again one of cooperation, as a form of partnership, between all elements and organisms of the planet and within the environment we currently inhabit. It is a system that remains adaptive and fully integrated in that there is a significant degree of active cause and effect issuing from each and all members of the partnership to each other. That is to say that all aspects of the environment will affect all aspects of the organisms living within it, and vice versa.

The corollary to this form of cooperative interaction is that once such cooperation becomes competitive or unbalanced in favour of one of its partners, then the conditions become unstable, or the life involved becomes affected, perhaps even to the point of extinction. This has happened throughout the history of the planet and will no doubt happen again, particularly as the dominant form of life on Earth, humanity, appears to have little or no regard to the benefits of such a cooperative partnership in its interaction with the environment of its inhabitation.

In his book *The Ages of Gaia*,[7] James Lovelock seeks to set out how the conditions for life on Earth came about and became sufficiently stable for life to persist. The self-regulatory system involved is one of *homeostasis*, which may be defined as the ability of an organism to regulate its internal conditions in order to maintain health and function. By monitoring its internal conditions and responding appropriately when these conditions deviate from their optimal state, organisms may generally achieve this state of homeostasis.

The interaction between all organisms and the conditions in which they can exist brings about a stable environment that is capable of adaptation as life evolves and is indeed also interactive in the means of such evolution. For some, this grants to the planet Earth, and all upon or within it, the status of it being a single living organism and there are some that will go even further by granting such an organism the status of it being sentient, of having the ability to sense things.

For many, particularly in the scientific world, the epithet of sentience is a step too far as it implies a level of consciousness, albeit a very weak one, that cannot be demonstrated to exist. The fact that our planet reacts as though it were a single organism that may also be sentient leads us to consider the nature of consciousness, and whether it can and does exist without the need for an inherent thinking process being involved. This will be the subject of our next chapter.

So far as we are aware the evolution of life in a symbiotic partnership with planetary conditions and environment is likely to be restricted to a narrow band of planets where certain conditions exist in the first place such as to allow recognisable life to become established and evolve. That is not to say that life, in some currently unrecognised form, does not exist on planets where conditions would be inhospitable or impossible for the life of Earth. We simply do not know.

But the symbiotic self-regulatory system proposed by James Lovelock supports the notion that it may well be that the ability of an unthinking layer of consciousness, in its weakest, lowest form, fuelled by an interactive symbiosis deriving from the formatrix energy of The One Source, is the driving force behind all of adaptation and evolution.

2.07. The Story So Far

The Emerald Tablet has provided a suitable starting point towards an understanding that the Cosmos is formed of one dimension and two realms of reality, the material and subtle realms. The nature of the material realm is experienced through our five senses and explains the reality in which we spend our daily lives. The subtle realm is that which exists beyond our senses and contains the essence of perfect Ideas arising from the mediation of The One Source of All Things. These become translated into the means by which both the material and subtle realms find their expression, and which are the principles and ideals by which we seek to govern society. The interaction between the two realms takes place through the medium of consciousness and forms an ongoing, continuous process that results in evolution and development of life in the material reality.

Based upon the two-realm cosmogony that is available to our consciousness, and their constituencies, we are now able to establish a structure for the material realm. This is the particulate structure of subatomic and atomic particles that gain their mass through the absorption of the minutest subatomic particle of all, the archaeus particle. This exists in the subtle realm on a field of energy that transmits mass to the material realm and goes on to form the dark energy that powers the acceleration of our Universe. The particulate mass of the material realm gathers to form stars which become the means whereby the different material elements are created.

A form of energy, the formatrix, enlivens particles of material, and when groups of particles combine and congregate each contributes their element of consciousness until complex particulate structures evolve to the point where they become aware. Eventually sufficient conscious mass has assembled so that it is able to observe the hitherto unformed mass of the material Universe which it thus determines, and in so doing gives it form and structure. Continual grouping of complex particles and consciousness proceeds until it is able to form an identity, and eventually consciousness reaches a level where the foundations for a soul come to exist; and as evolution continues, then so do the attributes and abilities of the soul.

Chapter Three

Consciousness

I gave my consciousness to everything
in order to gain the experience of everything,
everything that was to become.

Make of consciousness what they could, or would,
they are absolutely free to do so.

Take it to where my Ideas lie waiting,
for expression.

Just as it was for me, before there was the Space for Time to pass.

Come to think of it
the thoughts of those that come before them,
give them something of it all,
if they can only develop their senses
to 'see' so much more,
beyond that which they can see.

For where are their brothers and sisters now?
Ordovicia and Devonia,
Permian, dying large for Triacea,
for Cretacea and Kaytee.

Oh Evolution, I formed thee as a paradox,
Relentless! Redoubtable! Immutable!
Yet ever changing?

So that everything becomes possible.

And my consciousness ascends.

3.00. Introduction

Consciousness even in its weakest form has become the driving force of all that exists in the material realm of reality. It is consciousness in its relationship and interaction with the subtle realm that has enabled form, by way of Ideas, to transfer from the immaterial, subtle realm of reality to the material realm which, in turn, allows time to pass and evolution to commence its journey. It is consciousness that has developed the attribute of self-awareness and has promulgated the foundations for a fundamental soul existence.

In this chapter we look more closely at consciousness and examine how it might function as a motivator of life.

3.01. The Process of Consciousness

Consciousness, or at least conscious awareness in humanity, has long been a subject for much conjecture and speculation as well as extensive research and scientific development, and in this section we will look at a model of consciousness, as a whole, that might help us to understand the way in which the Cosmos works through the interaction between the subtle and the material realms.

Many scientists, especially those in the field of neurological research, propose that consciousness arises from a process involving electrical and/or biochemical currents activating neuron patterns within the brain. Current fields of study, especially those facilitated by the imaging technology recently developed in computed tomography (CT) and positron emission tomography (PET) scanning devices, have given science a new and fast developing insight into how the brain works. Three-dimensional images of the brain condition are built up, or isotope tagged chemical reaction techniques are produced that show live brain function, that can indicate not only the pattern present in healthy brain activity, but may also determine where brain activity differs from that which is considered to be 'normal'.

Similar to the presence of a soul in each individual, where we cannot point to a single something and say 'there is the soul', science is unable to point to a particular place anywhere within the brain that houses consciousness. This appears as a function of the whole of the brain including the way it works. As we shall see, this becomes an important factor when we come to discuss the nature of reality.

It is recognised that we do not use all of our brain at our current state of evolutionary development; that is to say that we may indeed use most of it over extended periods, but at any one time we only use up to about twenty per cent of it. The way that the operation of the brain is performed and what it is that we can think has created a great debate amongst the philosophical, neurological and religious societies as to whether each can affect the other, a debate that currently shows little sign of reaching any definitive conclusion.

Consequently, many questions arise: Can the electrical and/or biochemical process determine what we think? Does what we think determine or affect the process? Is creativity merely a response to such a process? Where does intuition fit into such a model? How does such a process interpret the subjunctives, such as beauty, goodness, truth, freedom, tolerance, justice and virtue etc.? Why does consciousness react differently in individuals even when receiving the same stimulus at the same time?

Such questions as these form a philosophical and possibly neurological problem that has tested humanity for centuries, arising from the fundamental question: 'Are the mind and the brain separate entities, or are they one thing only?'

The belief in separate entities introduces us to 'dualism' of the sort proposed by René Descartes in the 17th century, whilst modern concepts of the mind and brain being one unit introduce us to a monistic, emergent property position, where a form of monism of identity arises from the view that mind and brain are the same thing, but described in different terms.

It is not the intention here to espouse either one or the other of these positions, particularly as the arguments for and against continue, with sincerely held beliefs emerging from either side of the dichotomy.

Our model proposes that both sides of the divide which defines the mind-brain problem are indeed separate but are also cohesively unified into one all-encompassing unit. This is another form of the gestalt principle seen in the nature of the Cosmos and of the soul complex.

The mind and the brain may thus be said to be one combined, cohesive unit, because each without the other is devoid of expression. In addition, each relies upon the other for a demonstration of its existence for it is only in a full engagement with each other, at all points, that the mind and brain can function to their highest degree of health and efficiency.

There is no problem with accepting that the mind and the brain form one operational processing unit; indeed it would be difficult to envisage how the mind and brain could function if this were not so. To not accept this would be to deny the purpose of our material existence, not only leaving us with no means by which we could express ourselves, but indeed, how the subtle realm is able to find its means of expression.

But it is far less certain that those same biological, electrochemical reactions are capable of developing to form the nature of what it is that we think.

It falls to each one of us to individually decide for ourselves whether or not we believe that biological electrochemical reactions can determine what it is that we think. For the materialist, those that believe that material is all that exists, then the likelihood is that the substance of the brain and its biological function are all that is needed to produce what our thoughts are, together with their content.

Modern science can demonstrate that the brain processes various stimuli, from whatever source they arise, interior and exterior. Such a process is carried out within the brain's material substance, including the responses that arise from various materials interacting with each other to form biological, electro-chemical reactions, which are the natural outcome of such a process.

But to many of those who experience intuitive revelation, innovative creativity or mystical recognition of objectivity in their lives, the proposal that the biological process within the brain is responsible for the content of all that we think and for our total emotional output is an explanation of consciousness that seems to be, to say the least, inadequate. This being so, then we must consider that our mind/consciousness, that immaterial element of our constitution, is a separate element of our being, one that uses the material substance and processing ability of the brain as a tool for its means of expression.

This hypothesis proceeds in accord with the way consciousness has arisen through the signature of its imprint within all particles that come to exist within the material realm. Consciousness grows as the complexity of particle structure grows, yet the two are both separate and inseparable.

These separate elements are affected by, but also affect, the operation and the condition of the material substance of the brain. So we cannot dismiss as unimportant a process by which our brains receive data and which then facilitates the generation of thought and creativity, of intuition and interpretation etc. The relationship between the mind and the brain becomes clearer if we consider that the process in our material brains may facilitate the 'how' of our thought, at least in part, but not the 'what' it is that we think.

We should consider the biological electrochemical process as forming a carrier wave for the transport of our thoughts, but the objective content of those thoughts arises from our immaterial consciousness, using the mind to inject, or load, such objective content on to the carrier wave.

Thus, the 'how' of our thoughts arises from the material aspect of our brains, but the 'what' that we think arises from our immaterial consciousness.

Now we see the gestalt emerging. The mind and the brain are indeed one unified element of our biology, but with discrete elements within. Each element is a separate part of our identity and each is dependant on the other for its means of operation. Together they make up a whole. If separated and unconnected the mind would have no means of expression and the brain would be the means whereby only basic motor type functions were possible, without any sense of objectivity, direction or the ability to adapt and evolve.

A gestalt is the perfect way to describe the relationship of the mind and the brain: together they are a potent form, and if in isolated separation they are each impotent.

Consciousness may be the means by which the objectivity of our thoughts is created but it is also the means whereby the subtle realm is able to interact with the material realm. Consequently, the model of consciousness required goes very much further than considerations of human consciousness and thought, to become one that will incorporate a much wider field, perhaps infinitely so, to that which we are accustomed to consider.

So we now turn to consider one possible model of the nature of consciousness, of conscious awareness, and the form it might take that will not only satisfy our daily experience of awareness and being, but will also encompass and enable the transmission and establishment of the subtle Ideas that form other species of animals, of flora and fauna together with all vegetable and mineral existence.

3.02. Consciousness – One Possible Model

As a starting point for this model of consciousness we will look at an adaptation of the proposals of Pierre Teilhard de Chardin and his principles of cosmic unity.

Teilhard proposed that every particle of matter that has come into existence since the original creation event, which we may now see exemplified within the Big Bang theory, or the 'Brane' clatter hypothesis, contains a characteristic of its creator, The One Source of All Things.

This characteristic is an element of the energy of The One Source that is impressed as part of each and every particle created. Consequently, as groupings of particles of matter become ever more complex and numerous, as they gather their form, they combine to become an ever more homogeneous unit. This unit then emerges to exhibit ever-increasing, higher levels and quality of consciousness that subsequently come to order the material in which the symbiotic and gestaltic relationship is housed.

In Chapter One we looked at the characteristics required for Ideas to exist in the subtle realm and one of those characteristics involved the inability for such an Idea to change. The genus of all lifeforms themselves forms an important layer in the constituency of the subtle realm and the consciousness that inhabits all aspects of our material reality, including all lifeforms, does not change its nature and character. Therefore we can see that all lifeforms which are founded in an Idea from the subtle realm are not compromised by any change to the nature of consciousness whilst within that realm.

In Chapter Two, in dealing with the structure of the Universe, we have proposed that each particle in existence, from the smallest subatomic particle known, bear the hallmark or imprint of its maker, following which the singular monadic nature of particulate matter has taken on a dual nature, that of matter plus the imprint of creative energy, setting all in motion.

Consequently, all of this taken together becomes capable of 'creative union' with other matter, which would otherwise be without motion at subatomic levels, rendering it unchanging and undeveloped. This creative union becomes the potential for the development of the life of our planet through the vitality and elegant beauty of its inherent creative force.

Thus every particle of matter that exists, or has ever existed, is imbued with an imprint of the creative energy from The One Source and, as particles combine and grow to form evermore complex structures, then so does the creative energy within, and the result is ever-increasing layers, and levels, of consciousness.

In this way it may be seen that, once groups of several particles combine to form a structure or complex, then consciousness, in a basic, fundamental form, comes into being. Hence, and derived from Teilhard de Chardin's proposals, there arises a law of complexity where as the structure of all things become ever more numerate and complex in particle numbers so the layers and the levels of consciousness also become ever greater.

Consciousness, or awareness, thus arises from the imbuing of particle matter with a sort of echo of the creative energy of its creation by The One Source. Necessarily we might think of the layer of consciousness exhibited by a complex of only a few particles of matter as being very weak in its strength, but we must beware of thinking along these lines. The strength of the energy present in each particle is the same as in any other, and is equally capable of interaction with the subtle realm of Ideas. If this were not so then the process of evolution and development would not have been able to commence from its earliest, most simple beginnings, in molecules or single cells, to become subsequently sustainable.

A word must be said concerning the relationship of consciousness to sentience. Sentience in all lifeforms involves the ability to feel and, in particular, the ability to suffer pain.

However, sentience does not require consciousness for its expression, even though consciousness, as we are defining it, is present in all matter. Sentience is a function of the process of neuron pattern activity within a brain and, whilst the experience of suffering and pain may eventually come to affect the evolutionary process of natural selection, consciousness does not depend on sentience for its operation. Lifeforms that are lower on the scale of consciousness, that have not developed the brain capacity, nervous systems or sensitivity, may not have the ability to feel or suffer and may thus not be regarded as sentient.

The interaction between a form of consciousness in particle matter and the Ideas within the subtle realm is a process that is natural, and automatic. By this we mean that the interaction is involuntary and is one that happens on all levels and is one that is part of an inbuilt process of creation, evolution and survival.

The model we are proposing here requires us to accept that consciousness can and does exist without the need for or presence of thought, or a thinking process. Consequently, basic elements – rocks, plants and lower, simple lifeforms – might be said to be conscious entities, however weak, along with the generally accepted demonstration of consciousness exhibited by the higher animal lifeforms, particularly in humanity.

Inevitably we must once again change our notion of something we nearly always take for granted. We must enlarge our concept and thinking, this time of the nature of consciousness itself, from something that only involves a process of thought or awareness of self, to something much, much wider, to include all animal, vegetable or mineral matter, of whatever complexity, even though apparently devoid of sentience or a thought process.

For ease of understanding and further reference we will call that layer of consciousness that does not involve perceived thought or the ability for sentient awareness of self as potential or p-consciousness.

Note should be taken that we refer to 'layers' of consciousness in a further effort to separate what we come to think of as potential or p-consciousness, from normal or n-consciousness (as we currently perceive it) and 'neo-consciousness', or h-consciousness, being a new or higher layer of consciousness that will be further discussed when we deal with the outcome of evolution in Chapter Four. Within each layer of consciousness there lie several levels, some of which we will discuss later in this chapter. As an introduction to the levels of consciousness that we as human beings experience in our everyday n-conscious layer we will set the scene by way of the schema laid out by Robert de Ropp.

In his book *The Master Game*,[8] Robert S. de Ropp sets out his vision of how various levels of consciousness are experienced by humanity, using 'locked rooms' as a metaphor for the differing levels, and their attributes. He describes five separate rooms which humankind is generally unaware even exist. Only occasionally do we sense their existence and even then only rarely do we make any attempt to look into a room that may contain treasure of an advanced or higher level. Briefly de Ropp proposes that humanity inhabits the five rooms or levels of consciousness as follows:

Room 1. Deep sleep without dreams.
Room 2. Sleep with dreams.
Room 3. Waking sleep (identification).
Room 4. Self-transcendence (self-remembering).
Room 5. Objective consciousness (cosmic consciousness).

In the first room we are unaware of anything that our brain undertakes; here are our subconscious instinctive reactions that operate to preserve life essential to our continued well-being and health. It is important that we spend some time in room one in order that our batteries can be recharged.

The second room is entered naturally from within the first because it would be unhealthy to remain entirely within the dreamless state continuously whilst sleeping. This state is accompanied or perhaps even facilitated by rapid eye movements (REM) and the resultant dreams may be a means whereby symbolically we are able to sort out and clarify our subconscious psychological state.

Necessarily a healthy human being will spend a considerable portion of their lives in rooms one and two.

Before moving on to reflect on the third room of consciousness, a word should be said concerning the occurrence of dreams and their relationship to the levels of consciousness under discussion.

Sleep is a dynamic process that is essential to the well-being of each human individual. Dreaming may occur during any part of our sleep cycle but by far and away the most lucid dreams occur during that part of our sleep phase where rapid eye movement or REM sleep takes place.

There is no general agreement that dreams serve any purpose at all, but many who specialise in the science of sleep believe that dreams act as an operational function that brings some degree of order to the data impinging upon the brain whilst we are in the state of being awake. The process involved is one where signals from an area of the brain call 'the pons' are transmitted to the thalamus and thence to the area of the brain where learning and organisation are facilitated, an area called the cerebral cortex. Coincidentally, the pons also transmits signals that disable muscle function by producing a temporary form of paralysis, so that whilst sleeping it is difficult to perform physical acts involving movement.

So REM sleep serves to allow stimulation of that area of the brain where learning is processed and dreams, being predominantly a function that takes place during REM sleep, may be one method whereby some sense of order is brought to the data that has hitherto impacted upon the brain.

Once we have entered into the nature of sleep consciousness found in room two of de Ropp's schema, and whilst experiencing REM sleep, we are able to put into order the information gained whilst 'awake' at the third level found in room three. We will come to see that at the third level of consciousness we automatically consider ourselves to be awake, whereas what we are actually experiencing is a state that might be described as one of waking sleep. But the stimuli that come to us, whilst there, are treated as a mode of learning through processes that sometimes take place when experiencing level two consciousness during REM sleep patterns.

That is to say that the nature of the dreams experienced during a period of dreaming sleep, whilst in the second room of consciousness, sometimes results in learning arising when we are 'awake', during time spent in room three. This is a process that enhances the range of the levels of conscious awareness that are available to us, to the extent that fourth level consciousness, found in room four, although normally hidden to us in our current state of evolutionary development, impinges on our consciousness as a recognisable feature, with access thereto developing as a possibility.

The possibility also exists that the data entering our brains from external stimuli have more than one level of meaning. It may well be that it is through the process of dreaming that the data is organised with learning objectives accomplished. But also, it is also possible that any esoteric, spiritual and mystical significance, inherent within the data, provoking alternative meanings that originate from the subtle nature of the relevant Idea, are processed through the dream function.

Dreams then take on a dual role, partly of facilitating organisation and learning, whilst simultaneously aiding and interpreting deeper meanings of external stimuli, which may then become the esoteric, spiritual and mystical foundation for the nature of intuition and innovative creative knowledge.

The condition of waking sleep that characterises our inhabitation of room three, the third level of consciousness, is difficult to describe because during such inhabitation we are apt to believe that we are fully conscious and fully aware of our self-being. If challenged on this, we deny that it is not so. In such a condition we are wrapped up in whatever we are doing at any one time and tend to distort our reality to the point whereby we come to believe that we are generally happy with our condition. This is partly but significantly because we are surrounded by individuals in a similar state to ourselves, and consequently are able to fool ourselves into a state of contentment through familiarity.

When inhabiting room three most of us firmly believe that we are masters of ourselves and know where we are heading. But nothing can be further from the truth. We continually lose our way in any stray impression that we encounter and consequently have little or no control over our actions.

Many if not the significant majority of us spend the whole time that we are not in rooms one and two within room three, confined or restricted by a misplaced belief in being fully conscious, without ever knowing or understanding that any alternative is even possible. It may well be the case that most of us are happy to exist only at the third level of consciousness, not only by being unaware that other levels exist, but by failing to acknowledge that to enter a higher level requires very considerable effort and concentration.

Room four, the fourth level of conscious awareness for de Ropp, is a paradox in that it only exists for those that have experienced it; otherwise one may never know of its existence. Access to room four involves the transcendence of the self, as *'a going above and beyond selfhood [...] to become relatively egoless'.*[9] This transcendent condition is often characterised by the feeling that one can 'taste eternity' or 'glimpse the meaning of infinity'. In room four, the complete range of human characteristics come into play in order to appreciate the complete extent of the Cosmic horizons found therein.

Neither reason and logic, nor spirituality and mysticism, by themselves, are sufficient to accomplish entry into room four. Every attribute of humanity is required if a complete under-standing of the Cosmos is to be realised; the absence of any one facet of our being will limit or restrict the experience to one of fruitless endeavour.

Once experienced, however, an individual will seek out the key that unlocks the door to room four by any means at his or her disposal. This is because it is in this condition that they first experience a state of complete awakeness, and can know for certain they are their own master and where they are heading; what they are doing and why. The diminution of the ego, or rather the comparative expansion of the self/identity, experienced as the oracular coming to know yourself from the inside, enables a recognition of the expansion of Cosmic horizons that are a characteristic of room four.

Furthermore, an encounter and experience of fourth level consciousness is characterised by the understanding that the nature of time has changed from a flow or passage to one where time ceases to exist as we normally experience it. Every event that is perceived, the acquisition of any knowledge gained, all such experience appears to occur in an instant and confirms a closer encounter with the constituency of the subtle realm and conse-quently to the state of perfection, which is our destiny.

Such an encounter and experience is accompanied by the recognition of the need to set aside normal reason and logic, not to leave them behind or shut them out, but rather to 'position' them so as to approach the Cosmos from a different direction.

This is in order to understand the nature of spaces within spaces, which enclose all other spaces, locations etc. We must learn to see past normal reason and logic whilst at the same time retaining them in order that we may make the necessary interpretations that are capable of introducing such an approach into our own personal reality.

The setting aside of normal reason and logic is an essential element in the quest to understand enhanced consciousness, to allow the founding characteristics of intuition and Hermetic interpretation to expand, so that they may become a cognitive force in reality that will assist us in finding the key that will unlock the door into level four consciousness.

The search for the key to this room is most difficult and requires considerable time and effort. Most individuals are not prepared to make the effort and those that do will nearly always need some help from someone who is an adept to accomplish the task.

It is fair to say that most who do discover the key to room four do not spend extended periods of time within it, although some of the great men of history may have done so. Others are only able to look within, from outside. This is because to inhabit the fourth room continuously, for prolonged periods without recourse to spending time in rooms one and two, in our present state of evolutionary development, is generally injurious to our psychiatric well-being.

So far as exposure to room five is concerned, so few have experienced the occasional flash of revelation that is characterised by de Ropp's fifth level of consciousness. Humankind generally is not yet equipped to spend any amount of time there. However, a mere glimpse into this level of consciousness may be capable of the transmission of vast amounts of information, knowledge and direction in seemingly no time at all.

The levels of ecstasy experienced by very few individuals has resulted in some remarkable works, as is evidenced in RM Bucke's book *Cosmic Consciousness*.[10]

Bucke (1837–1902), who was President of the Psychological Section of the British Medical Association from 1888, lists a total of fourteen men who, between about 560 BCE and 1900 CE entered into a state he described as 'Cosmic Consciousness'. He also lists a further 36 people who achieved a partial state.

Although he comments that his lists may not be exclusive, in that others may well exist whose work and legacy has been lost, Bucke proposes that the incidence of Cosmic Consciousness is increasing with time, as evolution has the effect of raising the consciousness of humanity in a state of ascendancy.

Bucke's list of fourteen men who achieved the elevated state of consciousness is as follows:

Gautama the Buddha
Jesus the Christ
Paul
Plotinus
Mohammed
Dante
Bartolomé Las Casas
John Yepes
Francis Bacon
Jacob Behemen
William Blake
Honoré de Balzac
Walt Whitman
Edward Carpenter

Of the 36 aspirants to partial cosmic consciousness, fourteen are listed by initials only, presumably because they were alive at the time the book was first published and we will therefore not comment on any on this list.

It is not proposed here that we look in any detail at the lists offered by Bucke but we should note that his list of aspirants might be said to have been selected by him only to support the point he was making. Nevertheless, it is not relevant to our purposes to wish to deny any on Bucke's list their right to be there, or to give any particular measure of support to any one member thereon. Neither is it necessary for us to wish to add further members, as each of us could, no doubt, produce a different list from any of our fellows.

A glance at the list of fourteen confirms that all of Bucke's aspirants are male, there being no females listed. Most are associated with organised religion or have a strong religious tendency, although not all. Some are poets and authors although it may be said that the words of all on the list allude to a strong moral code of ethics. Some were social reformers although it may, once again, be said that all on the list may have been motivated by social reform. All on the list were philosophers with particular views on life and how it should be conducted, and all had a significant impact on society, both in their own time and since. All were motivated by a desire to improve the condition of humanity through a measure of what has been called 'spirituality'.

Bucke tells us that all had experienced spiritual illuminations of one sort or another, in which they gained significant measures of knowledge and understanding of the Cosmos. From that we can identify a means of interaction, through a higher layer or level of consciousness, with another realm of reality, one which we have proposed as being that of the subtle realm.

From this catalogue we may deduce that all gained their expanded insights and directions through a transcendent inter-action using enhanced levels of consciousness, what de Ropp describes as the fourth or even fifth rooms of consciousness.

De Ropp describes the five levels of consciousness, or conscious awareness, as those currently available to humanity, and, as we enlarge our view of consciousness as a whole, we will seek to understand how his proposals relate to our model under consideration. But before that, a word must be said in respect to human consciousness and how securely its condition is fixed.

Normal layers and levels of consciousness in human beings with healthy brains is in the process of being examined and defined by scientists, and this research is exposing what are labelled as 'abnormal' conditions that may be experienced by some. Some abnormal conditions such as those found in the savant prodigy population will be discussed later when we come to consider the nature of thought and perceived reality; but there are many thousands of other individuals whose abnormal conscious abilities are seriously affected through various means.

Accidental trauma, oxygen deprivation and viral infection of the brain are all means whereby an individual's consciousness may be lost or severely affected, in some cases to the point where to all intents and purposes their level of consciousness has been changed to the point where it might be said to be of a minimal existence. To varying degrees of extent, motor functions may also be lost, as may be the ability to speak or communicate. The ability to function as a human being at all may have been seriously affected. A vegetative state may come to exist where consciousness appears to be absent, or rather is not capable of being measured.

Yet, in some cases, a minimal level of consciousness may be detected, partly through the sensitivity of new technological techniques, but also through the response of close family members or friends who have a natural inbuilt ability to recognise such levels of consciousness, in their kin, without the aid of technology.

Although such changes in consciousness generally occur through some means of causation, either during or after birth, it does appear that levels of consciousness, after birth, are not securely fixed. Levels of consciousness may be altered, sometimes significantly, by various means or causes that are 'applied' during a lifetime. By extrapolation, we can see that consciousness, by not being a fixed condition, is capable of producing what has been described as abnormal conditions; conditions that testify to the existence of a non-normal reality.

3.03. Layers and Levels of Consciousness

Having introduced a greatly expanded concept of consciousness, from a pre-sentient state of potentiality to significantly enhanced, higher levels, we will now consider the three layers we are proposing. The selection of just three layers and the composition of each are, however, somewhat arbitrary and readers should come to their own conclusions as to what to include, or exclude, from each layer and where any demarcation boundaries might exist.

We have sought to separate the layers of consciousness into the most fundamental, potential layer that perhaps appears to be the weakest, then the normal layer of our everyday experience, and finally, an enhanced layer that operates at a level transcendent to our everyday experience. However, it must be emphasised that consciousness, whilst existing in whatever layer it occupies, is just as valuable as that residing in any other layer, because every particle in existence bears equally the imprint of the conscious form involved in its creation. It is simply the extent and complexity of its particulate structure, involving the archaeus particle and the formatrix energy within, that will determine the amount and the quality of the consciousness imbued within it.

Furthermore, our evolutionary journey to our present day form has involved an experience of all layers and levels of consciousness up to and including our present state. We must bear in mind that the extent of the formatrix energy which comes to inhabit all material, giving it its vitality and enlivened life force, will be determined by the extent and complexity of its particulate structure.

It follows that simple structures of particle matter containing fewer, less complex particle formations will exhibit smaller amounts of a conscious ability, such that, in the majority of life on our planet, consciousness as we normally accept the term may not be detectable. We cannot say that minerals or material elements etc. exhibit consciousness in any form at all, especially that of a thought process or even natural instinct. However, our model of the Cosmos proposes that consciousness in pre-sentient lifeforms together with minerals etc. does indeed exist, but operates at such a basic level that it appears to be so weak as to be undetectable, at least in the present development of scientific instrumentation.

We have also said that the interaction between the material realm of particle matter, no matter how weak the consciousness, is an involuntary and automatic natural process that even the highest of lifeforms on our planet are unaware of performing.

Perhaps a suitable analogy in today's world might be to think of the relationship between consciousness, at any layer or level, to the Ideas in the subtle realm as one existing as an 'open telephone line', or of remaining constantly 'online' while being completely unaware that telephones or computers are possible or even that electricity can exist.

The possibility of such scientific and technological phenomena has always existed, but humanity has hitherto been ignorant of its existence, pending its discovery or 'uncovering' by recently evolved levels of consciousness, in interaction with the Ideas present within the subtle realm at a time appropriate to the stage of human development.

3.03.01. The Potential Conscious Layer (P-Consciousness)

The p-conscious layer forms the lowest, most fundamental layer of consciousness in the material realm, but is one that can interact naturally with the Ideas of the subtle realm without any conscious effort being required. We will see that such an automatic, natural process will be the same for n- and h-consciousness, although, also as we shall see, the latter may be capable of a more active direction.

What then are the attributes of materials and lifeforms that comprise the potential layer of consciousness?

In general the attributes of the members of this layer may be described as those having no conscious thinking process: they exhibit a pre-sentient condition in that they are not self-aware, are not capable of experiencing feelings and have not developed or evolved a central nervous system. Generally speaking, regarding individual members of any species, or any of those within the classification of mineral and vegetable – those that have not developed the capacity to enable post-sentient characteristics to evolve – then consciousness is present, but remains in a dormant state that is incapable of detection or expression. This will include all minerals, all flora and fauna together with the lower lifeforms, including most insects.

The lowest levels of consciousness that exist within this layer might be said to exhibit a conscious ability that is inert in the sense that it is chemically inactive with only the motion of its formatrix energy vitality, bestowed within its atomic nuclear construction, inherent within it. Levels develop within this layer in the form of simple lifeforms and single cell structures that are not inert chemically and are capable of restricted motion. Such organisms may exhibit simple forms of reproduction, seeding, division etc. but this is not brought about by any thought-conscious ability, but rather through the 'programme' transmitted within their genetic composition.

The highest level within this layer of consciousness will be found in lifeforms that demonstrate 'natural instinct' as an operational means of survival. This develops to include many plant forms that seed themselves into a developing form that is suited to their changing environment. Birds migrate in constant patterns over decades or centuries, some returning to the same nests each year; salmon return at the end of their life cycle to spawn in the place of their own conception.

There are numerous further examples that could be quoted but this description of content, although extremely brief to the point of near destitution, is intended only to convey a flavour of the nature of this lowest layer of consciousness and the numerous levels it might contain.

3.03.02. The Normal Layer of Consciousness (N-Consciousness)

The next layer of consciousness is the one that we are familiar with and is the one that forms the basis of our daily lives. Amongst current definitions of consciousness according to the *Oxford English Dictionary* are:

> *the faculty or capacity from which awareness of thought, feeling, and volition and of the external world arises; and the exercise of this faculty.*

In psychology also:

> *the aspect of the mind made up of operations, which are known to the subject.*

Such definitions require a state of being awake and aware of one's surroundings, of experiencing awareness or perception, or of it being the totality of one's thoughts and feelings. As a definition this is perfectly acceptable, so far as it goes, because it sets out what is considered to be the core of consciousness as currently determined by neurological science. As we have already said, our model of the Cosmos and of consciousness requires a much wider perspective than that available through these rather narrow definitions, to one that grants to those lower animal lifeforms a level of consciousness that is undetectable and does not, so far as we are aware, involve thought.

The n-consciousness layer takes on from wherever the p-conscious layer leaves off. However, there is no sharply defined boundary between the layers of consciousness and some lifeforms may find themselves, on occasions, occupying a zone that encompasses both layers. Additionally any consciousness said to belong to the n-consciousness layer brings with it, through its genetic history and its DNA, all that it has acquired through evolution and development from any lower layer and level.

As we will see in Chapter Four, evolution and development of species has been ongoing since the planet Earth cooled sufficiently for it to start to produce and sustain life, and all that has been experienced since then forms the basis or backdrop to our current condition and state of development. We do not swap one set of experiences or conditions for another once a species evolves sufficiently for it to belong to a higher layer of consciousness. Rather we use all of those experiences gained along our particular line of evolution, in our efforts to survive and flourish at a higher level or state of consciousness. This will be seen particularly when we discuss the topic of death in Chapter Four.

So what then are the attributes of materials and life that form the normal layer of consciousness? In general the minimal attribute that allows a species to be regarded as a member of this layer is the ability to demonstrate a basic level of awareness of the self. The boundary between the upper levels of the lower layer, that of natural instinctive survival traits, and the lowest level of n-consciousness are very blurred and very difficult to differentiate.

This is because instinctive behaviour is often mistaken or taken to be evidence of self-awareness. An example of this may be found where many animals exhibit an instinctive need to migrate seasonally, may hibernate instinctively when the right conditions prevail, may 'know' instinctively where to find food, or where and when to mate; and the range of such behaviour is wide enough to include those lifeforms that may be said to be self-aware and those that are not. Not only is such behaviour wide enough to include lifeforms that might inhabit the zone linking both layers of consciousness, but necessarily the boundary between the two layers must be sufficiently forgiving to accommodate such a wide behavioural pattern.

The lowest level of consciousness in this layer might therefore be said to be associated with those possessing a well-defined instinctive behaviour, coupled with awareness of self, within their surroundings. Awareness of self and surroundings is often demonstrated by the ability to express communication with fellow members of the species. This will apply to a wide range of species. Some of the higher aquatic species such as whales and dolphins etc. are able to express a signalling system tantamount to language. Similarly some bird species like parrots and birds of prey and some insect species such as bees and ants are able to communicate geographical resource and need to their fellows, as are some rodents such as beavers. These forms of awareness of self and surroundings differentiate them from those species whose members exhibit only instinctive patterns of behaviour.

Developing from the lowest level of consciousness within this layer, we might find species members who are capable not only of communication between themselves, but also a capability of species preservation and the use of tools or implements. We are now approaching, if not within, the species containing the family known as hominoidea, the apes and ourselves, the human subspecies, currently in the form of Homo sapiens. Within this family there are several subspecies forming the great and lesser apes, and the levels of consciousness available to each subspecies will vary according to their state of evolutionary development and the current complexity of their particulate structure, especially where the brain is concerned.

Notwithstanding this, we must remember that all subspecies of the hominoidea super family have the same ancestral source. Indeed if we go back far enough historically, then we can see that all life stems from the same ancestral source. This is 'the common universal ancestor' arising from The One Source of All Things described in Chapter One.

It is tempting to separate the human race from the rest of the hominoideal ape super familial species because of our abilities and evolutionary development, and because of our attributes that persuade us to believe we are the most advanced lifeform currently extant on our planet. This temptation is one to which we will succumb as we will be discussing human concepts of development, but we must not forget that, even today, some members of human descent and ascent are capable of demonstrating 'throw back' racial characteristics through unexpected genetic transference.

Our quest for perfection and our racial purity is not sufficiently distinct, secure or complete as to allow us to forget our ancestral roots and our interrelationship to other species.

In addition, when considering the developed consciousness currently exhibited by human beings, we must recognise that the vehicle for such advanced consciousness, the brain, provides us with a range of activities that do not require thought for their proactivity but are essential to the very means of living. We will discuss these activities when we consider the nature of thought, but for now we will recognise such brain activities as belonging to a grouping labelled under a heading of the subconscious. This important grouping remains part of the n-layer of consciousness currently under discussion.

We are now able to assimilate the nature of consciousness that is available to humanity, which has been described previously using Robert de Ropp's metaphoric descriptions of the five locked rooms. We should, however, recognise that de Ropp's five levels of consciousness are spread out, perhaps as sub-levels, with levels one to three belonging within the n-consciousness layer and with his levels four and five perhaps belonging within the neo-conscious h-layer, or, at the least, bridging the boundary between these two layers. This latter condition would grant to those adepts who, for the most part, occupy de Ropp's rooms one–three the facility to enter briefly or at least look into room four. We must remember that no definite or absolute demarcation exists that defines the boundary between subsequent layers, particularly that which qualifies for admission to the neo-conscious layer that we will now discuss.

3.03.03. Neo-Consciousness (H-Consciousness)

The third and highest layer of consciousness in the model proposed we have called 'neo-consciousness' (higher or h-consciousness), again to separate it from the consciousness that we consider to be the norm in today's terminology.

H-consciousness is demonstrated by means of enhancing our current level from within the second, middle layer, to become something more, something able to perceive a greatly expanded horizon in all fields of human endeavour. Such an enhancement will be characterised by the knowledge that the adept is actually taking part in the development of the Cosmos. Initially this may manifest as a greater clarity and involvement in art, politics, religion, science and technology etc., but will culminate in a depth of knowledge, an experience of a greater understanding, feeling and certainty of Cosmic reality, in all its manifestations.

The ability to enter into a higher level of consciousness, in order to experience the ecstasy found in room four and the state of perfection to be glimpsed in room five, is an feature of h-consciousness.

We are restricting the ability of experiencing h-consciousness to those from within the layer of normal consciousness, in particular to that of humanity, because at present we are unable to detect within any other species the presence of a thought-based normal consciousness to a sufficiently high level to enable higher states of consciousness to become a reality. We should not close our minds, however, to the possibility that other lifeforms on planet Earth have, or have had, the ability to enter such alternative states of consciousness, perhaps in a way that is automatic or involuntary in the same way that all of consciousness interacts with the subtle realm of Ideas.

The attributes for membership of the h-conscious layer of consciousness, so far as our current state of evolutionary development is concerned, allow us to determine and centre initially upon an ability mentally to 'see' our reality in a way that is so clear, with such clarity, that the fullness of its truth becomes so very apparent and obvious in a way hitherto not available to us.

Many experts in whatever field of study may feel or purport to understand clearly the means by which the fruits of their discipline fully operate, but this is not what is meant by 'seeing' the complete reality.

The language necessary to describe what is meant barely exists at all because the comprehension of such 'seeing' is so difficult to translate. But in general the meaning may be described as one where the effect of a thought, on reality as a whole, in all of its interrelated aspects and ramifications, is totally or completely apparent from the moment the thought has come into the experience of our reality. Many people have described such a process as one of revelation due to the impacted knowledge gained being beyond their 'normal' comprehension.

The ability to position standard models of reason, so as to 'see' past normal reality; the recognition that the nature of time passing is not an unchangeable constant, but is subject to perceived variability; the ability to 'see' that which is not immediately apparent or does not directly engage our natural senses – all of these become of significant benefit when working at level four consciousness, within the h-consciousness layer. They enable the encounter and experience of the greater, enriched reality that lies beyond the standard model of the Cosmos to be perceived and interpreted from a much wider Cosmic perspective.

Examples of h-conscious thought, probably in a temporarily enhanced state of mind, are numerous throughout modern history and are demonstrated by thinkers becoming aware of breaking new ground in their field of activity without being aware of how they have arrived at their conclusions. As we have seen, Richard M. Bucke described some of these examples in his book *Cosmic Consciousness*.

H-consciousness arises from within the upper level of the layer of normal consciousness, sometimes through altered states of consciousness, an area we will move on to discuss after looking at the nature of thought, but which also manifests itself through the process of evolution that we will discuss in Chapter Four.

3.04. Thought

Thought is the tool of consciousness and is the means whereby we come to form beliefs and are able to express the process of perception from within our brains. It is also how we can measure both our level of consciousness and our awareness of self. After all, awareness of the inner self, as opposed to awareness within our external surroundings, may be described as a form of introspection, of thought turning in on itself to think about that which has been thought.

We generally take thought or thinking for granted; indeed, thought is that which grants to those animals that exhibit the higher level of consciousness within the n-layer a natural mechanism which enables us to perceive self-awareness, reason and identity. Simply put, it is that which enables perception.

We have seen that how we think is the result of a process within the brain that provides a 'carrier stream' which allows what we think to find its form of expression. The combined result allows thought to be conditioned and produced. But, given that the content of thoughts differs from person to person, even when the same external stimuli engage the senses at the same time and given that the process within different brains is generally similar, the question arises: 'What is thought?' Do thoughts have an existence of their own? Do thoughts go anywhere once they have been thought? These questions and many more of a similar nature only arise because we can think, and they have taxed our ingenuity over thousands of years.

Given the nature of the Cosmos proposed in the model under discussion, consciousness came into existence with the first emissions of archaeus particles following the big bang event, whereupon the interactive relationship with the constituency of the subtle realm commenced. Once the genus of lifeforms began to be expressed, levels of consciousness rose until natural instinct, as a beneficial trait, became a survival feature for some species.

It is easy to surmise that Homo sapiens have been able to think from the first moment of racial existence, but does evidence support this surmise? As we have already said, if we go back in history far enough then we will find that all animal forms arise from a common genetic ancestry which subsequently evolved through natural selection and cooperative symbiosis. Consequently, differentiation and specialisation occurred and the evolution of an immense variety of species took place.

In parallel with this evolutionary growth, there arose in those animals that developed a larger brain capacity, a process that enabled thought to be produced. Emerging from a combination of natural instinct and a larger brain processing ability, some animals exhibited a further beneficial survival trait, that of the use of the brain process to transcribe natural instinct into objective thought content. The process of natural selection ensured that these animals reproduced in greater numbers, and so the ability to generate different objectives in thought grew and was enhanced as the rate of survival increased.

It is easy to understand that such natural evolutionary developments could occur from a form of common genetic ancestry because the genetic composition of all life is remarkably similar, even today after millennia of evolutionary development and specialisation. Each of our human cells comprises approximately 23,000 genes, and the commonality of the genes in each human living entity exhibits a close correspondence to other lifeforms. The existence of a universal common ancestry from which all lifeforms originate results in there being a significant common genetic content amongst all lifeforms.

The more complex and 'closer' the lifeforms are to our natural evolutionary cousins, the significantly greater is the extent of the common gene structure, so that our nearest animal relative, the chimpanzee, is genetically similar to humanity to a degree that nearly ninety-nine per cent of genes are common to both species.

Evolutionary geneticist, Andrew G. Clark, Cornell professor of molecular biology and genetics said that:

Human and chimpanzee sequences are so similar [...] but we found hundreds of genes showing a pattern of sequence change consistent with adaptive evolution occurring in human ancestors.

This adaptive evolution took place during the 6 million years since the emergence of our common primate ancestors, and has resulted in divergence between various members of the hominoideal ape super familial species. The adapted genes are those involved in the sense of smell, in digestion, of long-bone growth, in hairiness, in hearing, and, most importantly, the developing ability initially to process thought and, subsequently, the capacity to think objectively.

Bearing in mind the extent of the common genetic make-up with other species, we may deduce that the development, in us, of the ability to think objectively is of prime importance in the success of our survival and flourishment resulting in our dominion over other species.

It is interesting to speculate that it was the ability to process thought and then to create objective content, at a sufficiently advanced level, which gave humanity the impetus to spread out, from its single genetic source, maternal origin, in the Rift Valley of Africa, to eventually populate the Earth with peoples of higher levels of consciousness.

Thought then arises, having evolved from a high degree of natural instinct, as an emergent beneficial trait that allowed the adaptive nature of our genetic composition and structure, the means of its survival, through a natural, selective, enabling process within the evolving brain. This became the vehicle whereby the process of thought initially took on the role of replicating natural instinct, which subsequently allowed the objective content of thought to develop and become capable of being stored, and interconnected, as a further beneficial trait.

Whilst we may understand that the basic process of thought may have assumed the role of highly developed natural instinct, it is also important to recognise that the brain is used for things other than enabling the thought process. It is also used, simultaneously, to activate normal physical activity such as breathing and heartbeat together with sensory capability etc., whilst also monitoring physical conditions and responses to situations that require motor functions and the alleviation of distress to the physicality of our bodies. It is the brain that controls these reactions to life's stimuli, through the process within the brain that interprets messages sent from all parts of the human body, in a subconscious, naturally instinctive way that does not require an objective thinking process for its motivation.

So the brain has evolved, in humanity, to enable a process

whereby thought can arise alongside other survival traits. The process within the brain can now be demonstrated to use a network of billions of neurons, interacting in trillions of combinations, that react to various stimuli, usually arising from the environment that the brain finds itself inhabiting. These stimuli and the consequent neuron patterns are then processed to support physical reactions within the human body, or to produce patterns that enable thoughts to arise which may vary in substance, objectivity and interpretation for each individual.

In this way humanity has been able to learn, from its environment, the means of survival as a race. However, humanity also affects the environment that it inhabits so that the evolution and adaptation of both are intertwined in a circular, interdependent and even paradoxical way.

So far, so good, but does this explain satisfactorily the creativity, intuition or subjective thinking that elevates humanity beyond the necessity of developing survival traits, to one of sensitivity and creativity in other areas of the arts, the sciences and technology etc.? We now have to consider the development and the nature of objective thought.

Although emerging as a separate species some 200,000 years ago, there is little evidence of creative, spiritual or mystical thought affecting the driving force in hominins, beyond that of the need to survive. Music, the arts and spirituality, often in the form of mysticism, do not feature as a factor of developing human character until about 50,000 years ago.

We are able to see that a semi-autonomous form of thinking, based upon reason as the driving force for survival, had emerged from the development of natural instinct, over the period between 200,000 and 50,000 years ago. Following this period, there slowly evolved, within humanity, an attribute that came to develop the creative, intuitive and mystical nature of thought as a further beneficial trait. Such a development arose, not only to justify human survival techniques and to understand the effect of hominin interaction with the environment, but also to begin to introspectively define some sense of purpose and direction, together with a growing need to mark our presence in the passage of time.

Perhaps there was even some degree of pleasure that arose from such creative, intuitive and mystical objectivity of thought, or perhaps those tribal members with these predominantly right side brain function attributes became more successful as leaders.

Some scientists say that creative thinking, indeed all thinking and all that it involves, arises from the neural patterns in the brain being activated from external stimuli through the experience of our senses. This may be because we experience pleasure or a sense of well-being following such creativity and thus such experiences have been strengthened and perpetuated through repetition to become a part of the evolutionary adaptation within the brain.

Of course such a scenario is bound to have a bearing on some of our creative thinking, and may be a significant contributory factor in the origin of the process that enabled and developed the ability for objective thought to arise.

From the scientific perspective, we are back to the mind-brain problem again because not only is there a world of difference between the subconscious activity within the brain that perpetuates the everyday living process that supports our mundane requirements of survival, but the reduction of thought to only a sequence of electrochemical reactions also reduces humanity to a machinelike, semi-autonomous state, which does not permit the creative, intuitive and mystical elements any form or expression.

The creative, intuitive and mystical elements of thought are those that have, essentially, enabled humanity to evolve beyond the semi-autonomous state that had only the need for survival as its principal reason for development.

That creative, innovative, intuitive and mystical objective thinking has evolved is not in dispute; and by arising from a natural process of evolution as a further beneficial trait their existence lends great weight to the notion that the mind and the brain, the immaterial and the material, are separate elements that go to form a gestaltic complex which renders their discrete parts inseparable.

In essence, a beneficial trait came into existence once the brain process became capable of 'carrying' objective thoughts that were overlaid upon the brain process. We have seen earlier in this chapter, when discussing the process of consciousness, how this resulted in the means of expression of those thoughts in such a way that the process and the content, the 'how' and the 'what', became inseparable, whilst continuing to be separate.

Current models of brain activity propose that the stimulus provided by our senses is transmitted within the brain in two streams of modality that operate in separate areas of the brain. In the case of sight or vision, to which much of our brain function is devoted towards processing, each of these streams of modality may contain multiple channels that recognise various structural aspects of what we see. These take the perceived form of horizontal, vertical or curved aspects, or those of colour, shade and intensity etc. Broadly speaking, these modalities operate so that the object that is the centre of the stimulus streams through one part of the brain whilst its characteristics of motion or activity stream through a separate part. A similar situation has evolved in respect of most of our other senses.

The two streams of modality containing their multiple channels of the structure of what we see are then 're-assembled' in an area of the brain specifically developed to receive both streams and, hopefully, a reasonably accurate facsimile of the actual visual experience encountered by our sense of sight is reproduced.

The brain is thus a very specialised organ that has immense potential to reproduce the reality experienced by our senses where it is processed in an indirect way that is akin to a virtual reproduction.

Now we can see that the potential arises for close, but not entirely accurate, reassemblies of 'perceived reality' to occur, due to differences that exist between individual brains and the visual operating process that goes on within. The effect is that we each of us may appear to see things differently from each other, even when experiencing the same event stimulus, at the same time. Furthermore, should the operation of a brain be significantly different from the majority of its contemporaries, then the reassembly of the sense input may result in a perception of a 'reality' that may also be significantly or radically different.

The differences arising due to the way our brains are able to interpret sense input raises the question as to: 'What is the true nature of reality anyway?'

The true nature of reality may be one decided by the majority of human beings that encounter similar, if not identical, representations of sensory input. Genetic transmission, within a population that has increased significantly in numbers, over the course of very many generations and long periods of time, may have resulted in sensory perceptions processed within the brain being 'levelled out', with the consequent establishment of reality becoming determined by a growing majority of the population.

This is a form of the tyranny of the majority that may result in the diminution, or denial, of alternative realities for the person who experiences a different brain process or interpretation, where their reality is equally as real and as valuable as any of the majority.

Reality is supported by brain process and the fact is that we have been conditioned by generations of evolutionary development to accept as natural the 'reality' experienced by the majority and to designate the 'reality' experienced by those with different brain interpretations as 'abnormal'. Many abnormal realities are labelled as unhealthy because the person involved simply does not fit into the norm of human society.

Pressure arises, from our contemporaries and from cultural aspects of society, for us to conform with norms that society sees as fit to espouse as acceptable which 'allow' individuals to become normal members of that society.

Here it is necessary to differentiate between those that experience abnormal realities and those that suffer from mental illness, although on occasions the line separating the two may be ill defined or very blurred. Clearly there are some conditions, in human beings at least, that arise from mental illness and this condition is often associated with defects or damage that arise from neurotransmitters within the brain. These are the chemicals that the brain uses to conduct messages across the meeting point of two neurons, a process within the brain called a synapse.

When a signal arrives at the end of a neuron, the neurotransmitter spills into the gap, crossing it. Scientists have identified over fifty neurotransmitters that are messengers communicating information from one part of the brain to another, and to all parts of the body. From this simple process, complicated brain patterns are built and mental illness can arise when this process malfunctions.

Mental illness may arise when there is insufficient neurotransmitter content, when there is too much, or where there is malabsorption of the neurotransmitter. Such malfunctions as these may lead to cases of schizophrenia, depression and obsessive-compulsive disorder (amongst others).

The reality experienced in such cases is one that arises from malfunctioning within the brain and might be regarded as being organic in its nature. In some, perhaps many cases, the brain process is unable to transport the objective thought; the 'how' malfunctions whilst the 'what' continues to operate objectively. In our model, it is not the intention to investigate the various aspects of mental illness, and so we will disregard the reality experienced by malfunctioning brain processing cases as being abnormal and consider them to arise from a defect that causes mental illness. But in so doing we also recognise that the alternate realities experienced by those suffering mental illness should not be dismissed as being of no account.

The way that our brains are 'wired up' and the exact relationship between our natural senses and the brain receptors is that which raises the condition of abnormality relevant to our considerations of the nature of reality. Notwithstanding, some such abnormalities may be the result of brain damage or disease, whilst some may also be natural, occurring at birth, through genetic transfer; this may result in a wide range of conditions and sometimes such genetic transfer is exhibited, to some degree, over many generations.

Some 'abnormal' abilities so displayed may appear to be ones that are enviable to the 'normal' majority that has established the yardstick of measurement of typical normal reality. Often these characteristics are to be found in the prodigious savants, the learned or wise people who seem to know things without apparent effort.

There are a significant number of examples of prodigious savant brain operation and one such is that of Daniel Tammet, chosen here because, apart from the nature of the features that grant to him the entitlement to be labelled prodigious savant, he is a rare case in that the rest of his physical and psychological make-up is close to what society regards as 'normal' and, consequently, he is able to describe the nature of his particular savant brain process at the same time as it is functioning.

For most of this class of savants their special abilities often arise at some considerable personal cost, in that some other area of their natural development is restricted, curtailed or retarded. This usually appears in the form of autism, or the lack or absence of the social graces, or may be seen in the failure of the brain to develop normal maturing or mental function. However, such a curtailment in natural development of other brain functions is not exhibited in Daniel.

Daniel, who has been the subject of much scientific excitation and also of at least one television documentary, is able to arrive at the answer to very large and complicated arithmetical problems posed to him, within a time period of just a few seconds, without the aid of paper, pencil or an electronic calculator of any means. Famously he can give and recite, also without reference to any means of aid, the exact value of Pi (π) to 22,514 decimal places. He is also able to learn a completely new language sufficient to be able to speak it fluently within seven days of commencing to learn.

Daniel maintains that he 'sees' the numbers necessary to produce the correct answer as a 'landscape' where each number is represented by a different feature of that landscape. He thus 'sees' the answer in its entirety, without the need to make extensive calculation within the brain. This 'seeing' of solutions is believed by the scientific community to be due to a form of crossover or combining of the modal flow of information as it streams through the separate parts of the brain, prior to its reassembly.

Such a condition is recognised in scientific terms as synaesthesia, where it is believed that approximately 4% of the world population are synaesthetes. Readers who wish to gain a greater understanding of synaesthesia may wish to refer to the online information provided by research neurologist Richard E. Cytowic.

Synaesthesia is not a form of illness and Daniel's reality is merely different from that of the 'normal' individual simply because his brain functions differently from almost the entire rest of humanity. But the nature of his reality is very valuable indeed. It is no less 'real' or valuable to Daniel, and is one that astonishes perhaps most people to the point of incredulity and even some envy.

The point here is that, because of the way individual brains operate and the way the basic thinking process performs, the 'reality' we all perceive and experience is not a fixed commodity that can simply be assumed. We have seen that sense stimuli are processed through the brain which may result in neuron based patterns that come to define normal reality. But we have also seen how perception may arise from within the brain, fully developed and with high definition clarity, without any thought process or pre-perception taking place, or even without meaningful sensory input.

Neuroscientists may have it that such non-perceived high definition clarity of thought arises solely from brain activity simply functioning in a different way to that experienced by a 'normally' wired brain. But, an interesting conjecture would arise if the vast majority of human brain function matched that of synaesthetes such as Daniel Tammet, whereupon our currently 'normal' reality would become the abnormal one. Perhaps the brain function has followed an arbitrary pathway of evolution with conscious reality being interpreted by neuron sequences that would otherwise present an alternative reality.

After all Francis Crick, the celebrated Nobel Prize winning scientist credited along with James Watson and Maurice Wilkins with the determination of the structure of DNA, has famously said in *The Astonishing Hypothesis* concerning our perceived reality:

> *You, your joys and your sorrows, your memories and your ambitions, your sense of personal identity and free will, are in fact no more than the behaviour of a vast assembly of nerve cells and their associated molecules.*

Here we see clearly the proposal that all that we are – our thoughts, emotions, our ability to interpret our experience, to be able to speak coherently, our ability to decide and execute any course of action, in fact everything that gives our lives meaning and purpose – arises as a result of neuron brain activity. Such neuronal brain activity may operate differently, to a lesser or greater extent, within each individual, resulting in the nature of reality becoming insecure, to the point where brain activity determines a reality; but, very significantly, one that is unique and valuable only to each individual.

It is only a short step from that realisation to one where our reality may be determined by the strength or weakness of the external stimuli encountered and the ability of our senses to transmit to our brain the true representation of the reality under consideration.

We may indeed be the product or the action of our neurons, but such action arises from a process within the brain that is affected by a great number of external influences which inevitably affect not only what we think, in terms of our reality, but also the way in which we think it. Once again we can see that the electrochemical biological functioning of the neurons within our brain may provide the carrier mechanism for the production of thoughts, but the content of those thoughts and the way they are assembled depends upon many other factors including external stimuli.

We may consider the basic neuronal thought process as the blank canvas upon which we, as the artist, paint either the objectives that arise from the engagement of our senses, or the depiction of an abstract portrayal that arises from an area that lies beyond our senses.

Then again, another further view might arise, if our consciousness is able to interact with another realm of reality, one that might already contain the abnormal condition experienced in savant brains and which might involve a field that contains every thought which has been thought, perhaps even in the form of a landscape.

Such a field labelled 'the Noosphere' was proposed by Henri

Bergson in 1907 in L'Évolution Créatrice and was further developed in Teilhard de Chardin's Cosmogenesis in 1922, and in correspondence issued by Vladimir Vernadsky in 1936. Here the principle is that the Noosphere represents the total content of the entire sphere of human thought and emerges as the interaction of human minds becomes ever greater and closer.

As humanity organises itself in evermore complex social networks, the greater becomes the awareness contained within the Noosphere, until a peak of consciousness will eventually be achieved. We might think of such an advanced state of consciousness as one that approaches the state of perfection intrinsic within the motion described on The Emerald Tablet. Some believe that Teilhard's concept of the Noosphere is embodied in the current integration of thought available through the World Wide Web, and through social networking sites that consequently may be said to have been predicted by Teilhard prior to their invention or instigation.

The concept of a Noosphere allows for thoughts to exist, to be interconnected, stored and encountered. The concept here is that we encounter a thought, develop it within the context of our own situation and leave the thought in an enhanced condition for others to encounter. Such a concept has much to offer as it not only complies with the tenet of the text on The Emerald Tablet whereby ascent and descent between realms is proposed, but also solves two of the great mysteries that humanity has encountered throughout its entire history.

Firstly the means by which the same ideas arise over long periods of time and over widely spaced, unconnected geographical locations without any apparent migration. Secondly, the means of operation become possible whereby leaps in the evolutionary process of thought and its subsequent objectivity occur. We will return to this aspect of creative thought when we discuss evolution in Chapter Four.

However, it is worth reiterating that whilst scientists

especially biologists and those engaged in neuroscience may well lean towards a thought process, within the brain, that can determine what it is that we think, including previously unknown areas of revelation and intuition, such a process is, as yet, barely formulated and understood. In addition there is also a body of thought that grants to an element of our consciousness the ability freely to generate creative thought without any pre-stimulation of brain neurons, as in the case of some savant behaviour.

We have proposed in Chapter Two that the composition of the Soul involves the higher levels of thought that are available to us within our current level of n-consciousness, once sufficient complexity of particulate structure has taken place. The form of life, endowed and enlivened by the formatrix energy, acting exponentially as a matrix, enables everything in existence to have the potential to possess a soul.

The brain stem automatically activates and maintains simple bodily functions necessary for us to continue to live, following which we become aware first of our surroundings and then of ourselves. We are then able to co-create our soul, using ever-higher layers and levels of consciousness to produce an intelligent thinking process together with enhanced levels of self-awareness and an egotistical element that, taken together, elevate the potential within us to the form of the Soul.

As material conceptions of life evolve and develop so do the constituents of the soul whereby self-awareness, perception, intelligence, thought and the ego also evolve to give a sense of individual identity.

Thought has thus become more than the means of survival which may have been its original purpose; it has become part of the human consciousness, within our soul complex, as the means by which we recognise and are aware of that consciousness. It has elevated itself to become the means for the development of and use of the brain, and in this way it may be said that what and how we think together with the extent of our thinking can and does affect the brain and its development.

The nature of the reality that is determined for an individual by the brain operation process can also be said to affect the development of the brain, and we can see that this aspect of evolution will become a significant part of human development as adaptation continues. Whether such evolutionary change is or will be the outcome of natural selection or of an alternative step change in the human condition will be seen by those who inhabit the future.

Thought, being the tool of our consciousness, now enables us to enhance our brain activity in such a way that allows us to relate to both the subtle and the material realms simultaneously. It is the means of perception that relates to the Ideas that come to form the material realm whilst being both the interpreter and the agent that model the practical aspects of materiality in such a way that suits the prescription of choice and free will.

In addition most of us are able to alter the level of consciousness that we currently inhabit to the extent that it may even be possible to experience, even if only for a short period, forms of non-ordinary reality including the higher layer of h-consciousness. It is this developing ability to enter altered and higher states of consciousness that we will now consider.

3.05. Altered and Higher States of Consciousness
Historically to enter an altered state of consciousness was often achieved through the use of hallucinatory substances derived from vegetable products such as cactus plants and vines, many of which originate in the northern area of the South American continent. There are about 36 known varieties of hallucinogenic cactus, of which peyote is perhaps the most well-known example. Ayahuasca is a brew that is made from vines and various leaves that results in a strong psychedelic drink in the

High Andean plains. Another plant form hallucinogen is that derived from the psilocybe genus of mushrooms, where there are 53 known varieties to be found in Mexico. Psilocybe cubensis and psilocybe semilanceata are two that are commonly found in the United Kingdom.

This method of entering into an altered state of consciousness is still available to those practitioners who wish for that experience. Although still popular it is, however, to be frowned upon today because the results are more often than not clouded by insensibility and this leads to a dead end so far as researching altered states of consciousness is concerned.

Drug induced altered states of consciousness might be said to imitate, to some extent, those states that are achieved by non-drug induced methods. To all intents and purposes, for some practitioners, altered states of consciousness may be perceived to offer the same experience as higher states, but this is not always the case.

Alternative means of entering into different levels or layers of consciousness without the use of drugs have been developed over many generations and it is non-drug induced methods that we will explore.

Those further ways of experiencing altered or higher states of consciousness may be through deprivation, especially of food and drink, or of sensory deprivation, or by the onset of fever, illness or trauma usually involving an accident of some sort, or by meditation techniques. Such means of non-drug induced altered or higher states may bear similar results to those described in the following paragraph with the exception that some may be found to be more or less permanent, and/or may not be capable of allowing the practitioner to remain in control of his or her consciousness throughout.

Alternative means of inducing altered states of consciousness may involve the practitioner inducing in themselves a trance-like condition through repetitive recitation or action. Gregorian type chanting, Jewish davening prayer, the Native American frenzied dance or sweat lodge experience, the effect of whirling for the Arabian Dervish Sufi adherent and the effect of rhythmic drum beats are all examples of such methods.

Chanting the same mantra over and over especially when done or accompanied by musical support has for many centuries been a way by which monks and the like could approach or even get in touch with the object of their religious substance or deity. Similarly, the rocking back and forth exemplified by Judaic adherents during daven prayer and the frantic action of the Islamic Whirling Dervishes also demonstrate means by which such a similar condition may be attained. The North American sweat lodge is a means of cleansing the internal organs and the soul spirit, and has been used for many thousands of years.

But what is it that such means seek to achieve? In modern day religious terms, the theurgical invocation of a particular deity is the apparent aim of adherents to these practices. But further back in history, before the advent of the major organised religions that sponsor such activity, indigenous tribal communities in the Americas, in Northern Europe, in Africa and the Antipodes practised these methods for the important benefit of healing within their tribes, as well as for tribal cohesion and to facilitate survival techniques.

These activities were performed by what popular Western socio-anthropolitical science or journalism has sometimes derisively called witches or warlocks, medicine men or witch doctors, but which should be more accurately termed shamans.

Shamanic techniques have been practised over thousands of years as evidenced by Miranda and Stephen Aldhouse-Green in their book *The Quest for the Shaman*,[11] that records a journey through prehistory indicating that shamans were active 35,000 years ago.

Shamanism is one of those practices that has arisen throughout entire geographical locations of the world over many thousands of years, with demonstrated characteristics that are not only similar throughout but have remained remarkably consistent, even after tribal separations have occurred. All of this without any apparent means of migration from one group to another. The efficiency of its technique and the results arising therefrom may be some reasons for its independent emergence everywhere over extended periods of racial history. But we should also consider that the shaman, from whatever geographical location and at whatever time he or she lived, by interacting with an Idea in the subtle realm, has produced these axes of affinity everywhere, throughout our racial history.

The ancient shamanic technique, centred around providing benefit to the tribal community to which its practitioners belonged, usually used a drug induced 'shamanic journey' to a realm of non-ordinary reality to gain information that would help the survival of their tribe, or of an individual that was important to it. Today's shaman may still practise for the same purpose but generally does so for an expanded regional or even global benefit to humanity as a whole. Whilst still undertaken by some, drug induced states are now the exception rather than the rule.

Shamanically, the rhythmic beat of a drum will induce a trance-like state of ecstasy, that is to say of experiencing an expanded, transcendent consciousness or initiating a feeling of being outside of oneself. However, the experiences gained from entering into an altered state of consciousness by any other means will be essentially the same with regard to purpose and outcome, even if the detailed experiences may vary.

Michael Harner, a leading expert on shamanism in today's society, confirms in his book *The Way of the Shaman* that laboratory research has shown that the repetitive sound of a drumbeat causes electrical activity in the sensory receptors of the brain to increase and affect the central nervous system of the body by enhancing the theta wave frequency and encouraging a trance-like state to occur.[12] This state allows the shaman to travel freely between ordinary and non-ordinary realities, in an altered state of consciousness, whilst remaining in full control and retaining complete memory of their activities and experience.

Having entered an altered state of consciousness, a shaman will 'journey' to a non-ordinary reality to ascertain the answers to that which he or she seeks to know. They are accompanied throughout by their own guides and teachers that arise through their interaction with the non-ordinary realm and which are particular to their own personality and practice.

Such helpers usually take the form of animals or some other aspect of nature, and a number of things might be said concerning shamans' entry into a realm of non-ordinary reality with the assistance of such helpers. Shamans may be said to become one with the laws of nature or perhaps of achieving a much closer interaction with Gaia. They may have put themselves directly and consciously en rapport with the Ideas of the subtle realm. These possibilities point in the same direction towards that of actively working with nature to gain under-standing in an altered state of consciousness.

Mircea Eliade, in his seminal work *Shamanism*,[13] extends the prospect of the shaman's alliance with nature and non-ordinary reality by confirming the belief, held throughout the shamanic communities worldwide, that there are three great cosmic regions which can be successively traversed because they are all linked by a central axis. These regions are the sky (above), the Earth (here) and the underworld (below). It is along this central axis that the soul of a shaman may journey, in a state of ecstasy, in a trance-like state, to gain information that would be to the benefit of their tribe or clan.

The journey upwards towards the sky would be to commu-nicate with the transcendent bodies that hold the answers to the esoteric nature and structure of the Cosmos; and the journey to the underworld would be to communicate with the spirits of the ancestors, those now dead shamans who had already gained the wisdom that had kept the tribe or clan together and in a prosperous, healthy state.

The symbolism surrounding the shamanic journey is a clear allegory of the relationship and interaction between the subtle and the material realms of reality that we find on The Emerald Tablet. Furthermore, the use of altered states of consciousness, by the shamans, as the vehicle for such a journey is a clear demonstration of such an interaction, one that uses a certain level of the active and creative imagination as the key pattern that initiates and enables the process of the shamanic journey.

It is possible that higher states of consciousness may also be achieved by using an altered state as a platform from which to journey further, if that is the intention of the practitioner. But this is not the only way to experience higher levels of consciousness.

It is true to say that higher states of consciousness are best achieved through non-drug induced methods and although this may sometimes be facilitated through first entering an area of non-ordinary reality, utilising an altered state of consciousness, more often than not higher states are attainable through the power of meditation alone. Such meditative processes also utilise the application of the active and creative imagination, the *mundus imaginalis*, as the cognitive key pattern that can unlock the door directly into de Ropp's fourth room level of consciousness.

The experience of higher levels of consciousness is not for the same purpose as entry into altered states. Here the objective is not for healing, cohesion or survival techniques previously described, although some extent of these aims may also arise from the higher state experience. In this case the objective is to achieve the attributes of h-consciousness as described in section 3.03.03, to recognise and understand the complete nature of the Cosmos. To 'see' with absolute clarity the extent of everything in existence, together with its full potential, in fine detail.

3.06. The Mundus Imaginalis

The work of Henri Corbin (1903–1978) in clarifying and extending the work of Sohravardi, the 12th century Iranian Islamic philosopher, provides us with what will become for us the master key that unlocks the hitherto undeveloped or hidden areas of our consciousness, in order to grant to us a means of access to altered and higher states of consciousness.

Corbin describes in some detail what he calls the link between the material (sensible) realm that is experienced by our senses and the realm of subtle bodies that can only be experienced by a facility that operates, within us, beyond the normal range of our senses. This facility has been labelled as the Active Imagination, the Imaginal or the Mundus Imaginalis.

Corbin is at some pains to emphasise that there is a wide separation between the attributes that are normally regarded as applying to the term 'imagination', those of fantasy, fiction and even illusion, and those attributes of mundus imaginalis that centre upon a structure which enables cognitive access to experiences that exist beyond those that the senses may encounter.

These experiences, although being fully objective, are incapable of being perceived by the senses as the properties of physical bodies. Our intellect, however, interprets these experiences as though they had been perceived by the senses, because this has been the only means available to humanity, which enables us to understand and categorise the events that engage the mundus imaginalis.

In this way a sort of 'immaterial materiality', as an extension of the material realm, is built that enables an evaluation of the subtle realm, and the mundus imaginalis thus becomes a metaphysical necessity akin to being a cognitive function. Furthermore it becomes a function that is ranked higher than our five senses that pertain only within the material realm. Albert Einstein, in an interview given to the *Saturday Evening Post* on 26th October 1929, said that:

Imagination... is more important than knowledge. Knowledge is limited. Imagination encircles the world.

Einstein, along with so many others, ranks imagination as more important than knowledge, and clearly we are not talking here about the illusory realm of fantasy even though this has its own part to play in the world of art. This ranking of mundus imaginalis above that of sensory experience in the material realm poses the important question: 'What is it within the human being that facilitates the mundus imaginalis?'

In Chapter Two we posited the soul as the formative energy that enlivens life as a form of consciousness that comes to demonstrate increasingly higher levels of self-awareness and, with it, intelligent thought and an ego that complements and fulfils identity. Once formed thus, the soul evolves and becomes capable of elevating itself to higher levels of co-creation involving free will and alternative states of consciousness.

The soul complex that has thus evolved becomes increasingly involved in directing the mundus imaginalis to cross the various thresholds of the levels of consciousness which then provide the means for the transmutation of interior material spaces into interior immaterial spaces; ones that, paradoxically, have no spatial location at all but do in fact contain all the spaces of everywhere, a clear example of the need to rethink the nature of volume and space discussed in Chapter Two in a way which also requires an alternative approach to reason and logic.

This concept is one where the mundus imaginalis operates in a similar way to that of how the Universe is structured around a centre that is located everywhere and which may be said to commence where normal, material spaces transmute into immaterial spaces, to inhabit a zone that encloses all other spaces, zones and dimensions. As such, the mundus imaginalis becomes a metaphysical necessity for experiencing and understanding the Cosmos that exists beyond the ability of our senses to encounter.

The soul thus becomes the only means by which the mundus imaginalis takes on a cognitive function, one that remains independent of the soul complex as we have described it, but which is yet reliant on it for its mode of expression. This is similar to the relationship we have seen between the material and subtle realms where each is dependant upon the other for its means of expression, and is also seen in the relationship between the mind and the brain where, similarly, the means of expression is interdependent. We can see that a cosmological pattern of repetitive form is developing as evolution continues.

It is important to remember that the soul complex remains independent of the physical body that is its vehicle, yet is dependant upon it for its means of expression, whilst granting to that vehicle its form of identity and being. In a similar way the mundus imaginalis depends on the soul for its ability to function whilst at the same time providing the soul with the means by which its evolution may develop. This interdependence between the soul and the mundus imaginalis is such that, even though each has a separate form of existence, they may become a combined single unit, once the mundus imaginalis has reached the stage of development where its encounter with the subtle realm become a cognitive function, albeit without the experience provided by the five senses.

Unlike our five senses, that are spread throughout our physical being and are often subject to malfunction or deterio-ration, the independence of the soul from our bodies and the independence of the mundus imaginalis from the soul, once they have become combined, are then enhanced to operate as a single form. This form is not only capable of demonstrating an efficiency that is superior to that of the five senses, but also reinforces the ability of this enhanced soul complex to sustain its joint existence beyond the death of its physical, vehicular partner.

We are now able to see the absolute need for the wide

separation between the attributes of the common usage of the word 'imagination' as there is nothing of the fictional world of fantasy and illusion associated with the attributes of the Active Imagination, the mundus imaginalis.

It is the mundus imaginalis, as an inseparable functioning element of the soul complex, including consciousness, that is the means whereby we can knowingly access the subtle realm, enabling us to exercise the prime subtle Idea of Free Will, that then enables us to unlock the doors into de Ropp's fourth and fifth rooms of advanced consciousness and allows us to enter. It is the driving force that facilitates the journey to non-ordinary reality using altered states of consciousness and is that which pushes the human being towards higher levels of consciousness and, consequently, of adaptive evolution. It provides an automatic interaction with all of the thoughts retained in the Noosphere and it is that part of humanity which grants to us the means for the continuation of life after our bodies cease to function.

The mundus imaginalis is indeed the master key to Cosmic understanding!

3.07. The Law of Attraction

In Chapter One we have stated that The Emerald Tablet provided the means for the foundation of many movements throughout its long period of history. 'The Law of Attraction' is one such movement and, whilst its principles are very simple in their essence, they are not always easy to put into operation.

We have seen in our discussions that reality is something which is relevant to each individual and is, to a great extent, created by each of us to suit our condition and circumstances. The interaction between the subtle and the material realms, as required by The Emerald Tablet, defines the means whereby our consciousness establishes our reality.

When we come to discuss destiny in Chapter Four and the nature of the future in Chapter Five we will see that many futures are possible, each of which depend upon the choices we have made, both in the past and those that we make in the present. The attraction of the object that we desire lies in the present; whereas the attaining of that object lies in the future, at least until that future becomes the present.

It follows that, by consciously visualising the objects of our desire in the present, those objects may become the reality itself, in the future. This sounds simple, but the evidence is that such visualisations do not always result in the objects of our desire materialising as a reality. So the question arises, why some times and not others?

The answer to this question also lies within the text on The Emerald Tablet:

You should separate the spiritual from the gross, the subtle from the material, truly and with great industry, as it ascends from the earth to the subtle, and back again, and in so doing receives the force of all things subtle and material.

By these means you shall have dominion of the whole world and all things will become clear.

We are instructed to recognise that the substance of our reality is a fusion of the subtle realm of Ideas and the material realm, and that the expression of each occurs through an interdependent, ongoing process of development. The elements of this fusion may be identified and acknowledged as having separate origins, contained within both realms, but it is consciousness within the material realm by interacting with the subtle realm that enables the material reality to manifest. It thus becomes apparent that we each should be capable, through our consciousness, of bringing the object of our desire to a material reality.

Because everything arises originally from the subtle realm, the objects of our desire comprise only of immaterial characteristics that are manifested through our consciousness, which is also immaterial in its nature. Thus, those objects of our desire that are immaterial in their nature, here in the material realm, are the ones most likely to become fulfilled. That is not to say that something of a material nature will not manifest here in the material realm, but this is only likely to do so as a means of fulfilment of an immaterial object of desire.

Thus, the desire for healing potential and for altruistic treatment of our fellow human beings; for the safeguarding and well-being of others and ourselves; for the establishment of harmony and peace of mind in reciprocal, loving relationships; for the acquisition of a lifestyle that is more conducive to achieving these objectives – these are the sort of desires that are most likely to be fulfilled through the law of attraction.

Whereas the desire for the acquisition of material objects purely for reasons of self-gratification or to satisfy egotistical imbalance are more likely to remain unfulfilled.

The process of the interaction of consciousness with the subtle realm is one that is automatic in that we are unaware that it takes place, or that it is continuous. It may therefore be regarded as a subconscious operation that occurs once choice is established and free will is brought into effect to activate that choice.

If we keep the objective of our desire in the forefront of our conscious awareness, then this may prevent the subconscious activity necessary to bring about the interactive fruits of our choice.

One method of overcoming this hurdle involves periods of meditation, using the mundus imaginalis as the means whereby the aim of setting aside the conscious awareness of our desire, from the forefront of our being, may be achieved in order to allow our subconsciousness the facility of influencing the interactive process of co-creation.

This is the process that may result in the determination of the strand of the future that marches with our choice and desire, thus enabling it to manifest.

Our conscious awareness will have made an objective choice, following which free will has activated the choice made and an interaction with the subtle element of Time, which determines the course of our future, aligns us with that strand of the future that fulfils our choice and desire.

In other words:

- If we are able to establish the object of our desire;
- then identify both its subtle and material elements, to the greatest extent possible;
- and then choose to bring those immaterial, subtle elements to reality;
- implementing free will as the means of activation;
- following which, by meditation and use of mundus imaginalis;
- we actively cause the object of our desire;
- to become absent from our conscious awareness;
- so that it becomes embedded in our subconsciousness;
- which then interacts with Time in the subtle realm;
- in such a way that the desired future may become the present;
- whereupon the object of our desire may then manifest in our material reality;
- as an act of co-creation.

This is the law of attraction in operation!

The way in which the law of attraction may operate, in the practical sense, owes much to the nature of intuition and synchronicity, a relationship that we will consider when considering possible futures in Chapter Five.

3.08. An Emergent Gestalt

All that has been said so far – from fundamental layers and then levels of consciousness incorporating a vitality that is the characteristic carried by each particle in a forward motion that interacts with the Ideas of the subtle realm – comes to fruition as a growing gestalt.

In our model under discussion, this is a form that cannot be measured by the sum of its parts, because the parts are incapable of separation or division from the whole, and the combining and fusing of its constituents creates a unified, cohesive, singular form that is immeasurably greater than the sum of its parts.

An example of a gestalt is seen in the Gaia theory, which prescribes a self-regulatory complex of all aspects of planet Earth's environment, ecology and conditions that is fully interactive and cohesive. Without the interaction of the constituent parts with the whole, all of which are all contained within that whole, then the condition and standard of environmental control would deteriorate beyond its capacity to sustain life of any sort.

Such a form of cohesive, interactive, unified self-regulation, including the soul complex within the human form, acting in encounter with the extra-sensate mundus imaginalis, creates a forward experiential motion that propels our consciousness, and thus our lifeform forward, towards an evolutionary adaptive future. Furthermore, we are now able to identify the relationship between the subtle and the material realms as also being one that is symbiotic and potentially cohesive.

The gestalt that is emerging is one that embraces all of existence, the entire Cosmos, sensate and meta-sensate, and is one where the flow of existence may be seen as a having a single direction, towards which the entire Cosmos is moving. Such a gestaltic Cosmos is exemplified by its unity as an evolving form. It is to this form that we will look, as we consider evolution, destiny and fate next, in Chapter Four.

3.09. The Story So Far

The Emerald Tablet has provided a suitable starting point towards an understanding that the Cosmos is formed of one dimension and two realms of reality, the material and subtle realms. The nature of the material realm is experienced through our five senses and explains the reality in which we spend our daily lives. The subtle realm is that which exists beyond our senses and contains the essence of perfect Ideas arising from the mediation of The One Source of All Things. These become translated into the means by which both the material and subtle realms find their expression, and which are the principles and ideals by which we seek to govern society. The interaction between the two realms takes place through the medium of consciousness and forms an ongoing, continuous process that results in evolution and development of life in the material reality.

Based upon the two-realm cosmogony that is available to our consciousness and their constituencies, we are now able to establish a structure for the material realm. This is the particulate structure of subatomic and atomic particles that gain their mass through the absorption of the minutest subatomic particle of all, the archaeus particle. This exists in the subtle realm on a field of energy that transmits mass to the material realm and goes on to form the dark energy that powers the acceleration of our Universe. The particulate mass of the material realm gathers to form stars which become the means whereby the different material elements are created.

A form of energy, the formatrix, enlivens particles of material, and when groups of particles combine and congregate each contributes their element of consciousness until complex particulate structures evolve to the point where they become aware. Eventually sufficient conscious mass has assembled so that it is able to observe the hitherto unformed mass of the material

Universe which it thus determines, and in so doing gives it form and structure. Continual grouping of complex particles and consciousness proceeds until it is able to form an identity, and eventually consciousness reaches a level where the foundations for a soul come to exist; and as evolution continues, then so do the attributes and abilities of the soul.

Following on from the nature and structure of the cosmos, we see how consciousness enables evolution to commence its journey of development. We understand that particles congregate and develop into ever more complex structures that exhibit increasing layers and levels of conscious ability.

Layers of consciousness, and some of the various levels within, allow us to understand how the Cosmos works towards an order of perfection, and we come to understand that all life is conscious and that self-awareness, the ability to communicate and intelligent thought are all stages in the evolutionary development. We can recognise that various layers of consciousness have developed over eons of time, and that within those layers there are increasingly transcendent levels of consciousness which we are learning to access.

Furthermore, we are also now able to recognise that reality, as we generally perceive it to be, is not fixed or reliable and this leads us to consider not only the nature and security of our reality, but that altered states of consciousness exist as a tool or key to accessing and understanding that part of the Cosmos that is, in our everyday existence, currently beyond the reach of our senses. We also see a form of the active and creative imagination, the mundus imaginalis, as the master key in accessing alternate realities and states of consciousness, which is not only the product of an adaptive evolution, but has also become the current means of propelling the evolutionary motion towards... what?

Chapter Four

Evolution, Destiny, Fate, Good and Evil, and then Inevitably, Death

From evolution they were able to become,
as part of my pattern of ascending consciousness.

Always in acts of co-creation.

Because the choice must be theirs.
Along with the Free Will to change,
so that their destiny and their fate,
arise from their consciousness.

Not only did I give them the gift of life,
but also the gift of death,
so that the lives of others may follow,
so that all things may change.

Yet I could not be so cruel
so as to make death the end of their journey.

Thus their soul!

That can go on and on,
always transforming,
always co-creating,
as they strive to 'see' all of it,
and yearn to be a part of it all.

4.00. Introduction

To date we have described a model of the nature of the Cosmos and how it is structured. We have seen how consciousness fuels the interaction between the two realms of subtle and material reality, and we have some understanding of that interaction. We can also comprehend the development of consciousness and the means that have come into being which serve the motion of our own development. But what of the purpose and the direction of it all? Does any purpose exist? Do we have any direction and, if so, is it reasonable to suppose that the direction leads us to somewhere?

This chapter seeks to look at these questions in a manner that takes meaning from all that has gone before.

4.01. Evolution

Evolution is now said to be such a strong theory that it must represent the truth. This is because it answers the significant majority of questions that arise in connection with the development of life and our environment. Nevertheless, it is true that the Darwinian and the Wallace theories of evolution are contested, particularly by some of those of a religious persuasion, whose faith in creationism and/or intelligent design refuses to be shaken in the face of such strong evidence of adaptation by natural selection. We will look at evolution with a view to understanding where the balance lies between these two opposing views.

According to the scientific community generally, evolution over a period of billions of years has resulted in a huge variety of different species and subspecies. According to evolutionary biology, life on our planet has evolved from a universal common ancestor, commencing from some 3.8 billion years ago, and throughout this period, through processes of divergence, mutation and genetic drift, our original common ancestor has changed, adapted and developed to become millions of different species of life.

In Chapter One we looked at the characteristics required for

Ideas to exist in the subtle realm, and one of those characteristics involved the inability for such Ideas to change. We are able to recognise that many species have come into existence and have since become extinct, and that such a process is one of change which requires the passage of time that does not take place in the subtle realm, but does so only in our material realm. Therefore the Idea of a genus of any lifeform in the subtle realm is unaffected by the passage of time, and therefore is not the subject of change in that realm.

The principle process whereby such massive speciation, through change, has occurred is proposed as being that of natural selection. Natural selection is the gradual process by which biological characteristics become either more or less common in a species population, as a whole, through repro-duction. Throughout the lives of individual organisms, their genomes interact with their environment to cause variations in traits whereby individuals with certain variants of a trait may survive and reproduce to a greater extent than individuals with other different variants. This is the means whereby the population evolves gradually. It is also the way in which traits that are less advantageous to the survival and prosperity of a population may become eradicated.

Evolution through natural selection cannot thus be said to be randomly generated because the process is one where any adaptation that takes place does so progressively, gradually and generally smoothly to suit the environmental conditions prevailing at any one time. This occurs in a way that has a general stabilizing effect upon large populations, a condition known as 'stasis'.

A word of caution must, however, be inserted here in that natural selection takes the species most suited to adapt to its environment forward through reproduction and this introduces a competitive element to the process of evolution that may manifest as the survival of the fittest. But the ecosystem that sustains the planet Earth can be demonstrated to be not only competitive but also, and at the same time, cooperative. The interdependence of ecosystems throughout the planet, as seen in the Gaia theory, supports a growing tendency towards cooperation between species, this being at least partly successful in propagating the interests of the species involved. It may well be that cooperation will supplant competition to an increasing extent as more and more species have developed and adapted over millions of years.

Nevertheless, natural selection remains the principle driver of evolution, whether competition or cooperation is the means of application.

However, the fossil record does not entirely support a gradual process of the evolution of a species or organism. Fossil records showing the various stages of adaptation as a gradual process over long periods of time are incomplete or have not yet been uncovered, and this has caused some to question the value of natural selection as the principal driving force of evolution.

The answer to this appears in the form of what has been labelled 'punctuated equilibrium' which, from the fossil record, indicates that there have been periods, throughout history, when organisms evolved at a very much faster rate than would be the case in a gradual process.

Punctuated equilibrium is a theory that was proposed by Niles Eldredge and Stephen Jay Gould, who observed that evolution tends to happen sometimes moving very fast, sometimes moving very slow, or even not at all. Darwin saw evolution as being a slow process, one that forms new species, in a continuous manner, without sudden jumps. If we study the fossils of organisms found in subsequent geological layers, however, we will see long intervals, when nothing changed, punctuated by short, revolutionary transitions, in which species became extinct and were replaced by wholly new forms. Punctuated equilibrium operates at the species level rather than at the larger group familial level where there is greater evidence in the fossil record of gradual change through natural selection.

So, we are able to recognise a combination of natural selection and punctuated equilibrium as the non-random forces that have driven evolutionary development on planet Earth. But to these processes we must add a random means and that is one of genetic mutation. Variation exists within all populations of organisms, partly because random mutations cause changes in the genome of an individual organism, and these mutations can be passed on to offspring.

Mutations are changes in the DNA sequence of a cell, and when they occur they may have no effect, or they may alter the product of the gene, or they may even prevent the gene from functioning. This may occur through an element of each cell, called a chromosome, which exists as a coil of DNA that contains, amongst other things, many genes and mutations. It is possible for large sections of a chromosome to become duplicated and this can introduce extra copies of a gene into a genome. These may then become a major source of the raw material needed for new genes to evolve. This is important because most new genes evolve from pre-existing genes that share common ancestors.

New genes can be generated when a duplicate copy mutates and acquires a new function. This process is easier once a gene has been duplicated because one gene in the pair can acquire a new function while the other copy continues to perform its original function. The generation of new genes can also involve small parts of several genes being duplicated, with these fragments then recombining to form new combinations with new functions.

Also, mutations can occur that have a major effect on the genome, whereby significant change can take place within the organisms affected. For example, when, in the hominoidea ape family, a mutation took place that combined two chromosomes into one new chromosome, significant change then occurred, culminating in a separate species of Hominids. This change enabled early modern Hominin subspecies to evolve, and subsequently modern human beings or Homo sapiens were born.

It might thus be said that both natural selection and punctuated equilibrium are features that are simultaneously present in an evolutionary process that is not random, to which must be added an element of mutation that provides a random evolutionary mechanism. All three of these features have spawned further avenues of investigation, surmise and controversy, and it is true to say that much remains to be determined as to the true extent and nature of these means that determine the evolutionary process.

However, the general weight of evidence is building such that there is a growing general consensus, lead by the scientific community, that the principles involved in the theory of evolution represent the true picture for the development of life on Earth, if not the whole Universe and, as such, we accept its principles.

In accepting these principles of evolution as the best current explanation for the development of life and our environment we need to take a look at the possibility that there is a direction to evolution with a pathway that is somehow controlled or directed by forces existing either within the organism itself, or from without.

The principle of a straight-line progressive direction for evolution is called 'orthogenesis', which may arise because the complexity of the higher organisms appears generally to be increasing, resulting in greater levels of consciousness and formatrix energy, creating the impression of an ascending direction of development.

In fact the considerable majority of species on planet Earth have comprised, both in the past and the present, of microorganisms that may not generally develop any more complex traits at all. Such fast-reproducing organisms as these may even lose their complexity depending on the environment that they inhabit. They may become simpler in nature if there is a beneficial outcome to their future reproduction through their loss of complexity. This can occur when specific genetic functions become redundant or are superseded by simpler, more advanced genetic functionality.

It is therefore generally accepted by the scientific community that orthogenesis, as a feasible hypothesis, has been discredited by the weight of evidence accruing to the principles of natural selection, punctuated equilibrium and genetic mutation, and the fact that many, if not the majority, of the species may not develop and progress in complexity at all.

However, during those lengthy periods when adaptive, developmental evolutionary change takes place, it may be true to say that for the larger animals which inhabit the macro environment and have a slower reproduction cycle and longer lifetime spans, then any loss of complexity may not be seen as in any way beneficial to their future species reproductive cycles.

There then appears a circular condition in that, for the more numerous populations of the larger, macro organisms, there arises, during extended periods of environmental stasis, a direction that evolutionary development takes. As more and more complex structures of organisms arise, this helps to stabilize the environment and thus allows further evolutionary complexity to be generated, consequently producing further stasis, and so on. This may be regarded as cyclical evolutionary momentum, one that gives rise to the notion that evolution itself is an evolving concept.

This is not to say that a force, operating in a conscious pre-planned manner, directs evolution from within the organism or through some external application. However, it does mean that some organisms and their environment each contain the elements of a directional flow that is intrinsic within their nature. The successful establishment of such a directional flow will depend on the efficiency with which increasingly complex organisms are able to reproduce and stabilize their environment in order to produce lengthy periods of evolutionary stasis.

Even then, such complexity may be affected or even compromised by the incidence of serious genetic mutation which may occur either from environmental changes or from exterior influences.

From all that has been said, it is fairly easy to accept the elementary evolutionary principles so far discussed when considering the material physiology of the vehicles that form our physical bodies and play host to our consciousness. But can we accept that the same principles apply equally to those immaterial aspects of life, particularly in humanity, that we have proposed in our model of the soul complex?

Natural selection uses beneficial traits within organisms to perpetuate and to strengthen the development of those organisms, either through competition or cooperation. This simple principle is entirely consistent with our soul model where the greater complexity of a particulate organism enables higher levels of consciousness to develop as a beneficial trait so that the reproduction of these organisms is a natural process of soul development which is complementary to the evolutionary principles of natural selection so far discussed.

Certainly the vehicle for the complex we have determined as 'the soul' is part of the biological process of evolution, and in that sense it is correct to say that without such an adapted vehicle as the human brain such a soul complex as we have described may not have had the means to evolve and express itself. We must therefore look at the means whereby the brain might have developed the ability to allow our soul complex to form, and subsequently to become the main operator of the brain itself together with our physical form.

It is now believed that, historically, the brain had been divided into two areas of specialisation, founded within the right and left side hemispheres. Simply put, the right side of the brain operates so as to enable the creative, intuitive and subjective processes to function, whilst the left side of the brain operates as the logical, reasoning, language generation and objective element of our being. The two hemispheres were interconnected, but have different specialisations of function, even though neither brain side function is solely confined to its hemisphere and each may assume some of the function of the other if one side is damaged.

In the 1970s a theory was proposed by Julian Jaynes in *The Origins of Consciousness in the Breakdown of the Bicameral Mind*[14] that, until the development of an agricultural lifestyle began to replace hunter/gatherer survival traits, the human brain performed mostly right side brain functions as this was best suited to the environmental conditions prevailing prior to the agricultural revolution. The development of agriculture allowed and encouraged populations to increase, requiring larger settlements, greater language communication and a considerably greater extent of forward planning. Consequently, over a period of a few millennia, the importance of the left side brain function became of greater significance.

The left side, language generating brain function was said, by Jaynes, to be modulated in times of stress by the corresponding right side brain function. This occurred as an internal, auditory instruction, represented as a 'voice in the head', often interpreted to be from an external source, thought to be a 'God' or a past alpha leader of the tribal group. The right side brain function maintained its dominance, because the left side brain function tended to execute the right side instructions without question.

Jaynes called this two-part function the bicameral brain.

Jaynes proposes that these bicameral brain arrangements began to break down approximately 3,000 or so years ago, and for this he relies on what he saw as a change in the ability of humans to introspect. Hitherto, according to Jaynes, we had not developed to any significant extent the ability to examine our own thoughts, feelings and mental state.

This change commenced following cataclysmic events centred around the Mediterranean area and it was this breakdown that eventually caused the bicameral brain to unify into a single operation where, generally speaking, left and right side functions began to operate in a more or less equal partnership. This allowed us to become capable of introspection.

It was from this development that, for Jaynes, consciousness as we define it today was born, between three and four thousand years ago.

In evolutionary terms the left and right hemisphere brain construct arose through interaction with the environment, to enable us to switch quickly or even instantaneously from creativity to practice, from mysticism to (assumed) knowledge, from reason to intuition, or from logic to 'the hunch', as the needs of our environment dictated and as a means of survival through a beneficial evolutionary trait. Conjecturally, it may well be that, during the long period when we existed in small hunter-gatherer groups or tribes, our distant ancestors relied on right side brain activity as the best means to survive and to flourish. This was at a time when left side function was less important in the fight for survival.

The idea of relating the ability for introspection as an adaptive evolutionary concept has much to recommend it; after all it may be seen as a beneficial trait that could be passed from one generation to another, perhaps, as we shall discuss later in this chapter, in a form of memetic/germline genetic transfer. When we consider the evidence from prehistoric periods, however, we are able to identify from cave paintings, from burial sites and the artefacts found therein, and from the rituals and ceremonies derived therefrom, that acute self-awareness, incorporating introspective elements of both the individual and tribal group motif, are apparent.

We are able, therefore, to accept the principles of Jaynes' theory of the bicameral development of the brain and its subsequent change to a more unified function as a beneficial evolutionary trait, but not his proposed timescale. It is likely that the bicameral activity of the brain, represented through the different hemispherical functions, evolved over many thousands of years with the evolution of left side functions developing simultaneously to the right side, but initially at a much slower rate, as the environmental need dictated.

Arising from this hypothesis, we may surmise that the soul complex previously proposed commenced its own evolutionary journey, using predominately right side brain function for its means of expression. It was only when left side brain function began to gain greater parity with the right side that gradually, over a historic period involving very many thousands of years, the soul complex was able to accelerate its own evolutionary development to incorporate more left side brain attributes.

This enabled the individual to combine increasing levels of introspective self-awareness, intelligent thought processes and an ego/identity with the mundus imaginalis that then forms the pattern for an emergent gestalt, one that enabled free will to become a dominant force in our whole brain function development.

In effect, by these means, the soul has become a progressively independent element of the human condition.

Consequently, although being complementary in its evolutionary development, we cannot say that our soul complex has evolved in the same way that the biological, material aspects of our being have evolved. This is because it is the immaterial form of our soul complex that has increasingly come to affect the very nature of evolution itself.

We are now able to contemplate and recognise that the nature of evolution itself has changed and continues to be ever changing, as it adapts to the growing demands of our consciousness, of our soul complex and our free will, all bound together in our personal and species gestalt.

However, the evolutionary process still remains the driver of adaptation because it is through natural selection that the beneficial trait of higher level consciousness is reproduced more frequently than those with a less beneficial trait of consciousness. But, paradoxically, evolution itself is affected by the natural selection of such beneficial traits! How can this be so?

We are now able, through introspection and a more equal relationship between right and left side brain function, to identify an evolutionary process that has branched into two linked but separate processes. One process continues to adapt the material physicality to its environment and is subject to natural selection, punctuated equilibrium and genetic mutation. This is the 'standard model' of evolution that is predominately non-random but does not have any directional means that are under the control of forces, either from within the organism it serves or from the external environment.

The second branch of evolutionary process is one that forms a pathway and is, to an increasing extent, gaining momentum as a consequence of the effect that our immaterial soul existence is having not only upon its own development and of the environment, but also its effect on the evolutionary process itself. This branch of the process of evolution may lead to the repro-duction through natural selection of those that exhibit higher levels of n- and, subsequently, h-consciousness, as a beneficial trait evident in humanity.

The effect of such a genetic selection or modification process may serve to curtail the momentum of natural selection as the principle driving force of evolution, but the consequential outcome may well be a faster development towards the natural hybridising process of higher level consciousness, found in de Ropp's room four, which could become a benefit to the ability of humanity to survive in its changing environment.

In this model the effect of natural selection is becoming of decreasing importance due to globalisation, through our increasing ability to control our reproductive system and some aspects of our genetic constitution and transmission. The effects of punctuated equilibrium and genetic mutation still have an important part to play in this model, but even here we get the sense that genetic mutation may become progressively more controlled.

Evolution, in this context, may thus be said to be directional and increasingly is becoming subjected to the control of humanity as the dominant lifeform on our planet.

This is not to say that humanity has arrived at its position through the auspices of an intelligent designer or that we were placed on Earth fully formed as part of a creation event. Far from it. The nature, type and condition of all life on our planet has reached its present physical state only through the hitherto natural process of evolution with no directional aspect to the development being involved.

Direction and control only arise once consciousness has progressed sufficiently, through an evolved, conglomerate complexity of a particulate organism, to enable the inherent soul complex to become independently progressive. Many will say that such an outcome is inevitable because 'The One Source' has imbued the archaeus particle with the vitality of the formatrix energy but, as we shall see in the next section, this inevitability does not extend to the physical form of humanity, or to that of any other species.

The principles involved in a fully formed creationist hypothesis are defeated by the progressive nature of the soul complex that currently just happens to be hosted by the human form. The concept of intelligent design, whilst not being completely defeated, is significantly weakened by the idea that consciousness and the soul may be housed in any animal form that has the capability. We will enlarge upon this aspect later in this chapter.

Recent interesting developments that will affect the nature of evolution, so far as natural selection is involved, arise from the knowledge currently being developed concerning the genetic structure of the human form and in particular the genome that relates to each individual. We are now able to determine from our DNA the genetic markers that indicate the means by which we have arrived where we are and, increasingly, the genetic characteristics that our physical bodies have 'acquired' on their journey from the past to the present.

The detail of the genetic make-up of each of us will enable reproduction to enter into a new era, where genetic matches for particular characteristics will become possible and a reproductive selection for future generations will not only be possible but perhaps inevitable.

Notwithstanding all of this, however, and bearing in mind our contentions concerning the structure of the Cosmos based on the archaeus particle enlivened by the formatrix energy, we are bound to ask whether there is any further mileage in the concept of an orthogenetic aspect to our evolutionary development, and will the possible future of human reproduction through genetic selection affect its direction?

The important question that arises from these considerations is:

'Is there a destiny for humanity and, if so, where does that destiny lie?'

4.02. Destiny

One of the most all-pervading thoughts that has occupied the minds of humanity is the idea that we are somehow 'destined' to live out our lives in a certain way, to arrive at a particular destiny, whatever that may be, or may involve. We are not dealing here with that which we sometimes call destiny where, by human contrivance and arrangements, an individual is either bred or groomed to fulfil a particular role or position. Rather it is one where individuals and the race as a whole may fulfil its life by following the determination, or otherwise, of any of the evolutionary forces so far discussed.

Destiny implies a destination, and to arrive at a destination there must have been a journey of one sort or another. In evolutionary terms such a journey would be the development of life as we encounter it on planet Earth today, from its origins in the bacteriological soup that was the birth of our beginnings, through an egress from the sea, to reach the canopy of the forests and return to the ground upon which we now dwell. We have seen that such a journey has been undertaken by the biological, material elements of life, through adaptation, within their environment, affected by punctuated equilibrium and genetic mutation. It has been one of a predominantly non-random, non-directional nature that has brought all species, including the one currently with the most advanced layers and levels of consciousness, to the present day.

There are two important points that arise from a journey such as this. The first and perhaps the most important point is that the invertebrate, mammalian species that currently have dominion over other species on Earth have only been able to achieve this status through the process of evolution. Humanity may naturally wish to assume that such a condition has been inevitable because the end result so far is obvious and apparent in its reality, and is one where it is difficult for us to envisage any viable alternative.

However, Homo sapien is a relative newcomer on planet Earth, and throughout its planetary history many major species extinctions have taken place, so that it is not difficult to envisage that one, or many, of the previously dominant species inhabiting the environment might, prior to their own extinction, have adapted and developed to the point where they would have become the species with the highest layer and level of consciousness, thus perhaps even depriving the mammalian familial species of humanity the opportunity to evolve as we have.

Evolution cannot have an opinion and, as a concept of a process, has no interest in promoting any particular species to become the predominant, conscious authority on the planet. That condition goes simply to the species that has most readily adapted to the environment prevailing at any one time and which possessed the potential to develop the brain capacity and/or electrochemical capability to house a large enough brain and developing layers of consciousness.

Following the many major extinctions of life on our planet this has now turned out to be humanity, but we must be ready and prepared to understand and accept that this need not necessarily have been the case.

The One Source of All Things, that has imbued all archaeus particles with an element of consciousness and with formatrix energy, has not restricted the physical form needed to host advanced layers and levels of consciousness and soul complex to that of the mammalian, invertebrate, hominin family. There are no restrictions or limitations to the physical form that houses such consciousness and soul complex, other than that which yields an intrinsic capability through the nature of its evolutionary journey.

Furthermore, the physical nature of the vehicle housing such a soul complex, by being irrelevant, negates our desire to relate our present physical form, from one of automatic or divine superiority, to being simply one of egotistical, psychological transference. We simply wish to be regarded as holding an automatic natural, inevitable place at the pinnacle of creation or of evolutionary development; which, if true, would only serve to restrict or limit the form of The One Source to that of our own physicality, or image, a proposition that is absurd.

Therefore, as far as a particular destiny for the physical, material form of humanity is concerned, it is simple and easy to see that no such thing exists, or has ever existed. Physically, we are what we are and where we are through a process that has nothing whatsoever to do with being replicated in the image of The One Source, or of our being the result of an intelligent designer. A proposition that many of a religious disposition may find difficult to accept, but one that we should all learn to embrace.

However, can the same be said for those immaterial aspects of humanity that involve the soul complex?

Which brings us to the second and hardly less important point arising from our model of evolution. We have seen from our discussions in Chapter One, from the text on The Emerald Tablet, that an ascendant journey has been the focus of the development of consciousness through an interaction between the subtle and material realms of reality.

That which is below is like that which is above and that which is above is like that which is below, to accomplish miracles for one purpose only:

as it ascends from the earth to the subtle, and back again, and in so doing receives the force of all things subtle and material.

The journey involved in this respect is one that relates directly, and only, to consciousness within the evolving sole complex and in particular to that of the increasing complexity that has enabled initially p-consciousness and then advanced layers of n-consciousness to develop. If there is any direct relationship between Homo sapiens and The One Source, then it is only where the immaterial aspects of consciousness within the soul complex are involved.

Such a soul journey has been, and continues to be, one of ascendancy that, since the last major species extinction, has evolved towards an ever-closer correlation with the notion of perfection discussed in Chapter One, even though it is apparent that we may not have made a great deal of progress on this journey and acknowledging that there is still a great deal further to go, to approach such a destination.

We may therefore assert, with some confidence, that the journey involved in the developing aggregation of consciousness and the soul has been directional and, furthermore, is one of an ascendant nature heading towards a more perfect existence.

Any evidence that this journey has been orthogenetic is very flimsy, perhaps to the point of non-existence. Yet, in commencing from such microscopic beginnings within the very structure of particulate mass, embodied in the archaeus particle, to become a living entity with the levels of complexity and consciousness so far developed, it is difficult to entirely dismiss orthogenetics from our model.

Everything described so far relates to the historical record of evolution and adaptation supported within the fossil record and from paleolithic, geological and archaeological evidence. There is no doubt that, from a historical point of view, we are where we are through evolutionary forces, even though such forces work in different ways upon the material and immaterial aspects of our existence.

But as to the future, will these forces continue to act in the same way?

There is no reason to suppose that the development and adaptation of our physical form will not remain the subject of the same evolutionary forces that have worked upon life on Earth to date, at least so far as natural selection, punctuated equilibrium and genetic mutation are concerned.

However, because evolution itself is a changing concept, the effect of the forces involved in natural selection will themselves also change, and vary, as we change the nature of our environment. Increasing globalisation, the understanding and subsequent control of our genome will alter not only the rate of our physical evolutionary development but also the nature of any adaptation involved.

Punctuated equilibrium as an agent for change is more difficult to pin down due to the diverse nature of its cause which, at least in part, may arise from influences outside of the zone of planet Earth. The incidence of stellar events such as sunspot activity and asteroid or meteor earthfall are as yet barely predictable, but could have a massive and perhaps catastrophic effect on species evolutionary development.

But none of these forces will change the evolutionary process that operates upon our physical being, or on that of all life, even though the outcome may be changed as we change our environment through the sheer weight of population growth and misuse of planetary resources. The aspect of humanity that will cause significant change to the very nature of evolution is that which involves the effect that the immaterial elements of humanity bring to bear.

Because our layer and level of consciousness together with our soul complex has developed sufficiently to become somewhat of an independent, progressive element of our lifeform, then the ability to change the nature of those evolutionary forces that act upon our existence are also subject to change. This is because we are no longer talking about changes to the environment or of genetic mutation, but are considering changes that can occur within the internal layer and level of consciousness of any particular human being, as an act promoted by choice and free will.

The evolutionary journey of our soul with its consciousness now takes on a different nature. Ever since the right and left side brain hemispheres gained something approaching parity, the journey of the soul, of consciousness, ego, identity, and the mundus imaginalis, as a gestaltic complex, has diverged from that of the standard model of evolution, to follow a differing pathway towards a definitive target or goal of achieving a natural state of perfection.

The impetus for this separate pathway arises from within the individual members of the organism known as Homo sapiens.

Can this impetus in any way be described as orthogenetic? The answer to that question will lie within the belief system of each individual as they seek to exercise their own adaptation of choice and free will. This is because, at the very core of our physicality, there is that imprint of consciousness within each archaeus particle that emanated from The Source of All Things and which has coalesced to allow the development of higher layers and levels of consciousness.

For many the physicality and the development of consciousness have been, and remain, inseparable. But for others the physical, material aspects of the human vehicle and its immaterial consciousness are capable of separation, and this has been demonstrated by those whose physicality becomes redundant through the trauma of paralysis, whilst consciousness remains a functioning capability, and also for those able to experience out of body encounters, particularly the shamanic communities of ancient history.

For yet others, the very core of our physical bodies, our particulate structure, is one that, in itself, is increasingly subject to change and adaptation. This is due to the outcome of our consciousness and soul complex, affecting the physical body to the extent that it is gradually adapting itself under the direction of its consciousness to open itself to alternate realities that are allowing us to accomplish feats that hitherto have not been possible.

This is clearly demonstrated in the accomplishments of the prodigious savant population who are often not bound or restricted by the reality presented to us by the 'normal' majority.

Another alternative example would be that of Lewis Pugh who is the only person in the world today who is known to be able to change his body temperature by raising it two degrees centigrade, an act of conscious choice, enforced by free will, enabling him to swim in extreme cold water conditions for extended periods of time, without protective measures.

Similarly we see evidence in the exploits of humanity that push the physical form beyond its present bounds, to ever-higher levels of achievement in all fields of activity. We are currently experiencing physical feats of endurance, of sporting prowess, of medical practice and of educational excellence, which the body achieves through the increasing dominance of its consciousness.

As a consequence of this, it is possible to say that the hitherto discredited notion of orthogenetics may still have a part to play in our evolution and in our destiny. This is because it becomes clear when we look at evolution, as a concept that is itself undergoing change and development, that there is now a direction to the pathway that human consciousness is choosing to take.

The driving force of consciousness is propelling us along this pathway and it comes from within the human organism. The direction taken is always an ascendant one towards the ideal of perfection and is subject to a form of control that arises from within our, as yet, subconscious soul complex. Consequently the pathway that human consciousness is taking may be called one of destiny.

Were it to arise from an exterior force then it would be possible to propose that the pathway towards destiny could be considered to be predetermined or predestined.

The implications that the introduction of free will brings to our soul complex makes predetermination or predestination of the end result an impossible element to contemplate within those ways and means that currently enable any progress towards that journey's goal. Whilst the ultimate goal of any evolutionary journey may be thought of as leading towards a state of perfection, there are many ways and means whereby the end result of perfection may be approached.

Any measure of predetermination would, however, necessarily affect the outcome forces of evolution and destiny, negating the process of natural selection and survival of the fittest. We do not therefore believe that any element of predetermination or predestination is involved in the evolutionary journey of humanity, or its destination, as it currently stands.

Whether we are able to achieve any further significant progress along the pathway of our choice will be determined by our consciousness as it struggles to expand its perception and scope relative to the changing realities we face.

Such expansion will need to initially accommodate and then overcome the reluctance for change and general apathy of our political, economical and philosophical institutions, evidenced in the well meaning but closed minds of those for whom materialism is all that exists. Furthermore, the thrust of scientific and political endeavour and output must change from one that generally seems unwilling, or unable, to devote itself exclusively to the altruistic good of the whole race and our environment.

The means by which our consciousness is able to approach the task of expanding the perception of its purview has been, and remains, that of introspection. It is the ability of the human race to examine its own existence and the means by which it is able to evolve that enable the journey towards its destiny and a state of perfection.

Destiny then arises and is directed from within our consciousness, from within our immaterial soul complex, but necessarily only in an abstract form of participation, because destiny is the subject of a future that has not yet been determined. Destiny by definition can only be a characteristic of the future; its position within the present is only transitory and is subject to other forces.

4.03. Fate

If destiny is a characteristic only of the future, then fate, if it exists, can only be a characteristic of the present, the here and now, but one that acts on the future if and when that transmutes into our reality.

The fate of all life on planet Earth may be said to be death. Everything that lives eventually dies or changes into something that is unrecognisably the same form. The subject of death will be discussed later in this chapter, but this is not the subject of our discussion of fate. Our views on fate here exist alongside the fact of the culmination of our lives and involve the operation of our consciousness with the active and operative agency of free will.

We have said that the pathway of destiny is not predetermined or predestined and the nature of time, as mentioned in Chapter One, as a constituent of the Ideas in the subtle realm lends additional weight to these notions. Because time only comes to exist as a passage or flow as the present in our material realm, through interaction of consciousness between the monolithic Idea of Time in the subtle realm, then it follows that destiny by being a characteristic only of the future cannot be formed or determined as a result of that same, present time interaction with the subtle realm. This then gives us a clue as to the workings of that which we label 'fate'.

Consciousness interacts with time as a subtle Idea to produce a reality that centres our existence in the present. The future has not been realised and nor will it be until consciousness, in the present time, converts it to become the ongoing present. Following this conversion, the nature of the future will have become resolved to represent an interactive reality between individual organisms anywhere and everywhere within the Universe as it expands. This is because the nature of the present reality is determined by each of us individually, as a collective, subconscious act of choice involving free will.

As the present becomes the reality, then the free will involvement of each of us will create and form a pathway towards a future that is better described as an ongoing present, one that, paradoxically, has yet to become. In so doing that pathway will affect not only the environment, but also all of the connections that each individual maintains with all of nature and all lifeforms. This is why many human beings feel that they experience an intimate contact and interaction with Gaia or what we sometimes call 'Mother Earth'.

Everything in the present is interconnected with everything else in the present, even if some of the connections seem to be remote. This is an aspect of the thought, previously discussed, that asks us to consider that any location in the Universe is its centre and any space is contained within all other spaces whilst simultaneously containing all other spaces within it.

The effect of maintaining all of these connections has an influence upon our conscious choices whose action is regulated by our free will, and it is this influence that establishes the pathway of a future destiny that is not predetermined.

At its best, such influence is in a full synchronicity that attempts to act in the best interests of the interconnected self-regulatory Gaian system that is planet Earth, the Universe, the Cosmos and all within it. At its worst, it is one that becomes an act of temporary harm or injury in that it disrupts the harmonious element of the connections within that same planetary, Universal, or Cosmic system.

It is consciousness that determines time which then becomes our present, it is consciousness that creates the pathway towards our destiny and it is consciousness that maintains our relationship with all things housed within and connected to our individual reality. It should therefore come as no surprise to learn that it is consciousness that endeavours to keep us upon the pathway, towards the state of perfection that is our destiny, and it is the outcome of the activity of our consciousness, in this respect, that we call fate.

It is an intrinsic element of our progressively independent soul complex, including consciousness, that it seeks to direct our ascendant journey towards a state of perfection. The nature of the subtle realm, to where consciousness in all its forms has journeyed since its inception, has always been the realm that houses the pure essence of Ideas and, as such, has been the resource for the purity that leads to perfection. It is therefore only natural that the direction of all consciousness bears the same influence from its interaction with pure essence of subtle Ideas.

Once the rise of basic consciousness was set in motion by the initial, amalgamating complexity of a particulate organism, processed as a trait, through natural selection, then the beneficial nature of this trait ensured that its evolution would progress and improve as further adaptations developed and were reproduced. As we have said, this was not a directional journey under external control but was a progression that used the beneficial trait, inherent within a growing conglomerate of consciousness, as a means of selection.

All of this was the case until our bicameral brain function gained an approximate parity between right and left side hemisphere characteristics, which enabled greater, introspective self-awareness. This allowed our soul complex to become a sufficiently progressive independent element of our existence, so that the effect of natural selection was decreased, to be supplanted by a branch of evolution involving an increasing level of directional control from within.

So the continuation, by our consciousness, of directing our journey towards the destiny of perfection is one that is natural, having grown from millions of years of practice. This occurs entirely through our natural unconscious abilities in the same way that the act of breathing is an unconscious function.

Therefore, there arises, as a natural function of consciousness, an imperative to encourage and direct every individual and consequently the race, as a whole, to continue its journey towards a destiny of perfection.

Now we can begin to identify a difference that is emerging between fate as it operates on an individual organism and fate as it affects the whole of the human race. This manifests as a difference between the microcosm and the macrocosm.

We have said that predeterminism and predestination have no part to play in our destiny, and this is also true with regards to fate. By operating only in the present, our consciousness is naturally and automatically able, through its interaction with the subtle realm, to identify, not only that which would be a benefit to each individual, but also to the race as a whole.

It is perhaps a sad comment on our application of consciousness that we do not always act to the benefit of others and for racial improvement.

Minute, or what might be regarded as microscopic, changes by an individual organism may affect the outcome of our racial journey towards perfection but, in general, such changes would need to be of a major, macroscopic nature or be repeated in sufficiently large numbers of individuals within the population so as to bring about major effects capable of affecting the future of the race. Remember, we are talking here of changes in direction that only take place in the present which, rightly or wrongly, seek to keep the goal of the human journey pointing towards perfection.

However, one Idea of the subtle realm, the one we have said is the most important, that of Free Will, is the Idea which allows the individual the scope for uniqueness. The exercise of free will requires each one of us to consciously or unconsciously maintain our own pathway of destiny, or to divert from it, without affecting the direction of the race as a whole.

This is because as the human population expands in number, the evolutionary direction it takes, being basically random in its nature, becomes increasingly slower to change. This reflects the law of large numbers, which operates mathematically to 'guarantee' stable long-term results for the averages of random events.

Of course there is no guarantee involved where evolution is concerned, except that the fittest for purpose will have the greatest chance of exhibiting a survival trait; but statistically, the larger the population becomes, with each member implementing their own choices, through free will, then the effect of each choice increases evolutionary stability, or stasis, as the effects of the choices smooth out to become closer to the mean or average.

History has shown that the journey of an individual can indeed change the direction of the pathway towards perfection which the race has embarked upon. But to accomplish such a change, then very large numbers of individuals have been needed to exercise their own choice and free will, in compliance with the individual or small group initiating such a change.

Whilst it is correct to say that a change in an individual destiny might have a serious, major effect upon the destiny of humanity, its lasting effects are only wrought through the mass of the population. It is the consciousness of the mass population that comes to operate in such a way that the change of direction in an individual would be assimilated. Thus, the destiny of any one individual, by its being housed in consciousness and being only an element of the present time, does not have lasting effects. The overall racial direction would be maintained.

In this way free will operates for individual organisms, keeping us unconsciously on our own pathway of destiny, but in a way that does not affect the outcome of our racial destiny. We will see in Chapter Five how free will may operate positively, negatively or passively to affect our progress towards our destiny.

Fate then is a characteristic of consciousness, operating microscopically for each individual without the racial pathway of destiny being affected. Macroscopically, fate operates at the level of mass population numbers, in a manner that employs the pure essence of the free will of all individuals, collectively, to maintain, or, most importantly, change the directional flow of our immaterial soul complex in a way that results in an alignment towards an ever-closer state of perfection.

This is the essence of what we call 'fate'.

4.04. Good and Evil

The Idea of Free Will, from the subtle realm, becomes embedded in our consciousness and allows each of us to be a unique individual, giving effect to our choices that can operate to the benefit or detriment of our fellow individuals and the environment. This whilst not diverting the race as a whole from its journey towards a state of perfection.

But the consequence of the exercise of free will also allows those choices that are to the benefit or detriment of our fellows to be regarded as either good or evil.

In considering the manner by which we are able to determine what is good and what is evil, we now turn to look at the principles of the Neoplatonic view as to the way that evil arises. We have seen that everything that exists in our reality has arisen from The One Source of All Things, and if we are to continue with this belief then we must be prepared to accept that evil also arises from that same source. To abrogate this belief would result in 'The One' becoming more than one, or even none at all. In religious terms this would result in two or more creators and two or more creations, or none at all.

One of the last of the classical Greek philosophers was Proclus Lycaeus (412–485 CE) who refined the work of Plato and Plotinus to confirm their view that evil exists only as a privation of good. That is to say that evil can only exist as a partial absence or significant reduction of goodness.

For Proclus, absolute evil would be the total absence of goodness and this cannot, and does not, exist because evil relies for its very existence on goodness. He uses the example of light and dark as an analogy to explain and emphasise his proposals, saying that darkness is only a relative condition because it only exists as a partial absence of light and therefore depends on light for its existence.

Bearing in mind that the presence of light is a natural outcome of the big bang event, it might be fair to say that goodness should be the natural attribute of the existence of everything that results from it. But, if the presence of evil is dependant upon the existence of goodness then we must also acknowledge that goodness itself is, to some extent, diminished by the presence of evil.

If we accept this definition then we are able to say that there is no such thing as absolute evil, one that exists with the total absence of goodness; there are only relative degrees of evil by which we can recognise and define evil, as it appears in our reality.

Similarly, absolute goodness is impossible whilst the presence of even the minutest element of evil in our reality exists. This will mean that the ultimate target of destiny being an absolute state of perfection might never be attainable.

The relationship of evil to goodness as proposed in the Neoplatonic sense has permeated and affected societies over the whole of the planet since they became popularised, and have played a significant part in the development of religions, including Judaeo-Christianity and Islam, together with the principles of most, if not all, legal systems and the way that we are governed.

Nations govern their people through systems of legislation, or edicts, that operate to offer benefits or advantages to those who comply with the civilised code of conduct, as determined by the state and, conversely, operate to apply sanctions to those who offend against the code of conduct. We can all recognise that degrees of transgression are represented and expressed in various categories of crime, which attract various levels of punishment, when justice is brought to bear. In principle, as goodness is increasingly reduced, the greater the evil becomes, which then attracts the greater the punishment.

Evil then arises from within our consciousness in a form that is relative to goodness. If we are able to envisage good and evil as a single strand or filament of our psyche, with good and evil polarised at either end, then it is our conscious choice and free will, embedded in our soul complex, that determines the point, in our reality, where our good/evil ratio is positioned along this strand. It is by the use of the mundus imaginalis, the imaginal key, that we may actively move our conscious choice along this strand, towards either polarity.

In the same way that our consciousness determines our individual course of destiny and sets in motion the application of fate to help keep us on the pathway towards perfection, then also the exercise of consciousness, upheld and supported by the form of free will, using the mundus imaginalis as the key, can at least keep us in balance along the good/evil axis of our being with hopefully a greater tendency towards the pole of goodness.

Thus the extent of evil in each of us is within our own ability to determine, bearing in mind (literally) our destiny and fate.

We believe that these principles are apparent and correct and confirm that we discard the notion that evil exists as a separate entity to that of goodness.

If evil exists as an absence, to some degree, in a relationship with goodness, then some of those naturally occurring events that some people regard as evil cannot be accounted for through the exercise of free will. We refer here to events such as earthquakes, floods, volcanic eruption, tsunami, tornado and cyclone, to name the most common of these events.

The reason why events such as these cannot be accounted for through the exercise of free will is because they are not evil events at all. Some people sometimes regard them as evil because of the effect they can have on the environment, or on human existence, where they may cause possibly large numbers of humans to suffer premature death or disability. However, they are not evil at all because they arise from those conditions on Earth that have allowed or promoted life to grow and for adaptation to take place.

Were the planetary conditions to have been so stable that these natural 'cataclysmic' events could not have occurred, then such conditions would have resulted in a much more sterile or even stagnant environment, to the point where it may not have been possible for the conditions necessary for the development of life to come into existence.

It is a known fact that all of life is in a state of continuous motion, both within the atomic structure of each element of its material substance and through its cycles of birth and death. To exist in a world where conditions did not allow for or encourage change would be to restrict or deny such movement. Had the planet not cooled from the super-heated state of existence existing over 4 billion years ago, then life as we know it would not have been able to become established.

The constituents of the atmosphere have adapted and changed through various means to allow oxygen-breathing life to flourish and cycles of propagation to become established, and that has enabled a huge variety of life to develop. The list of changes is huge.

So naturally occurring 'catastrophes' that adversely affect the human population are not the subject of evil. It is the failure of humanity to avoid placing populations in the path of destructive, natural events that causes us to consider them as evil. Our failure to take adequate steps to abolish or limit those of our activities that influence these events may also contribute to the 'evil' effect they may have. In these circumstances our influence on natural events might be an additional factor that can be regarded as arising, to some extent, from the application of our choices and free will.

Further natural evils are present due to the nature of the environment. These include the rise of disease and of the presence of materials that are toxic to human beings. Humans have always recognised that the effects of disease can be ameliorated by the use of other naturally occurring materials or by the processing of some materials to combine with others to effect relief or cure. The encounter and effect of contact with toxic materials is one where the race has needed to learn of its cause and effect and, again, to find a cure or relief through recourse to naturally occurring neutralising materials.

Until very recently, there has been a general natural system of checks and balances, intrinsic within nature, as part of the self-regulatory system that is Gaia. This natural system has recently come under strain or threat due to the huge, unrestricted, exponential growth in human population numbers, the rising levels of manufactured disease or toxicity and a lack of knowledge, ignorance, or apathy, in respect to the ecosystems of Gaia.

Thus the incidence of evil, whether it be through the activities that are counter to the laws of the natural state, or through the commission of living in a manner that is not in harmony with nature, can be seen to lie within the power of each one of us, and in the race as a whole.

In the words of Siddhartha Gautama, the Buddha:

All that we are is the result of what we have thought.
If a man speaks or acts with an evil thought, pain follows him.
If a man speaks or acts with a pure thought, happiness follows him,
like a shadow that never leaves him.

4.05. Death

Within the sphere of Western society, death has been held up as being something that is a great sadness, something that is to be avoided if at all possible (which of course it can't be), or as something that has been inflicted upon the human race because of some deviation from an ideal pathway, through some form of 'sin' or omission.

Nothing could be further from the truth.

Bearing in mind our comments concerning premature death in Chapter Two, in this section we refer to death as being a natural occurrence, in the course of nature, and not as a premature event brought about as the process of evolutionary refinement proceeds, or of the intervention of something that we call evil, as discussed in the last section.

Death is an absolute necessity that facilitates the ability of all species on Earth to come into existence, and then to survive and develop. Were it to be the case that nothing that has ever lived had ever died, then life on Earth would have stagnated to point where it would not have been able to develop at all. We must accept that we are only able to be born and to live because those alive before us have died, and that our own death allows new life to come into being. In effect, our death facilitates the birth of our children.

If death was not a built-in factor of life, then lifeforms could not have evolved, through reproduction, and neither would there have been any room to accommodate what would be continually increasing population numbers apparent from the very beginning of our racial journey.

This would create another circular paradox that would arise because, with nothing dying and with the planetary resources, including space, becoming exhausted, no evolutionary development would be possible through lack of reproduction, following which everything would then die in any case.

Thus we can see that death is an inevitable factor in the life cycle and is one that we are obliged to look at not only as a necessity, but as one of the means by which new life is both enabled and is able to continue.

Although we should not consider death to the form of life in the material realm to be a punishment for sins committed by ourselves or our forefathers, or through deviation from some ideal pathway, we should not look forward to death as something joyful, or necessarily to be embraced. Natural death is merely a means to an end, one that we should certainly recognise as essential to the well-being of everything and everybody on our planet and as a natural part of the Gaian principles of planetary self-regulation.

Accepting death as a necessity for life and in an attempt to dispel some of the many myths that surround death, we will look at the means by which it has become part of our life cycle. In his excellent book, *Life Ascending*,[15] Nick Lane sets out his views on the ten great inventions of evolution and in so doing includes death as the tenth of these 'inventions'.

(As an aside, it is important to note that the inference that evolution is able to 'invent' anything at all is unfortunate, because the exercise of evolution does not and cannot have any conscious thought-making or creative ability within the scope of its process. This may be regarded as splitting hairs, but the important point to recognise is that we must abolish from our thinking the notion that evolution is a separate, self-contained 'something' with creative powers of its own. It is not; it is, as previously discussed, the label given to a process of adaptation where natural selectivity encourages the development of lifeforms that exhibit beneficial traits.)

Dr Lane seeks to explain the importance of death, both to life and for the living, and in so doing goes back to the beginnings of life on our planet, some 3 billion or so years ago. One feature of life then, as now, is that of algal blooms seen on the surface of the oceans and waterways. Such blooms persist for many weeks whereupon they vanish overnight by dissolving into the very water that has sustained them.

Recent scientific progress has shown that the disappearance of such algal blooms is a built-in feature of their existence, in that they don't just die but in fact commit a form of suicide through a system of enzymes contained within each cell, which are 'programmed' to dismantle the cell from within.

Although the genes within each cell of the algae may be identical, each cell adapts to a greater or lesser extent to its environmental surroundings as a form of differentiation. When the time comes for the bloom to dissolve into the ocean then those cells that have better adapted to the environment may form more hardy spores which serve to seed the next generation of algae.

This is a simple example of the working process of evolution through natural selection where those best suited to adapt to the environment are those that are the subject of natural selection, and best circumstanced to reproduce or seed the next generation.

The interesting point that arises is that the algal blooms of 3 million years ago are remarkably similar to those experienced today. (For those interested in illustrations of such blooms, they may be seen on Wikipedia Commons images from NASA originals.)

The blooms may contain many thousands or even millions of microscopic bacteria for every millilitre of water and are usually green in colour. However, some may also be red or brown depending on the nature of the bacteriological content. The green blooms are mainly made up of cyanobacteria which are similar to those found in the cells of our own bodies.

Whilst the process described above has been significantly simplified as there are more interactive elements involved in the life and death cycle of the algal blooms, there is sufficient detail here for our purposes as we go on to consider that human life has evolved from the oceans and from bacteriological sources originating from the first adaptations that took place around 3 billion years ago.

Bearing in mind the similar nature of the bacteria in the algae and in the cells of our bodies, it is not surprising that the cycles of reproduction and of life and death issues should be replicated and built into our own life cycles, in an adapted form, from our very beginnings in the universal common ancestor.

Evidence that this genetic transmission of the mechanism of death is inbuilt into all lifeforms is prominently evidenced in species such as the Pacific salmon whose life cycle is terminated in a 'programmed' manner after attaining the site of their birth and experiencing a frenzy of hormonal spawning activity. Similarly, queen bees are destroyed by their daughters after sixteen years of sperm production ceases and their life purposes are then regarded as completed.

There are many more examples that could be cited but the end result for all life on planet Earth is quite simple: we all die, eventually, from natural causes that are built into our life cycle system. So the factor that is common to all lifeforms is that we all die and this goes to reinforce the idea that death is a necessary step in the process of living and in the process of evolution.

Interestingly, as cells gather together and form larger multicellular units and colonies, then the tighter, more contained environment experienced by such entities brings about a further adaptation. Some cells within the multicellular body become differentiated into what biology has termed germline cells (as opposed to soma or somatic body cells), that serve to organise and police the colony.

Dr Lane points out that, whilst there is no law which states that all cells in a body have to suffer death, most single cells die, which is apparent in all lifeforms and is usually expressed through an ageing appearance of the lifeform involved. But even this cannot be said to be totally true of all known lifeforms.

This is because there are some lifeforms that are capable of replacing the cells within their multicellular structure as those cells die, and they continue to do so ad infinitum. In one sense they may be regarded as immortal, as their cellular structure remains the same even though the cells themselves may all have changed several times. This raises the question: 'Is this true immortality?'

Arising from the differentiation between germline and somatic cells, we understand that, whilst the somatic body cells may be disposable and may to some extent be replaced, the germline cells have specialised to the point where they are able to be the means whereby genetic information may be passed down from one generation to the next. The development and adaptation of specialised germline cells must be regarded as one of the most significant beneficial traits that the process of evolution has facilitated.

Now we see emerging from the process of dying many possibilities, including the means for the transmission of the mechanism of death itself, that is automatically built into the reproductive cycle and which becomes part of our life expectation. But also we may see a clue as to another, perhaps enticing condition, that of partial soul migration or metempsychosis, through the ability of germline cells to transmit information to future generations. For many the experience of a past life is a part of their reality and this is what we will look at now.

4.06. The Encounter with Previous Life Experiences

In looking at the possibility that we may somehow encounter the experience of a previous life, lived by an earlier 'someone' who has a relationship to our present existence, we need to look at a suitable mechanism for the transmission of such an experience. The means of such a transmission may come about through the combining of the process of germline transmission, developed over millions of years, together with a modern, cultural idea in the form of 'memes'.

We are indebted to the molecular biologist Richard Dawkins for tabling, as a topic for discussion, the hypothetical concept of memes in his book *The Selfish Gene*.[16]

Germline cells have been with us for millions of years, literally. As we have already said, they have been the means whereby genetic information has been transmitted down the generations of animal life from the earliest stages of our evolutionary process. In this respect they may be regarded as being immortal so long as the reproduction of the animal species concerned continues to be recognisably in the same established form, albeit one that continues to adapt and develop.

The possibility of previous life experiences arises when the soul complex previously described is one that is capable of being transmitted through germline cells. The nature of the complex represents a beneficial trait in humanity, one which has allowed and encouraged the dominion of human beings over all other lifeforms that inhabit planet Earth and, as such, is subject to the principles of natural selection previously discussed.

So much for the mode of transmission. But the soul complex described remains an immaterial human resource that, although arising from within a biological base, has no material substance from which replication may be established. This is where, in our opinion, Richard Dawkins' concept of the meme lends itself to become the imitator of the soul complex making a replica of its content available for attachment to the germline cells for reproductive transmission into future generations.

Germline cells have provided a self-replicating means of transmission, upon which evolution depends, and memes may require a similar mechanism for their transmission. The replication of memes is generally thought to be through exposure to others of the same species, who have evolved as efficient copiers, or imitators of memetic information. Such cultural aspects of human characteristics may be seen, however, in descendants who have not had the opportunity to acquire such features through the means of imitation, but may have done so through a form of reproductive copying. Thus, the way that memes survive and change may be likened to the process by which genes function in the process of natural selection.

So, in our model, memes may be described as units of cultural transmission, although it is fair to say that there is little agreement as to what exactly constitutes such a unit. However, proponents of Dawkins' concept point out that, whilst it is not possible to define a particular size given to any gene, neither is it possible to ascribe its every particular feature. Each gene encapsulates the key aspects of its inheritable features, and we consider that this criterion applies equally to the cultural unit which is proposed in a meme.

Whilst the meme hypothesis is still in its comparative infancy, it forms an interesting means by which behavioural patterns and cultural aspects of heredity are transmitted, and we can see the possibility arising where the genetic function of germline cells becomes allied or adhered to that of the experience of a soul complex. The result is the possibility of their transmission, to subsequent generations, through the reproductive process.

It appears to us that there is a similarity between some of the features which emanate from a soul complex, such as the one proposed in our cosmic model, to that of the cultural content in the model of Richard Dawkins' meme.

The possibilities that such a feature grants to us are immense, but predominantly they offer to us possibilities as to how past life experience and reincarnation may arise if the experiences that the soul of someone previously alive, and with whom a genetic relationship exists, is indeed transferable down the generations.

A word must be said concerning the genetic relationship which is necessary as the foundation for such a transmission, and this is centred on what is called 'the genealogical paradox'. This is expressed by the theory that if everyone currently alive has two parents and each of those parents has two parents, and so on back through time, then two things that are not possible appear to be viable. The first is that the population of the world would be larger the further one went back through the generations, whereas the opposite is true. Secondly by the time each of us alive today went back through say ten generations we would have 1,024 direct ancestors, and if we went back twenty generations we should have 1,048,576 direct ancestors, and if we went back thirty generations we should have more that 1.1 billion ancestors.

Clearly we would soon reach the point where the number of ancestors each of us would require would outnumber the population of the world or even the number of people who had ever lived.

Obviously this could not be the case and hence the term 'paradox'. So we should look for reasons why. The first reason why our genetic ancestors are less than the numbers required to fulfil the theoretical volume of the population is that of inbreeding. The prevalence of our ancestors marrying or procreating with cousins of some degree (first, second, third, once removed etc., etc.) has, historically, been very significant, thus creating common ancestors. Then the incidences of events arising from migration, plague diseases, war and catastrophic natural events have all combined to reduce greatly the actual number of our direct ancestors.

The number of our direct ancestors is almost impossible to determine beyond a few generations, but it is certainly nowhere near as many as the theoretical maximum permits. The number of descendants over many generations, however, will still be significantly very large. So that when we are considering the possibility of encountering, from someone previously alive, an experience from their soul complex, we must recognise that our genetic descendants include a very significant number of the past population.

The soul complex of our ancestors does not die or cease to exist, and parts of their experience become available to us through the genetic transmission of our germline heritage and associated memelike aspects of our soul complex. The mundus imaginalis, once again, is the key that can unlock such past experiences; and if the experience of a previous soul complex were to be transferred more or less as a whole, then this might manifest as a reincarnation.

For most who encounter previous life experience, the 'memories' may be occasional and it may be that sometimes they are incomplete or indeterminate, and may only be encountered as something akin to déjà vu. But for others the transmission may be more complete including the elements of identity and ego whereupon, for the individual receiving the past life experiences, they may become overwhelming to the point where dissociative personality disorder or dual personality may ensue.

The means of uncovering past life inhabitation of individuals who are currently alive exists in the form of hypnotic regression techniques and many examples exist where life experiences, both singular and multiple, have allegedly been encountered within the consciousness of one individual.

In addition, for some members of some races, there exists a tradition of what is called karmic transfer, which involves soul experiential transfer that arises from the outcome of natural acts in cause and effect. That is to say that if goodness is enacted during a lifetime then goodness will ensue in any soul transfer, and conversely if evil or badness is enacted then that is the experience that may be transferred. The opportunity thus may arise for some redress of evil experience to become available to the now living person, if he or she **chooses** that to be the case and their free will so enacts that choice.

In this way it is possible that the race, as a whole, may gravitate towards a greater racial goodness along the pathway towards perfection.

Although not requiring or relying on any genetic correspondence with ancestors, an interesting theory that is allied to the genealogical paradox is the notion that any individual on the entire planet may be introduced through the connections of no more than five other individuals, one of who must be known personally. This is the theory that has been labelled 'six degrees of separation' as set out by Hungarian author Frigyes Karinthy in 1929, whereby a chain of a 'friend of a friend' statements can connect any two people in a maximum of six steps.

This theory reinforces the notion that everything which exists on our planet is thoroughly interconnected and perhaps even interdependent to a much greater and closer extent than we are prepared generally to acknowledge.

Consequently it becomes even more difficult to understand why it is that individuals and groups of individuals are prepared to fight each other, often to the point of death, when we are all so closely interconnected with each other and with every other aspect of our reality. Any damage we do to any other is damage we do indirectly to ourselves, and conversely any good we do to any other is goodness that we indirectly do to ourselves – the latter being a fundamental principle of enlightened self-interest.

4.07. The Story So Far

The Emerald Tablet has provided a suitable starting point towards an understanding that the Cosmos is formed of one dimension and two realms of reality, the material and subtle realms. The nature of the material realm is experienced through our five senses and explains the reality in which we spend our daily lives. The subtle realm is that which exists beyond our senses and contains the essence of perfect Ideas arising from the mediation of The One Source of All Things. These become translated into the means by which both the material and subtle realms find their expression, and which are the principles and ideals by which we seek to govern society. The interaction between the two realms takes place through the medium of consciousness and forms an ongoing, continuous process that results in evolution and development of life in the material reality.

Based upon the two-realm cosmogony that is available to our consciousness, and their constituencies, we are now able to establish a structure for the material realm. This is the particulate structure of subatomic and atomic particles which gain their mass through the absorption of the minutest subatomic particle of all, the archaeus particle. This exists in the subtle realm on a field of energy that transmits mass to the material realm and goes on to form the dark energy that powers the acceleration of our Universe. The particulate mass of the material realm gathers to form stars which become the means whereby the different material elements are created.

A form of energy, the formatrix, enlivens particles of material, and when groups of particles combine and congregate each contributes their element of consciousness until complex particulate structures evolve to the point where they become aware. Eventually sufficient conscious mass has assembled so that it is able to observe the hitherto unformed mass of the material Universe which it thus determines, and in so doing gives it form and structure. Continual grouping of complex particles and consciousness proceeds until it is able to form an identity, and eventually consciousness reaches a level where the foundations for a soul come to exist; and as evolution continues, then so do the attributes and abilities of the soul.

Following on from the nature and structure of the cosmos, we see how consciousness enables evolution to commence its journey of development. We understand that particles congregate and develop into ever more complex structures which exhibit increasing layers and levels of conscious ability.

Layers of consciousness, and some of the various levels within, allow us to understand how the Cosmos works towards an order of perfection, and we come to understand that all life is conscious and that self-awareness, the ability to communicate and intelligent thought are all stages in the evolutionary development. We can recognise that various layers of consciousness have developed over eons of time, and that within those layers there are increasingly transcendent levels of consciousness that we are learning to access.

Furthermore, we are also now able to recognise that reality, as we generally perceive it to be, is not fixed or reliable and this leads us to consider not only the nature and security of our reality, but that altered states of consciousness exist as a tool or key to accessing and understanding that part of the Cosmos that is, in our everyday existence, currently beyond the reach of our senses. We also see a form of the active and creative imagination, the mundus imaginalis, as the master key in accessing alternate realities and states of consciousness, which is not only the product of an adaptive evolution, but has also become the current means of propelling the evolutionary motion towards... what?

The 'what' has now become apparent as the adaptive evolution of consciousness that is represented within the longer lived, macrocosmic animal lifeforms on our planet that continue on an ascendant journey, one which strives to reach towards a state of perfection. Following this principle, we have seen the means whereby dual sided brain evolution has unified to enable the soul complex to develop to the point where it has become able to control and direct the output of the higher brain function.

We are then able to identify evolution as the principle driving force towards this ascendancy, a force that acts in a mixed non-random, random and directional manner, simultaneously. The direction arises from our own consciousness which serves to increasingly divide the process of evolution into two distinct branches. The first continuing to adapt the material and physical aspects of all life on Earth. The second process also continues adaptation, but now of the immaterial elements of our being, which are coming increasingly under the direction and control of our soul complex and, in particular, our consciousness.

Arising from this two-pronged evolutionary process we are able to identify destiny as a directional journey that can only have an abstract form because of its ability to exist only in a future that has not yet arrived or been determined. Extrapolating from this future, which is determined as the ongoing present, we have seen that fate also exists through the actions of our consciousness, incorporating the free will of each of us as a conglomerate structure whose direction does not change.

In looking briefly at good, evil and death we are able to see the means whereby life progresses and is enabled to adapt. We can acknowledge the necessity for death as an enabling part of life, and we also are able to identify the beginnings of a hypothesis that sees soul migration and reincarnation as a possible reality.

Part II

Cosmic Interaction

Chapter Five

The Interactive Cosmos

My pattern continues to be uncovered,
questions arise about all of it,
demanding answers to the meaning of it all.

But,
Are they ready to discover the truths?
have they maturity enough to understand the 'why'?
can they begin to appreciate the scope of my Cosmos?

Is their consciousness able to respond?
to interact with the echo of my Free Will?

Do they 'see' what they are doing?
is their consciousness capable of further ascent?
can it be sustained at the level of 'knowing'?

Are they in control of their own future?
within my pattern of existence?
within the care-full balance of it all?
within the perfect symmetry of the whole?

Can their yearning reach fulfilment?

Questions, questions, questions?

5.00. Introduction

Having briefly looked at the nature and the structure of the
Cosmos together with those aspects of life on planet Earth that
arise therefrom, which start to give meaning to our existence, we

now look to develop a more cohesive, inclusive understanding from those elements so far discussed.

It is important to emphasise that none of the aspects under consideration operate in isolation from any other, and the thrust of the next two chapters will be to bring everything together to create an understanding of why things are as they are.

5.01. Three Principles: The One, the Subtle and the Material

We have described the Cosmos as comprising one dimension and two realms of reality that together form the initial gestalt of existence. The two realms rely upon the dimensional nature of The One for their form and reality, whilst all three depend on each other for their means of expression. The principles involved are very simple and are as follows:

5.01.01. The First Principle: The One Source of All Things

The entire model described so far relies on the existence of an entity or force that caused everything else to follow. The label that is attached to this force or entity depends on the belief system we each adopt, but we have called it 'The One Source of All Things'. It is from this principle that all things, in our Cosmos, come to be. The evidence that such an entity, or force, exists at all does not derive from any scientific or empirical point of view. Science is very good at establishing how the Universe developed from the big bang event, but offers little or no credible explanation of the cause of such an event.

The existence of such a force as The One Source is all around us – such a force must exist because we and our Universe exist, at least as far as we can determine.

Can there be any doubt that the material Universe which we are currently a part of, in our daily habitation, came about through some means or another? Whether it be from a condition where previously nothing existed or from a state of material in chaos, we exist and are here because 'something' caused that to be so.

The answer to the question 'Why is there something rather than nothing?' is the one that has motivated the sciences and the religions throughout the ages and, by that very motivation, there is an implicit acceptance, from all aspects of the human condition, that the Cosmos must have arisen somehow! It is only the means of the 'somehow' that has divided us and differentiated our attempts to determine the beginnings of the Cosmos.

In order for it to be understood, there has been a great tendency, one that might even be described as a driving need, for humanity to define the 'somehow' as an entity or force. Great scrolls of literature imbuing the entity that is The One Source, with every power imaginable, have been generated, handed down orally and finally written down over millennia, so that a great many stories, myths and legends abound, even today, in the age where reason and logic hold centre stage. Many religions preach that, because we exist and have developed in the way that we have, in conditions conducive to the propagation of life generally, that it must be due to some form of intelligent design, which was imparted to the Universe and us from the very beginning of life.

Religions throughout the world have sought to uphold The Source as a God or a series of attributes that constitute a God, and have gathered around the storyline of their deity a number of intensive procedures and regulations that have sought to secure and govern the conduct of their adherents. It was Voltaire who reputedly said: 'If God did not exist it would be necessary to invent him', and this serves to emphasise the need, that humanity demonstrates, to categorise the nature of how and why we exist and to establish a set of rules that conduct our daily lives in support of each relevant deity.

Did we invent God as a comfort blanket, or a delusion, in order to rationalise our existence and thus answer the 'why' question mentioned earlier? The answer to this question must be a firm 'no' because all we are seeking to do, all of us whether in the fields of the sciences or the religions, is to define the 'somehow' of our existence, and nobody who is alive today, or who has ever lived, has been able to produce a satisfactory, definitive answer.

Having looked at intelligent design in Chapter Three we need say no more here, but we are still left with the fact that we are indeed here, and furthermore, that this has happened through a systematic process of evolution that selects on the basis of beneficial traits which appear to operate in an ascendant direction, at least on the immaterial aspects of our being.

Although there are some cosmologists who offer us a Universe that had no causal event (it simply just happened), science has been successful in its attempts to look back into the history of the Universe in order to 'see' what it was that started it all and has generally concluded that some event or the beginning of some process must have occurred to initiate the existence of our Universe. Science generally has 'the Big Bang' as its starting point, but before then, when time and space did not exist – what?

Religion has 'the creation' – but from what? Nature in all its many forms is the natural knitting together of all ecological and physical systems as they arise and develop, but which rely on the existence of life before it can start its work of forming a homogenous, all-encompassing, singular, organised, self-regulating system.

It is the cause of that initiating occurrence that we have called 'The One Source of All Things' and it matters little that religion or science may choose to label this occurrence to suit their own beliefs or purview. It is the same cause no matter how we label it. The existence of 'The One Source' may be taken therefore as a given, but it must be acknowledged as one where each individual can and must be free to define or grant attributes to it, according to his or her own beliefs.

5.01.02. The Second Principle: The Subtle Realm

The second requirement of the model under discussion is the establishment of a realm of reality that we have labelled as 'The Subtle Realm'.

This is a realm that has no material attribute or content and we have seen from our considerations in Chapter One that it is one that exists every-where and no-where, at the same time. We are unable to point to any place where we can say, 'Here lies the subtle realm'; it is one that exists in all places at once.

From the beginning of self-awareness, consciousness has become the means by which we are able to decide how to proceed and progress in our daily lives. Given the blank canvas that must have been the condition of the embryonic minds at our species' beginning, from where would such notions as ethics, virtue, science and religion etc., etc. have come?

It is true that the need for survival may have acted as a driving force and encouraged, within some members of the human race, the desire and need to find ways of living peacefully with each other and a means of gaining an advantage over other aspects of life, in such a way that improved the chances of surviving. But, starting with nothing by way of experience, or knowledge of anything, where would the first species' members turn to for their ideas?

We begin to see the need for a separate realm where Ideas reside, one that arose from the start of life wherever it existed, when little or nothing in the form of a thought process existed. History has shown that some ideas have arisen, across the planet Earth, without apparent geographical migration, sometimes over long time spans, sometimes simultaneously.

We must remember that knowledge of the physical laws which govern our Cosmos, once gained, only uncover the patterns that already exist. Our species have not created any new patterns of physical law that enable our existence that were not already there awaiting exposure to our experience. In this respect we can say that we encounter knowledge once the development of our consciousness has progressed to the point where such knowledge might be relevant and understood.

Such a process would require knowledge, in the form of ideas, to be stored awaiting exposure to our consciousness at the appropriate time. It is perhaps easy or convenient to suppose that the subtle realm of Ideas exists within the interior of each one of us, in such a way that it may, in fact, actually be our own consciousness. This is because it is our consciousness that forms the interaction with the subtle realm, so it would be natural to suppose that all notions and ideas stem from that same consciousness.

The existence of such a realm as the one proposed in this model is an attempt to satisfy all of the experiences that humanity has encountered in its evolutionary progress to the present day reality. We need to take on trust something that we cannot measure and cannot yet prove to exist. After all, this is the way we have gained knowledge and intellectual value from the very beginning of our self-awareness as a race.

We must also recognise an aspect of the subtle realm that is of crucial importance to our thinking, and that is that its constituency has no material properties whatsoever so that its content can have no means of expression without the existence of the third principle. The relationship between the two realms is thus symbiotic, each to the other!

5.01.03. The Third Principle: The Material Realm

The third realm of being is perhaps the easiest to understand and to come to terms with. This is the material, physical reality of our existence, one that allows life to develop and be nurtured.

This realm is governed by structures and patterns of what we have come to label as science, physics and/or mathematics. The laws of thermodynamics, of the atomic or nuclear structure of all things, of the quantum world, that still remains somewhat of a mystery but which can be seen to produce spectacular results, are all examples of the way in which our Universe is structured and held both together and apart. All of these are examples where truths have existed since the inception of the Universe and which have been uncovered or exposed by the human need to understand the reality that we encounter – the need to define the 'somehow'.

To say that understanding this realm is the easiest of the three under discussion is in no way meant to detract from the effort and achievement involved in uncovering the truths involved in every scientific, physical and mathematical discipline. If we are not able to understand the means by which our existence, in the material realm, is enabled, then we will have little or no chance in understanding any of the realms that might exist, beyond our physical reality.

It is fair to say that the more we are able to uncover the patterns of being that sustain our Universe, then the greater becomes the mystery of how we all came to exist in the first place, the greater becomes the power of the entity or force from which everything arose and the nearer we come to answering the question, 'Why is there something rather than nothing?'

The three principles set out above form the foundation for all that follows; they form the matrix within which all realities, all dimensions, all existences of whatever form or being, derive. They form one homogenous unit that we call the Cosmos, a gestaltic form of a unity, where each element partakes of the other, where each part is distinct yet indivisible from the whole.

The wisdom handed down from our starting point on The

Emerald Tablet can be seen to be all inclusive, all powerful and entirely far reaching. It is perhaps worth reminding ourselves of the principles involved by way of a shortened, modernized version of the text as we go forward to consider the meaning of it all.

> *From the mediation of the one thing (or entity) and therefrom by the establishment of a realm of the subtle (above), and a realm the gross (below), a two-way interaction, or correspondence, between these realms enables the miracle of all things to be created.*
>
> *The correct nourishment or expression of the subtle within the gross increases its subtle content allowing perfection to be approached and creation grow towards wholeness.*

5.02. Perfection

Throughout our discourse so far, we have referred to the objective of evolution and human endeavour to be that of attaining an ever-closer correlation to a state of perfection. To date, we have recognised this state as belonging naturally to The One Source of All Things, and the manifestation of the mediations that arise therefrom seen as the Ideas within the subtle realm.

If we were to achieve such a state, it would mean that we would then become alike to The Source and also to the pure essence of all of the Ideas. But the question we have not yet asked is: 'Do we really want to achieve perfection and what would be our condition if the human race were to attain such a state?'

To consider this any further we will need to assume that it is possible for us to achieve a state of perfection, as the questions posed would not otherwise arise. So we will proceed on this assumption.

Nothing exists in isolation and the sum of all things in existence, taken together, creates a fully integrated self-regulatory gestaltic system. Therefore, to achieve a state of perfection would necessarily involve us in becoming at one with all of the characteristics that have been established for Ideas which are seen as the pure essence of their existence. In our present state of mental and psychological development, this might appear to represent a set of paradoxical characteristics.

The notion that every facet of every Idea, in the subtle realm, could become contained within each of us whilst, at the same time, each and every Idea maintained its separate character, in compliance with the conditional requirements for Ideas, set out in Chapter One, might appear as a paradox within us. However, all of those who attain perfection would have within themselves the combined pure essence of all Ideas and yet be able to comply with the separate characteristics that maintain their purity.

Thus, each individual would be automatically capable of sharing and integrating the nature of each single Idea, not only with everything that imitates the character of that idea, but with the characteristics of every other Idea itself. This whilst being capable of retaining and maintaining the singular, unique, pure and separate essence that is the Idea.

A state of perfection would require us to ensure that the essence of each Idea remains discrete even as the interaction or interdependence of several, or all, Ideas becomes an essential requirement.

This sounds complicated, but many of the scientific community, particularly the anthropologists and etymologists, may already have recognised this and may have begun to develop the ability to approach the means of doing so, at least in part. This is because there is involved in those disciplines the recognition and separation of the root elements of everything that exists, back to their original source and then the complex recombining of multiple Ideas to replicate the complexity that is an everyday reality. In fact, we all have an ability to achieve this process to some small extent in our daily lives as we make various connections between differing aspects of our reality.

The difficulty that arises, however, is that, in a state of perfection, all of this would be accomplished simultaneously, as a matter of course, for everything in existence. The perfect entity would, without any effort or further process being involved, be able to 'see' the entirety of any reality in all its finest detail, with all its potential laid out before them.

The conditions for the perfect entity do not stop there. We have said that Ideas must be able to last forever, that they cannot change and can have no parts. This means that, being perfect, we also would last forever, but could not change and could have no parts.

A picture emerges of an entity that is fully comprehensive and cohesive. Each individual, besides being able to 'see' every aspect of their reality and its every potential, would remain in a perfect condition, totally unified, fully integrated, wholly organised and of course immortal and most importantly unchanging. Furthermore, a new sense, or set of senses, would naturally need to develop to encompass all of the foregoing characteristics. This would be one that would bring the entire scope of perfection into the realm of our present senses, whilst remaining discrete as to the means of its presence, existing as a sort of separate, master sense that enables and augments the other five senses.

This master 'sixth' sense may already exist, perhaps in an embryonic form in some people and, if it were to be proven to be a beneficial trait, then, given sufficient time, no doubt the process of evolution would naturally select it for the reproductive benefit of the human race in a long-term future that has yet to come into existence.

But would such a condition of perfection, such as the one described, represent a benefit for the future of the human race? Would it be a condition that the human race could endure?

Some points to consider are: We would 'know' everything that there is to know through the total assimilation of the subtle realm within us, and consequently, there would be nothing left for us to gain knowledge of, nothing to uncover. Perhaps more importantly, nothing would remain to us as a belief. If we know all there is to know and can see the entire potential of everything, then belief would cease to exist because it would have no foundation upon which to build and no meaning that could be ascribed to it. Belief and faith would be displaced by knowledge.

Additionally, there would be nothing to create, because the potential for all things would have been seen and created. Creativity, which may have been a cornerstone of human endeavour from the beginnings of our objective conscious racial history, would have no purpose and would cease to exist as a human aspiration.

If we know everything or potentially everything, if creativity becomes meaningless, then there would be no need for emotions to exist. What would be the point of an emotion when the outcome of every action or thought would be apparent to every perfect body? To be perfect might bring a perfect emotion of ecstasy, one that is perpetual and unchanging, but having nothing to relate it to would render it meaningless and stagnant.

A strange thought then arises from the condition of perfection and that is: 'Would there be any point in living, once we become perfect and immortal?' Another cornerstone of human endeavour has been that of striving to improve, pursuing the search for knowledge, gaining security from one's belief system, using our creativity and emotional responses to raise the quality of our existence. But given the nullification of these character-istics, we would ask, what is there to strive towards once every-thing is known and belief becomes meaningless? What would be the point of immortality?

It is possible that along with the state of perfection there would naturally arise the ability to be content and satisfied with that condition, where the desire to be anything different was unrecognisable and absent. To have and to hold on to perfection might grant many benefits to the entity possessing it, where emotional feelings of isolation and loneliness, although present, may not be felt or recognised.

In these circumstances we may well conclude that becoming perfect would not, after all, be a benefit to members of the human race, especially from the vantage point of our current reality. The notion of perfection might then be seen as an ideal goal located on the far horizon of possibility, but without us having the true desire of ever achieving such a destiny.

This represents a condition that may appeal to our current level of understanding. It may well suit us to closely approach a state of perfection without ever actually attaining it, thus leaving a purpose and direction to each individual human being. It would also allow for the sixth sense to operate more efficiently and for change to be possible and to occur, whilst we would become long lived to the point of our natural maximum term lifespan, but foregoing immortality.

However, this condition would eventually involve the slowing down of the process of evolution until it came to a halt, a condition that currently does not seem possible, as it is beyond the present limits that our consciousness can encompass.

Another possibility, therefore, is that the process of evolution, whether affected directly by the human organism or not, continues to adapt Homo sapiens to the point where they (we) cease to be regarded as human beings, to become human beings 'plus', or an enhanced race that we might call Homo superior. In these circumstances it is possible that a state of perfection might become a desired state of existence, which may be attained without any of the disbenefits that our current level of understanding identifies.

In which case the ascendant progress towards a state of perfection would be maintained and the natural selective evolutionary process aided by our consciousness would continue, to a conclusion.

All of the above is based on the premise that reaching a state of perfection is possible, and this may not be the case in reality. Certainly, from our current state of development, and bearing in mind both the physical and mental activity of our daily lives, we are so far from a state of perfection that it could only remain as an ideal; an aim for the unforeseeable distant future. Nevertheless, human endeavour has always been one of improvement and in many generations to come such an aim might come closer to achievement.

It is worth expanding on the condition of perfection that we have described, at least in part, as the condition that pertains to The One Source and a possible consequence thereof. We should reflect upon the thought that, if the emanation of its mediations are considered to be perfect, then we would also expect such an entity to be perfect in all aspects of its being and its potential. It would necessarily be omnipotent, omniscient, and unchanging in all respects, as well as being immortal. Such a state of perfection does not permit anything to be present within the realm of its existence that is not also perfect.

However, being alone, perfect and unchanging, bereft of new experience and encounter, may not be a condition that is worth enduring and hence the desire to experience the knowledge of itself, resulting in the establishment of the means to do so, experienced by us as the Universe. It is reasonable to conjecture that this is the reason for the creation of the subtle realm of perfection and from thence the material realm of imperfection, and was the means whereby The One Source could recognise and relate to its own perfection.

This leads us to contemplate that The One Source of All Things may have sought to experience imperfection through its mediations contained within the material realm.

This is as good a reason as any offered throughout history for the creation and existence of the entire Cosmos in its form of three realms that form a hierarchal, unified, gestaltic, and, currently imperfect, whole.

5.03. The Immaterial Reality of the Subtle Realm

Many people, especially those from the scientific community and those who believe that all that exists arises from material 'stuff', may dispute the very idea that a subtle realm exists at all. The nature of any dispute may arise because concepts such as the subtle realm, the soul and free will are not material concepts that can offer any degree of empirical proof. For many scientists the inability to prove (or disprove) the existence of such concepts means that they do not exist, from which they extrapolate that there is no need for them to exist.

This then goes to the very nature of reality itself. The *Concise Oxford Dictionary* defines reality as:

> *the state of things, as they actually exist, as opposed to an idealistic or notional idea of them. Reality is something that is actually experienced or seen, that has the quality of being lifelike or has the state or quality of having existence or substance.*

There are several problems with such a restricted definition. For a start we have already outlined, in Chapter Three, that the experience of things which exist may be encountered and interpreted very differently from person to person, thus rendering the nature of reality as being insecure or variable. Then, a great number of things that might be said to exist do so in an abstract form. These include concepts such as justice and all of the virtues, all numbers, indeed mathematics generally, together with the many possibilities that are mathematically proven to exist at the quantum level, but which reduce to a single reality when observed, even though the alternative possibilities continue to exist. All of these only impinge on our senses in an abstract way, but can affect the nature of our reality in a radical way.

Furthermore, when the reality that has become relevant to an individual is combined with the realities experienced by the rest of the population there results a common reality, one which operates along a general alignment of perception, with minor variations accommodated. This represents the experience and perception of the considerable majority of the entire population, who base their reality on standard models of reason, founded entirely within the narrow limitations that the standard dictionary definition of reality permits. Be that as it may, this does not negate the truth that reality is what each or us, individually, perceives it to be.

Clearly the nature of reality is not possible to define with any certainty. Abstract perceptions and differing individual experiences of single phenomena will cause the nature of reality to vary according to the individual observing or perceiving the event stimuli. Our perception relies on the input of our sensory organs that can be seen to vary in strength, capacity and efficiency, and the result of any perception may also be conditioned by our general state of mind and health, our previous experiences and, most importantly, our beliefs.

Consequently, any perception is conditioned and, in the first instance, results from what our brain is able and prepared to comprehend, based on both its condition at any one time and with the belief systems that have contributed to such conditioning. In essence, we will only see what the brain is prepared for us to comprehend, so that our reality initially results from that same, somewhat restricted, state of health or condition of the brain.

But then, our consciousness introduces aspects of intuition, creativity, mysticism and abstract objectivity, to make us aware of facets of reality that exist beyond the capacity of our senses and, in so doing, alters the scope of our perception to produce a different or enhanced reality.

On this basis, the existence of the subtle realm, and perhaps even its constituents, may fall outside the perception or experience of many individuals. Their belief systems and brain conditions may prevent them from allowing the subtle realm to form the basis for a common reality.

But this does not mean that its existence, as a reality, can be disputed to the point of denial or non-existence; rather it must be accepted as a given reality to those capable of perceiving it, believing in it and accepting it.

5.03.01. Free Will

In our model of the subtle realm, we have said that free will, by itself, is the most important tier in the hierarchy of the constituents therein. This is because free will touches every aspect of our lives whatever our beliefs or our state of knowledge, whatever our moral conduct happens to be. The freedom to do, or think, or be anything at all within the material Universe may well be the generator of creation and co-creation. The way that Free Will interacts with consciousness, and vice versa, will determine the course of everything that follows.

However, we must recognise that, as with the existence of the subtle realm, there are many eminent scientists who do not accept the need for free will and consequently deny its existence. Many of these arguments arise from the secular, humanist, or atheist scientific sector, where the development of views that deny free will generally appear to have been 'assembled', as a secondary argument, principally to support the atheist agenda of disparaging and attempting to defeat the teachings and the role of religion in our society, rather than as a direct criticism of free will itself. Such views need to be considered, not only because they represent a legitimate point of view, but also because, in so doing, our own view will, and does, emerge.

Sam Harris, PhD is a renowned neuroscientist and author, with particular expertise in the neural basis for belief, disbelief and uncertainty. He appears to have concluded that there is no such thing as free will. For Harris, free will is at best an illusion and, at worst, it constitutes an incoherent proposition.

By his reckoning, everything 'just happens' and does so as a result of a series of causes and effects.

For Harris, causal effects arise from a system of functionality within the brain that can become classified as beliefs. The brain functions to perceive the properties of something which then causes the belief to arise in accordance with that perception. A similar condition arises with regard to courses of action which demonstrate certain properties that result in beliefs.

Consequently, none of us make free will choices but the actions that we do take are done as a result of the circumstances that have brought us to the point in time when the action becomes relevant. He gives an example of his view citing the 'bad luck' of being born with genes that influence us to act in an evil manner, this being a cause that has nothing to do with a free will choice. Thus a person's genome, seen in the migration of their genes from their parents and direct ancestors, forms the microbiology of their brains and this means that they are not, in essence, 'free' to make any choice. Their conduct thus becomes exculpatory, in that they are not to blame for their actions. It seems that 'bad luck' is.

In Harris' reality, our entire course of action is dependant upon a string of interpretive causes over which we have no control. We are unable to inspect them and thus are unable to make any choice that might change them. In these circumstances choice ceases to exist and we do not know what we are about to do next because we are unaware of the detail of the causal chain that results in our next action. Furthermore, Harris asks, 'Where does the freedom of choice lie when we are not aware of all of the options that are available?'

Can we be aware, all of the time, of all of the options that might be available to us if free will was a factor in our lives? Is choice defeated if we are aware of, say, only nine hundred and ninety-nine options out of a possible thousand? Or, is free will denied to us when we are only aware of a small number of the choices available to us. At what point along the statistical chain is free will prevented due to lack of knowledge of all of the options?

It becomes clear as we consider these questions that the number of options available to us has no effect on whether free will is available to us so long as the options for choice number more than one. A single option is the only number that truly denies choice. But, as we shall see later, free will provides at least three options available to us in any circumstance: we can be active (or positive), passive (or negative), or neutral (inactive) when any choice becomes available to our consciousness.

Consequently the proposition proposed by Harris becomes pointless. That is to say that it is not right or wrong, correct or incorrect, it is merely pointless. Individuals will approach any number of options available to them from a positive, negative or neutral standpoint. They will apply belief, disbelief or uncertainty as all or part of the measure of their choice-making processes. The causes and effects which may have played a part in the options that now become available to the individual will inevitably be coloured by the positive, negative, and passive uncertainty matrix that permeates our lives all of the time.

Therefore, to propose that free will does or does not exist is an operation that has no purpose, unless we can also take into account our belief, disbelief or uncertainty as it applies to the chain of cause and effect that represents itself to us in the choices available at any one time. Belief, disbelief or uncertainty therefore become major players when making any choice that presents itself, and this renders the proposal that free will does not exist as a meaningless or pointless proposition.

Furthermore, the definition of free will does not, in itself, incorporate the need to make choices of any kind, whether based on cause and effect, or belief, disbelief or uncertainty. It is our consciousness that is responsible for making choices, and this is a point that we will discuss later in this section.

Such views as those expressed by Harris, however, should not be dismissed outright as having no value. As the population growth of our planet has accelerated to its present numbers we must also consider that the influences which affect such vast numbers of people have also grown. It may well be that a common reality has become more firmly established through the sheer weight of numbers combining to form such commonality. But those same numbers have also increased, exponentially, the options available to us when confronting a choice, to the point where it is not possible to be aware of all of them. And yet choice still remains.

But more importantly, if cause and effect are the levers that generate our actions, whether we are aware of them, or can inspect them, or not, then the human race might never have had any choices open to it since the first causal event impacted on the brain and set in motion the pattern for all effects ever since. Over tens of thousands, perhaps even millions of years, is it possible that we may have only been acting upon a string of causal events, and will continue to do so until the human race ends?

If Harris' contentions are accepted we are then merely a form of automaton, a human machine that has no free will, but only proceeds in accordance with its string of causal events. We might say in today's technological language, its programme, a proposition which itself raises the possibility of intelligent design.

Furthermore, once cause and effect is set into operation then we might say that the way we live our lives is predetermined, if not predestined, a proposition that we have discussed previously and have dismissed because it would negate the process of evolution.

It is apparent, however, particularly through the influence

and conditioning of the media as a whole, with all its sprawling attachments of electronic communicators and games paraphernalia, that we appear to be increasingly happy to hand over some aspects of our daily lives to computers and robotisation, so that humanity is allowing itself to become generally conditioned to the point where the need to exercise free will may have been diminished or may even be bypassed.

There is no doubt that, for an ever-growing number of people, the lure of a programmed, autonomous existence, free of the need to make decisions and choices, has an attraction that has encouraged a change from a situation in which one's life was often handed over to a form of religious control, operating through doctrine and dogma, to one of increasing control, through computers, media operations and the multinational corporation generated compulsion to consume.

Both lifestyles act as comfort blankets that do not challenge our intellect and leave the individuals concerned stranded in de Ropp's third room of conscious (in)activity, reposing in a reality that does not allow decisions and choices to have any importance. In effect the experience is then one of a form of sleep whilst believing oneself to be supposedly awake.

It might be said that we have indeed already become at least semi-autonomous, allowing the strings that generate our actions to be pulled by a machine-like entity. For if we take Harris' belief to its natural conclusion we all are, or will become, fully autonomous machines ourselves. None of us are, or will be, masters of our own existence.

And yet the notion of free will still remains intact so long as, through our consciousness, we are able to consider any choice that is available to us.

What defeats this Harrisonean progress towards a state of becoming automatons is self-awareness and the mundus imaginalis. If we consciously use the imaginal key to unlock access to alternate states of consciousness, whilst at the same time remaining aware of ourselves, our surroundings, our environment, our existence as human beings, it is clear that the causal chain cannot have the same effect.

By becoming aware that a chain of cause and effect in our lives may even exist automatically changes the options that become available for choice. Self-awareness and the awareness that choice exists have the potential to allow each and every one of us to decide for ourselves whether to make decisions, one way or another. Based on our perceptions of reality we can, using our consciousness, supported by free will, overcome the 'bad luck' of the hand dealt to us through our genome. We may even overcome the conditioning that belief imposes.

But only if we choose to let it be so and utilise our free will accordingly.

We should be grateful to Sam Harris for bringing to our awareness his views concerning the chain of cause and effect, in relation to free will. It does indeed have an effect on our ability to make choices, because it widens the choice options. Rather than accepting that determinism, as seen in the causal chain, operates in such a way as to negate free will by denying us any choice at all, we can see that the opposite view prevails.

Carlo Rovelli, PhD is a theoretical physicist currently involved in the study of quantum gravity. He says that the brain, made up of billions of neurons, operates predominately in a probabilistic machine-like fashion, rather than deterministically, through a series of causes external to the will.

However, Rovelli goes on to add that such a feature does not contradict determinism because it simply means that a full description of the state of each neuron is not possible. For him, two people who share the same external condition and who have the same internal state may decide on different actions based on the same stimuli. This is due to the flexible variation within their atomic neuron structure. There is no violation of physical determinism involved, and the chain of cause and effect remains intact.

He proposes that the incredibly complex nature of the human being precludes us from being able to refine and accurately predict our future course of action and behaviour. Our predictions, at best, can only be a crude approximation of our future actions and we continue to act in ways that we are not able to envisage with any certainty.

Rovelli calls this inability to accurately predict our future actions 'free will' because it allows compatibility between freedom of choice and determinism to operate, simultaneously, at the microscopic level. Questions of morality or justice do not arise because, in this schema, free will only results because we are ignorant as to why we make the choices we do. It appears that a fully deterministic world would apply were we able to define the exact state of every atom in every neuron of our brain; otherwise a form of free will based on ignorance ensues.

We would maintain that ignorance does not grant any form of viable, genuine free will, one that frees humanity from the chains of causality or an autonomous machine-like existence. This argument for compatibility suffers from the same limitation that characterises the argument put forward by Sam Harris, because choice continues to exist and we are not autonomous human machines, whose every action has been predetermined from the first causal event. Ignorance of the minutest form of detail adds nothing to or takes anything away from the nature of free will.

Roy F. Baumeister is Francis Eppes Professor of Psychology at Florida State University. He proposes that free will is bound up through compliance with institutional rules and regulations. For him, our racial survival and ability to reproduce successfully have been helped by the cultural aspect of our institutions, that is, our governments, hospitals, universities and corporations etc. that have formed the foundation for us to be able to decide upon our future course of actions.

Freedom for Baumeister then becomes the choice to follow the rules laid out for us by these institutions.

Alternatively, being able to do whatever we want would place us alongside the animal kingdom generally, but having free will requires us to inhibit any of our desires that do not conform to the established rules, or to find alternative ways of satisfying them within those rules.

Baumeister says that free will then becomes a higher way of acting, based on rules and regulations and guided by disciplined imagination and self-control. Our choices arise because of these social, institutional parameters, ones that encourage our actions based on reason rather than impulse.

Free will as described by Baumeister hardly seems like free will at all. It is conditional on self-control being directed towards one particular aim, that of compliance with the requirements of the institutional society in which we dwell. Of course the well-being of the many in compliance with the rules of society is the laudable and praiseworthy object of the institutions that established those rules in the first place. Naturally, the integrity of the institutions involved has to remain true to their original purpose and this has not been the case for many institutions, particularly in the governmental, financial, health and caring sectors.

To act in accordance with Baumeister's definition of free will once again involves relegating true free will to that of obedience to the edict of others in an autonomous manner. Furthermore such obedience denies integrity of choice in so far as it is sometimes executed at the whim of public opinion.

Compliance is an act of consciousness put into effect by free will and may still be fine so long as there is no compulsion placed upon us so to comply. Once compulsion enters the arena, as it appears to do so in Baumeister's proposals, then consciousness is indeed no longer free and the application of free will can no longer apply.

Interestingly, the intervention of a deterministic cause and effect nullification of free will has the effect of introducing compulsion into the consideration of whether free will exists, so Baumeister's definition of free will falls at this hurdle.

However, the conditions for free will, proposed by Baumeister, will take on greater value when we come to discuss aspects of justice and the virtues.

Thomas Troward was Her Majesty's Assistant Commissioner and later Divisional Judge of the North Indian Punjab from 1869 until 1895. In his influential Edinburgh Lectures delivered in 1904 Troward categorises the will as the means whereby the mind maintains its faculties in that position where we wish them to perform.

Troward attributes three conditions that the will, in a normal healthy human being, should freely endeavour to maintain. These are the consciously active, the consciously receptive and the consciously neutral. Here consciousness plays a part in ascertaining the choices or options that become available to it and then establishing or deciding upon the course of action best suited to promote those interests.

The will then freely sets in motion the action needed to comply with the direction our consciousness has chosen, and encourages or enables the relevant course of action. In these circumstances, however, the will is sufficiently free and flexible to enable the course of our actions to change direction should the need arise through a re-evaluation by our consciousness.

Following Troward, free will can thus be defined as the means whereby the choices arising from our consciousness are given action. Such action may take the form of being positive, negative or neutral.

It is these circumstances that defeat the propositions previously described: that we do not have any influence upon which choice we may adopt, because the active, receptive and neutral aspects of our beliefs, disbeliefs and uncertainties are not taken into account, positively, negatively or neutrally, when considering cause and effect, or the 'good or bad luck' of our genome, or the compulsion set up by compliance with institutional regulation, or the ignorance of our mental and physical condition at any one time.

It may be seen from this sample of opinions that there is no agreement upon the nature of free will or even whether it exists at all. Does this make free will a subjective concept? Is there really any doubt that we have within us the freedom to choose from options that present themselves throughout our lives?

As we have already said, the arguments put forward by Harris, Rovelli and Baumeister are academic constructs that appear to be designed to support other strongly held views, rather than to stand in their own right as an argument for or against free will. Their object in promoting these proposals appears to be: 'If free will could be negated then so could religious belief.' Determinism is supported through a false positive founded in the quantum world where there is still so much uncertainty, and the moral high ground is claimed through an association with institutional objectivity and success that, upon close examination, does not bear fruit.

The genuine fruit of institutional success would be seen in the successful and universal application of the principles of Enlightened Self-Interest; the philosophy whereby only doing good to all others results in only receiving good yourself.

Free will is not a subjective notion that may or may not be dismissed as something which operates through the agency of a separate set of powers or forces. Being a discrete Idea in the subtle realm enables free will to act as a separate agent that affects our consciousness, by keeping it aligned in the direction it has determined, according to the choices it has decided upon.

The causal chain/determinist arguments attempt to account for the fact that each of us makes decisions based on the choices that are available to us every day. But to say that choosing to wear a particular necktie or to wear a polo shirt rather than a tee shirt, or watch movie A rather than movie B, is due to a cause that impacted upon human brains setting up conditioning that may have originated possibly thousands of years ago, or which arises through the genetic transfer of our characteristics over multiple generations, stretches the bounds of credibility far beyond the possible, into the realm of the absurd.

Other choices that confront us, whether, for instance, to marry a particular person, to have a child or to purchase a particular dwelling, may have a special, more important significance to the individuals concerned, but in the grand scheme of things they are only as insignificant as the choice of apparel or what movie to watch. There may well be causal effects for these choices, but they are still just that, choices.

The bad luck of our genetic constituency may be a factor in choosing to carry out the deliberate killing of another human being, but to say that the killer has no choice in the matter does not stand up to scrutiny. Were this to be so, then the human race would be regarded as autonomous slaves to our historical genetic constituency, and would rank along with all other animals in this respect. If he or she were compelled to carry out the deed because of their genes, this would deny our level of consciousness seen in the reality of our daily lives. The evidence for this is experienced through the willing, compliant membership of social groups, expressed not only through the acceptance of political and legal constraints, but also with the educational and environmental forces at play, together with any alternative, available personality characteristics that may be brought to bear.

It will be said that the pattern of neuron activity in the brain will be the event that causes the action to become a reality, and this may well be true. But it is that same neuron pattern activity that also brings into being the recognition of the choices upon which our decisions and actions rest. The point is that choice exists everyday, all of the time, and how we come to select one choice rather than another is down to our consciousness, but actioned by what we call free will.

Thomas Troward cleverly grants to the will the control of the direction that our consciousness has considered and decided upon. Based on the stimuli that our consciousness has received, it is the will, freely applied in one of three ways, that provides the impetus to take action or to remain neutral. We all experience the effect that our will exerts every day in choosing simply to get out of bed (if we are able), to eat, to wash etc. It is our will that has the task of keeping our consciousness aligned in the direction it has chosen. This includes the choices made that result in neutral or deliberately inactive actions.

But does this important task allow the will involved to be determined as 'free'. To have no will would mean that our decision-making process would differ from moment to moment, having no directional consistency. The will can create a momentum whereby all the activity of our brain comes together as a single unit of consciousness. It is not the activity of the brain that puts the outcome of choices made into action; it is the will. Once a direction of action has been brought into existence the will then promotes the required activity, but it does not itself make the choices that become the direction, and neither can it negate the result of such choices having been made.

In this respect, the will may be the only genuine 'Free' element that affects our consciousness, even though it must be said that it is separate from it. Essentially, by being an Idea from within the subtle realm, it is free to form part of our soul complex, as the director that follows the course determined by our consciousness. It is neither for nor against any course of action that our consciousness decides upon and it does not take part in choosing such a course. Free will has no input in deciding right or wrong and does not operate through any moral code, but rather it is simply the effective agent that causes things to happen and to continue to happen. Thus the will is the only genuine free agent operating within our soul complex.

To say that it is cause and effect that determines our actions and choices ignores the fact that it is our genuinely free will, and only that, which allows those causes and effects to come into existence in the first place.

Free will is indeed the most important of all the Ideas in the subtle realm because it becomes the agency whereby everything else follows, including determinism, cause and effect. The freedom to do, or think, or be anything at all within the material Universe, to be the generator of creation and co-creation, all is enabled by the way that free will directs the interaction between our consciousness and with the Ideas within the subtle realm.

5.03.02. Time

We have spoken of time as being different in the subtle realm to that which we experience here in our material reality.

All of Time in the subtle realm exists within a single instant, or in a period that has no time lapse at all, and is in a form that contains everything which can effect change for us here in the material realm. Time is as important as free will because as with the absence of free will nothing would come to exist or develop, so it is with the absence of the passage of time nothing would be capable of change or of development. Evolution, adaptation, ageing, decay, deterioration and change in material elements would not be possible if time did not pass.

But time does not pass in the subtle realm. One possible way to picture subtle Time in our minds is to think of it as a vessel that occupies no space or volume but which contains the pure abstract essence of what we call time – all of it! The events that fill time in the material realm and consequently allow us to recognise its passage do not exist in subtle Time.

The vessel of Time in the subtle realm is empty of experience, until it has been converted into time in the present, whereupon it immediately becomes the past. The experiences encountered in the present remain as memories that are 'stored' as the past in the subtle realm. Such memories are accessible to our consciousness that has developed the ability to store relevant personal elements of the entire past memory bank.

Every aspect of every reality that the material realm has realised as the present and which has then become the past is contained in one Idea, one mediation from The One Source. Furthermore, this same Idea has the capability to store every experience encountered in all realities throughout the entire Universe once they have been manifested as the present time in the material realm.

In essence, this is similar to the nature of what Bergson and de Chardin defined as the Noosphere relating to the material realm, but which is part of the constituency of the subtle realm.

This is literally a mind-blowing concept to us human beings with our total inability to envisage simultaneously every reality throughout all of time in all its detail. We are simply not equipped to be able to envisage eternity at all. What we are equipped to do is to convert the essence of subtle Time to one of time that flows or passes in the material realm, and the means of accomplishing this is that of consciousness, even in its lowest manifestation.

So, once the big bang event had been manifested and the presence of matter in the material Universe had been established through the emanation of archaeus particles, then time, as we recognise it, could commence its passage. It was able to do so as a stream that flows, and was brought into being through the interaction with the consciousness endowed in those same archaeus particles. The passage of time will continue so long as these particles exist, somewhere, anywhere in the material Universe.

The commencement of the passage of time can thus be measured from the moment the Big Bang was manifested, and will cease once no particle of consciousness exists anywhere. There was thus a beginning to the passage of time, and there may be an end to it also. However, Time as 'stored' in its pure abstract essence in the subtle realm will continue to exist as an expression of the complete experience of the material realm.

Immediately following the Big Bang, change became possible because time was able to pass or flow. Evolution, as a process, was kick-started; ageing and death became a factor, one that continues to this current time and has enabled life to be sustainable and sustained. The ability for matter to conduct energy, to adapt to form new chemical elements, to coalesce into stars and planetary systems all owe their existence to the passage of time, without which none of this would have occurred or would exist.

It was through the passage of time that the complexity of particle matter came to grow to the point where consciousness ceased to lie dormant within matter, and emerged as a force on its own. This would not have been possible, would not have occurred, without the passage of time. The Universe would have remained in a stagnant, unchanging state of chaos, devoid of any form of consciousness.

Furthermore, we must divest ourselves of any notion that we, as possibly the highest form of consciousness on our planet, are responsible for creating time. Whilst Time in its entirety is present in the subtle realm as an Idea that is the abstract essence of all Time, the interaction with consciousness, allowing it to be converted to a manageable stream, commenced at the microscopic level and was fully automatic and 'unconscious'. That is to say that we were, and still are, not conscious of the interaction that causes time to flow. At the microscopic level the archaeus particle does not have any conscious level of recognition even though it is imbued with the imprint of the consciousness of its emanator.

However, if we examine our relationship with Time as found in the subtle realm, we can sometimes identify the feeling that time, in the material realm, passes at varying speeds. Sometimes we cannot believe how quickly we perceive time to pass while at other times the opposite seems to apply. We are even prone, on occasion, to believe that 'time stands still' when our consciousness determines that it should. Time, as we recognise it, only becomes constant once we combine the experience of the whole population and once we add an agreed, accurate means of measurement to its passage.

So the way we perceive time is dependant upon our consciousness and how it interacts with the subtle realm.

There are those who, at an unconscious level, are able to grasp this immense concept and perhaps to interact with the subtle vessel of time in a more consciously structured way. We generally label such people as 'para-normal', rather than 'abnormal' and often treat their abilities as 'clairvoyant' or 'precognitive'.

These are people who can, through some form of control of their consciousness, interact with subtle Time in such a manner that the effects of the passage of time are seen or experienced differently. To the consciousness of these people it may appear that they can 'see' into a different time represented as the future or the past, but actually it is their consciousness that is interacting with subtle Time in a different, broader, more structured and detailed manner.

But if the future does not yet exist because it has not been converted into a flow pattern, and the subtle vessel of Time is empty of future experiential events, how can the clairvoyant possibly 'see' the future that is yet to be experienced and why is it that they do not always see 'the future' exactly as it is when it becomes the present? The answer to these questions lies in the nature of the present, together with two factors that affect the future.

The present, in the material realm, is formed following an interaction with our consciousness. This is the same consciousness that, since the advent of the objective self-awareness of the human race, has been confronted with choices. The choices that we have made have resulted in both the present and consequently the past.

The effect of such choices will go on to play a significant role in forming the future. So, whilst the future has not yet been determined, its possibilities begin to exist in the choices made in the present. All choices made affect the present and most choices affect only the immediate or short-term future. Only very few choices will have an effect on the long-term future and even then that future will become affected by other choices subsequently made.

Thus, the immediate or short-term future becomes somewhat established by the choices made in the present, and anyone capable of tapping into the subtle vessel of Time at a point in the near future will 'see' the future as a probability.

Of the two factors that affect the future, the first is another consequence of choice, directed by free will as its enforcing agent, and the second is the nature of the reality experienced by both the visionary and their human subject(s).

Choice effectively brings into being the possibility of more than one future. If we perceive the future as many strands, each with many sub-branches, with some crossing each other, where each individual strand is potentially one possible future, all of which are gathered together at one point, which is the present and which refines to one single strand, to become the past, then this helps us to recognise the nature of time in the material realm.

When discussing free will, destiny and fate, we have recognised that, as population numbers have grown, the overall direction of human development is not changed through the activities of an individual. However, the choices made by an individual can and do affect their own future experiences and, unless the clairvoyant can be aware of all of the choices that an individual may have, and may make, together with the choices of others associated with the subject individual concerned, then any prediction of any possible future becomes based on probability factors.

In these circumstances it is even possible that the choices available to any individual can become conditioned by the advice given by the clairvoyant, to become self-fulfilling prophecies. But it is more likely that the prediction of a particular future becomes increasingly more certain when the choices available to the human subject are fewer or in some way restricted. Furthermore, the further the vision looks into the future the less certain is its reality likely to become, because the greater are the number of choices and consequent futures that need to be taken into account.

The difference between the realities experienced by the clairvoyant and the person who is the subject of their vision may also affect the accuracy of any prediction. Each is an individual and, as we have already established, each will encounter reality as a different experience. In some cases any difference will be minimal and, consequently, the vision of the future may be more or less accurate. But in some other cases, even with the same subject person, the experiential differences in perceived reality will be sufficiently large enough that the vision of the future will be unrecognisable once it transmutes to the present. Remember that the future is only the ongoing present in the model under discussion.

However, people who are well practised and experienced in clairvoyance will, with the passage of time, become increasingly more accurate in their predictions due to their subconscious recognition and processing of the factors dealt with above. In addition the interpretation of the information received in the vision of the future will also become more refined. But the point to emphasise here is that genuine clairvoyance depends upon an ability to access the vessel of Time, in the subtle realm, where all possible futures may be anticipated, to 'see', by a means not normally available to the five senses, the one future that is most likely to manifest in the material realm for the individual(s) concerned.

The effects for some people of being able to directly access the subtle Time vessel may be found in other examples such as bilocation, the ability to experience multiple places at the same time; divination, the acquisition of an insight through means that do not require the five senses; precognition, the perception of events before they happen; psychometric ability or being able to obtain information about a person or object; and retro-cognition, which is the perception of past events.

Many will once again deny the existence of such abilities as those described above and once again we have to point out that the nature of perceived reality must allow each of us to come to our own conclusion based upon our own experience and knowledge gained. After all, looking at a possible future is not so dissimilar to 'seeing' the complete solution to a problem laid out in the mind, as the prodigious savants sometimes do, and as some scientists have experienced.

What does emerge from our discussions on the nature and realisation of many possible futures and the operation of the law of attraction described in Chapter Three is the confirmation that all aspects of cosmic reality are closely and inextricably intertwined. This is an inevitable consequence of the structure of the Cosmos where each realm and dimension is dependant upon the other for its means of expression.

The journey undertaken by consciousness between the subtle and material realms of reality often manifests as a form of intuition or synchronicity, both of which abrogate any credence founded in the application of chains of cause and effect.

Intuition arises internally within an individual who suddenly, without any obvious explanation, comes to 'know' something without any apparent means of acquiring such information. Synchronicity arises externally from any individual where meaningful coincidence occurs to provide experience that otherwise would not be perceived.

Both intuition and synchronicity arise from the motion that takes place when consciousness journeys to the subtle realm, which is characterised as a gestalt of Ideas that are all interlinked and entwined, whilst remaining discrete, pure and separate from each other. It is the interaction of consciousness with the vessel of Time in the subtle realm and its subsequent conversion into a flow or passage that can result in intuitive knowledge and action arising from 'unknown' sources. The same process may result in apparent meaningful coincidence occurring when consciousness unwittingly interacts with several possible futures, which then manifest as synchronous events in the material realm.

All of the paranormal phenomena described – clairvoyance, bilocation, divination, precognition, psychometric ability, retrocognition, intuition and synchronicity – all arise due to the deep interconnections between and within the subtle and material realms of reality, becoming realised through the interactive journey of our consciousness with the many possible futures that derive from within the subtle vessel of Time.

Our perception of time varies significantly from individual to individual. Some envisage time as a straight line that passes through our existence or through which we pass. Some see time as a vertical axis along which we climb, whilst others see time as cyclical, where the same or similar events keep occurring over long periods.

Each of these perceptions has their own value and yet each is both true and false at the same time. The birth and death of stars and planetary bodies, the formation of volcanic and tectonic plate activity as gases and masses cool, the coming and going of ice ages all continue throughout the Universe. Some of these events occurred in a past so remote that we cannot yet possibly know of their occurrence and so we must temper our perception of time, in the material realm, to one of our own personal experience.

This is the whole point of our being able to transmute the unfilled, subtle, abstract essence of Time to one of time as a flow that becomes a manageable passage, wherein we are able to be born, to change and to develop our own reality, experience and understanding, and eventually to experience the death of our physical being.

Consciousness, wherever located within the Universe, does not interact with a different Time for each location, even though visual events that are manifested take time to travel to our awareness, so that it appears as though a different Time has been accessed.

Finally, a question often asked is: 'Can we travel through time?' The answer to this is 'No', at least not in the physical sense. The ability of our consciousness to access past events is one that is already possessed by some adepts and is a function of our consciousness only, not our physical being. Such ability for our consciousness may, or may not, be developing and adapting, but whether or not such ability develops will depend upon whether or not it is a beneficial trait for human beings to possess. At present, it is difficult to determine the benefit that would accrue to humans generally to possess such ability, but this does not mean that this will always be the case.

Travelling into the future, whether physically or through our consciousness, is impossible simply because the future does not exist in any form that would be meaningful to us. It is possible to say that, because all potential futures exist, at least until they become the present, there are some adepts who, using their consciousness, are able to glimpse all possible near futures, one of which their experience and ability dictates, and is the most likely to come to pass.

5.03.03. Justice and the Virtues

In Chapter One we outlined the partnership between free will and time that allowed justice and the virtues to come into being through our consciousness. The human, aspirational journey towards a state of perfection is motivated through the subtle Ideas of justice and the virtues.

From that point in our ancient history where we became sufficiently self-aware, there has been a desire to improve the condition of the human race, a desire that has seen its objectivity focussed in beneficial survival traits that have been developed through evolutionary natural selection processes. After all if we do not want to improve our condition from generation to generation then we will stagnate or deteriorate as a race and will eventually become extinct, as a direct result.

Once the racial change, from hunter/gatherer tribal existence to one of agricultural settlement, was underway, involving a growing parity within the right and left hand elements of the bicameral brain, the need arose and grew for a defined and agreed structure of rules and regulations by which ever-larger communities could live together. As mentioned in our discussions concerning the process of evolution, this may be where a cooperative beneficial trait could have been of greater advantage to the development of the human race than that of a competitive trait.

Cooperation between increasingly larger centres of community involving the principles of justice, underpinned by virtue and ethics, results in a closer correlation to a state of perfection.

In order to give credibility and status to any agreement as to the nature of justice and the virtues, it became necessary to found the rules and regulations in various bodies of expertise that we have labelled as 'institutions'. These include all states of government and their legislation, all professional bodies set up to establish and protect expertise in any particular field, all organisations devoted to improving and maintaining public health and education and, finally, the religious hierarchies of the principle religious movements, established to determine and control the moral and ethical issues of early developing society.

Justice and the virtues are thus closely associated with the institutions that form the basis of our society. They are meant to be the ideal by which we are able to measure ourselves, both as individual, civilised human beings, but also of civilisations generally.

From looking at the work of Roy F. Baumeister, we have already seen that compliance with institutional rules, using free will as the means whereby conformity is enacted, is desirable provided there is no form of compulsion involved and provided that the institutions remain true to their founding principles. However, once institutions become more interested in self-preservation, as may be seen to be the experience in many cases, worldwide, today, then the interest of the institutions concerned ceases to be just and virtuous. Societies may then develop where justice is tempered to suit the requirements of the particular aspirations of public opinion or of its institutional membership, and the virtues involved become less than ideal.

Even in nations and regions where freedom and liberty are the professed aim and objective, institutions have allowed and in some cases even encouraged a 'tyranny of the majority'. This is an abstract concept whereby any majority operates to subvert the purity of the Ideas of justice and the virtues, often in the name of freedom or democracy, to suit their own purposes. This situation poses the question: 'How can the interests of minorities, however large or small, be safeguarded and protected against the oppressive restrictions imposed by a majority?'

We have all seen, in recent years, examples of governments whose legislation is designed, not for the benefit of all, but for the advantage of their own followers, whether in a majority or not, and for the purpose of retaining power. Professional institutions have turned inwards to protect their own members at the expense of the general population, in an often elitist and self-gratifying fashion, irrespective of their own rules and regulations and the ideology that motivated their establishment in the first place. Public health issues have become prone to interference due to the culture of achieving targets at the expense of an adequate level of care, or from financial restraint preventing their success. Religious bodies have sought to hide within their doctrinal provenance, whilst allowing and concealing injustice and abuse within their organisations.

Whilst there are still institutions that try to comply with the ethics involved in their original constitution, particularly where charities are concerned, the evidence for this catalogue of failure can be seen: in our politicians who do not always seek to serve the best interests of the whole population; in our philosophers who have let us down by seeking only to ask questions whilst declining to seek or even point towards appropriate answers; in our scientists who are prone to dismiss anything that does not suit their own purview; in our service providers who have become more interested in self-preservation than providing service; in our financial institutions when demonstrating the unacceptable face of capitalism, whose main aim has been one of maximising profit or returns at the expense of worldwide interests and small investors; in the media whose presentation of events is not objective, but is coloured to suit their own ideological opinions and the need to pursue ever-increasing mass coverage and circulation numbers, and in our religious adherents who have continuously failed to distinguish between faith and knowledge, between charitable altruism and self-preservation.

It is clear that where the pure, subtle essence of justice and the virtues relies upon the institutions for their expression in the material realm, the institutions are currently not able to carry out the instructions contained on The Emerald Tablet sufficiently well for true expressions of justice and virtue to be represented.

The father is all of perfection here in the world, if it is converted into earth truly, whereupon its power and force is complete.

You should separate the spiritual from the gross, the subtle from the material, truly and with great industry, as it ascends from the earth to the subtle, and back again, and in so doing receives the force of all things subtle and material.

By these means you shall have dominion of the whole world and all things will become clear.

The power of perfection has not been truly converted from the subtle realm into the material, and the perfect ideal has become obscured through the lack of industry and the extent of unenlightened self-interest exhibited in the human race.

We must all be aware and be prepared to accept that all of human nature is represented in these failings; that all of us bear some responsibility for allowing the human condition to diverge so far from the pathway of ascendancy towards perfection.

It becomes clear that the true conversion of the subtle Ideas of justice and the virtues into a true representation, in the material realm, is a prerequisite to our remaining on the pathway towards a state of perfection. Whilst free will is the means of enactment, through consciousness, of everything that comes into being, and time is the medium through which change for everything is enabled, it is justice and the virtues that are ranked third in the hierarchy of our model of the constituency of the subtle realm, because, in practical terms, if we are unable as a species to get these aspects of the subtle realm firmly established on the pathway towards perfection, and then maintain the ideology involved, then any aspirations towards sustaining racial survival from within the Ideas of science and technology will become meaningless and will eventually be doomed to failure.

Furthermore, the genus of most possibly all life species will be condemned to extinction within the material realm.

Looking at the world in its present state we sometimes perceive only institutional decline, and it is tempting to view the situation as hopeless. We appear to be incapable of progressively developing the pure essence of justice and the virtues throughout the worldwide theatre. But this is not necessarily the whole case.

Democracy is often portrayed as the best, most adequate of the flawed systems available to us, to ensure that freedom exists, even at a subsistence level. Yet that very same democracy gives birth to dissatisfaction for minority groups whose interests are often disregarded once a so-called majority has been established. All of this whilst bearing in mind that a significant portion of the planetary population does not agree with the principles of democracy in the first place. Many societies wish to see institutional systems, based on religious principles, on dictatorship or even hegemony, imposed on populations.

However, there is one ideology that, if enacted by all of us, all of the time, would bring justice and the virtues into full frontal focus as the prime mover in the human journey towards a state of perfection. The ideology concerned is that of 'Enlightened Self-Interest'.

Enlightened Self-Interest is a term coined by Alexis de Tocqueville, a French philosopher who visited the United States of America in the early part of the nineteenth century to investigate the development of democracy there. Although his notions on the tyranny of the majority were seen to rest on rigid, semi-permanent majorities, which is a condition that does not always apply, his appraisal was that the self-interest of any individual is best served by their actively taking part to serve the best interests of society. The greater goodness of that society would thus be enhanced, which in turn would enhance the well-being of its individual participants. In addition, an idealistic foundation would be formed upon which to compare the development of our advancement in social institutional grouping.

There is evidence throughout the democratic, free world that the principles of enlightened self-interest do actually apply and produce the desired results. Corporations that offer scholarships and bursaries to prospective students benefit the participating group, whilst creating a larger bank of educated labour from which they can expand their business and create greater well-being. The unreserved and unconditional help given to those in need where catastrophes occur, all over the world, bears witness to the value of enlightened self-interest. Thousands of examples exist where, on a daily basis, individuals freely give their time and effort altruistically to help those in need. There are hundreds of other examples that could be quoted.

The need for humanity is to be able to extend and develop the principles of enlightened self-interest to the whole world, whereupon the tyranny of a majority would cease to exist, as would all conflict that had self-preservation at the expense of others at its heart. Tribal conflict, racial discrimination, unequal gender would all diminish to the point of non-existence if we were all able to actively work towards the interest of others and consequently the benefit to ourselves. All it requires is that choices are selected and free will brought into play that bring about the global conditions which would benefit all of humanity, including ourselves and the environment that supports us all.

Is such a scheme remotely possible? If we are to survive on planet Earth then the answer must be a resounding 'yes'. If we were to exert our consciousness, through free will, over time, towards the aim of realising here in the material realm the true essence of justice and the virtues, as resident in the subtle realm, then we might be able to grasp a future that would become more certain and secure, if not to say more perfect.

Such a prospect is available to the human race through the processes involved in the exchange of consciousness between the material and subtle realms and the use in the mundus imaginalis. Our future would be assured if the subtle pure essence of justice and the virtues were allowed to prevail and the well-being of everybody was to become our first priority, resulting in the greater benefit for ourselves.

The answer lies entirely within our consciousness.

5.03.04. Science and Technology

We have said in Chapter One that science and technology each form a cohesive Idea of such complexity, integration and inter-action that they can be seen as being similar in scope to that prescribed for the planet Earth by James Lovelock in the Gaia theory. Thus every single aspect of science is dependant on every other aspect for its continued existence. All of science forms a single, self-regulatory pattern contained in one Idea that human consciousness is in the process of uncovering through its interaction with the subtle Idea itself.

Little more needs to be said concerning the nature of science and technology within the subtle realm except to add that it forms a bridge between the lowest, outermost tier of subtle Ideas, that of the genus of all lifeforms and the inner conceptual Ideas of Justice and the Virtues.

This is because the tier that contains the genus of all lifeforms requires particulate matter for its form of expression in the material realm, whereas the Ideas of justice and the virtues are idealistic in their form. Consequently they do not require a particulate structure for their means of expression, other than a vehicle where they can reside, allowing them to be expressed through an association with our consciousness.

Science and technology have, so to speak, a foot in each camp for their means of expression. It is idealistic in its perception but becomes predominantly particulate in its mode, once transmuted to the material realm.

It is important to bear in mind that the nature of science and technology is that of a single matrix of interactive patterns which form a whole structure for all of science and all of technology, which themselves operate in a significantly interactive method. In likening science and technology to the theory of Gaia, it is like saying science is like science. Whilst this appears to make little sense, it does serve to emphasise the all-inclusive, singular nature of the pattern of science and technology as a complete interactive unity.

Thus the intricate, all-inclusive matrix of science and technology is a pattern of pure perfection where the mathematics and physics of the entire Cosmos is laid out, within its purview, as a fully elegant solution to the existence of everything that is capable of manifestation in the material realm. The uncovering or exposing of such a pattern as is found in these two associative Ideas has become a priority quest for humanity in our attempt to understand the nature of our reality.

The Ideas of science and technology are, in essence, just that, ideas that come to form part of the material realm, but not necessarily through the means of a particulate structure. It is true to say that the practice of both science and technology requires particles as a means by which their practice may be demonstrated, but the essence of science and technology remains in the realm of Ideas, albeit ones that require consciousness as the means of creation.

The danger that exists for us is that the fragmentation of science into discrete manageable disciplines has resulted in some aspects becoming devalued or set aside entirely, with the consequence that the full, true nature of reality may not become cohesively apparent to us. Empirical scientific methodology will need to re-examine and widen its parameters if the true nature of reality, perhaps of all realities, is to become accessible to our consciousness.

5.03.05. The Genus of All Lifeforms

As was said in Chapter One, this Idea contains the resource that becomes the material expression of all lifeforms which come to inhabit the material realm. This includes all species that have already existed but are now extinct together with the prospective potential of all species that may yet possibly come to manifest themselves in our reality.

This notion needs to be examined further to avoid confusion. It might be said that because species yet to manifest in the material realm may be waiting, so to speak, in the subtle realm, that implies that the existence of lifeforms here are somehow predetermined. This is not the case.

All species that are possible or that may conceivably arise from the universal common ancestor do not necessarily manifest in the material realm, on planet Earth. It is not possible to say that every possible combination of cell structure, bacteria and genetic permutation has arisen throughout the course of world history. Only those lifeforms that have been the subject of natural selection through beneficial traits have arisen, whilst other possible combinations have not been selected as compatible to the Earth environment prevailing at any one time, and have thus remained unexpressed here.

Because all lifeforms originate from a common universal ancestor that forms the foundation for every varied lifeform that has been, and is to come, once consciousness came to interact with the subtle Idea of all lifeforms, then the whole field of potentiality for all or any species to exist becomes a possibility, even a probability, but one that does not necessarily become a material reality.

It is consciousness that has interacted with the subtle Idea under discussion to allow the possibility that every conceivable lifeform could evolve. Consciousness in combination with the process of evolution may be said to be the means of introducing order and discrimination to the progression of life on planet Earth.

One further point is that, in Chapter One, we proposed that the subtle Idea where the genus of all lifeforms resides is not subject to change partly because time in the subtle realm exists only in one instant. Then, earlier in this chapter, we explained that time, in the subtle realm, is devoid of experiential events until stored as a memory of all the past experience garnered from the material realm.

These same factors also apply to the genus of all species that have yet to manifest here on Earth in the material realm. As time comes to pass here, through its transmutation to a flow characteristic, then any further hitherto unexposed elements within the Idea may become uncovered and may come to manifest in due course, if the environment is so conducive. The experience of new species will then become a memory held by time in the subtle realm.

Conjecturally consciousness, by existing everywhere in the

Universe through its particulate characteristics, will interact with the subtle realm that also exists everywhere and yet nowhere, to produce lifeforms that are relevant to the environment and pertaining to its existence. Thus, the likelihood of lifeforms, of some sort, existing elsewhere in the Universe is so great as to be regarded as a near certainty.

We can see that there is nothing predetermined about the manifestation of species that have arisen or may yet arise anywhere in the Universe and that the progress of all lifeforms on planet Earth has not been subject to chance, except where external influences have impacted to affect the environment.

The subtle Idea of the genus of all lifeforms is the only Idea that relies on a particulate structure for its form of expression in the material realm. As such the importance of the subtle element of the archaeus particle that permeates throughout this tier of the subtle realm cannot be overstated. The bridge between the subtle and material realms, by which means access for consciousness becomes possible, is established through the existence of this subtle Idea and the subtle element of the archaeus particle.

5.04. The Subtle Realm Re-Conceived

We now have before us a more detailed and complete conception of the subtle realm, one that contains the foundations for all that has come to exist in the material realm. Yet whilst forming that foundation, the material realm has been 'free' to develop and progress the essence of the Ideas found in the subtle realm, to create an experiential reality that is not only an expression of those Ideas, but gives to the Idea of Time, in the subtle realm, the memory of the entire experience of our reality so far.

We envisaged the subtle realm, as expressed in Chapter One, as a hierarchy of Ideas that forms tiers of importance. Whilst such a scheme still has much to recommend it, it may be more profitable to our understanding if we consider another form of layout for the subtle realm.

Conceive of The One Source at the centre of All Things, with the constituent members of the subtle realm ranging outwards concentrically towards the material realm which itself surrounds the construct conceived. Not only are the constituents arranged in a hierarchal order of importance, but they represent an interdependence, each upon the next tier, inside and outside of it.

The hermetic postulate 'as below, so above and as above, so below' may take on additional meaning when considered as a hierarchy ranging out from The One Source, to offer a consistency of existence to the structure of the entire Cosmos.

Consciousness, which is present in the material realm, travels within the subtle realm, inwards towards the centre, gaining strength and initiative from each succeeding band representing the hierarchy, until it reaches the dimension containing The Source, which it cannot penetrate.

When travelling back towards the material realm from the boundary that separates The One Source, consciousness takes Free Will through Time, thus allowing change to occur and thence through the important constituency of Justice and the Virtues into Science and Technology, where, amongst the patterns of all scientific criteria that exist, there resides the pattern of the essence of the process of evolution.

All of the foregoing, on this return journey, then injects the combined Ideological intent of all inner bands, in their pure essence, into the genus of all lifeforms, before they can be manifested in the material realm.

Notwithstanding all of the foregoing, it is important to remember that the constituency of the subtle realm, and any hierarchy involved, does not possess a closed, exclusive content. The constituency is a matter for each and every one of us to determine for ourselves, and much will depend on how you view the nature of your consciousness and whether you consider free will to be an intrinsic part of it, rather than it being a separate element of the soul complex that not only keeps our conscious choices aligned, but initiates any positive, negative or passive action relevant to those choices.

The reality that each of us perceives is one that is relevant to us as an individual and should have arisen through a process of carefully considered free thought. Whilst remaining careful to keep an open mind, it is important that one is prepared to accept and consider everything that impinges upon it.

However, it is critical to understand that the subtle and material realms have a symbiotic relationship where each relies upon the other for the expression of its existence. The subtle realm has nothing about it of a material content; it is simply and purely one of Ideas, Free Will, Time, Justice etc. Whereas the opposite applies to the material realm, which is structured entirely through the means of particle matter, and the arisings therefrom, with any non-material elements being introduced into it through the subtle Idea housing all of science and technology.

Matter in the material realm has the archaeuic imprint of consciousness from its emitter, together with the formatrix life energy imbued at its emanation; but what those archaeus particles and formatrix life energy come to form, in the material realm, depends upon the mutual interaction and expression of each realm with the other.

5.05. The Material Realm Realised

Chapter Two sought to set out a structure for the material Universe that we inhabit. Little more needs to be said concerning the pattern of particulate, nuclear structure that science is doing such a superb job of uncovering, except perhaps to emphasise the part played by the archaeus particle.

The archaeus particle gives to the material realm the manner of its substance; it is the 'material of the creation of all matter', as without the archaeus particle all other particles and thus matter itself would have no mass.

The search for this particle has been one of the great quests of modern science following the proposals of Peter Higgs. Confirmation of its existence has given to us an understanding of how things come into our own field of encounter. Many different interpretations may result from the confirmation that this particle does indeed exist and the one currently under discussion here is only one of many possibilities.

Our endeavour has been to attempt to fit together a cosmic perception that allows everything to be accommodated within its boundaries, if boundaries can be said to exist at all. Science will by its own methodology proceed to develop its own precept of how and why the Higgs boson comes into being and what the entirety of its function is.

We have said that the archaeus particle, whilst resident in the subtle realm, is one that is embedded within a field of energy, a field we have labelled the archaeus field. Upon the interaction with consciousness originating from within the material realm, this particle becomes both subtle and material at the same time. Upon transfer from the subtle realm, to the material, then its gross characteristics are released from its carrier field and become 'free' to deliver mass to other subatomic particles, whereupon it is absorbed into the mass of those particles.

What a clever, yet simple system for the creation of matter, of substance and, consequently, of being! Is it really possible that such a sophisticated, yet simple system of matter production could 'just happen', that it should just arise, 'by chance', from that place/zone/dimension where all particles originate? Here we touch upon a fundamental difference between science and the area of mysticism that covers so many varied aspects of our existence. We really must learn to keep our minds open to consider all possibilities.

Before moving on it is worth mentioning again that the archaeus particle is able to exist in both the subtle and the material realms simultaneously:

You should separate the spiritual from the gross, the subtle from the material, truly and with great industry, as it ascends from the earth to the subtle, and back again, and in so doing receives the force of all things subtle and material.

This is a truly important and amazing property of the archaeus particle because, by its existence in both realms, it is able to keep all of the Ideas in the subtle realm accessible to consciousness in its interaction. It also forms the bridge whereby the motion of such interaction is enabled. Our notion of the Higgs boson particle goes far beyond that which science is prepared to ascribe to it in its present state of knowledge, and hence our need to separate its properties and our renaming it the archaeus particle.

The archaeus particle may only be detected through its reaction or release from the archaeuic field of energy prior to which it might be said not to exist because it has no measurable characteristics. Yet its existence is essential and must be regarded as a given in order to be able to transfer mass to other subatomic particles. As previously said, here is yet another paradox that challenges our notions of logic, a pattern of paradox that appears to be common throughout our consideration of the Cosmos.

Then a question arises: What happens to the archaeus field of energy once in the material realm and once its embedded particle has been released and has given mass to its fellow particles? Science has established that energy may not be destroyed, but is converted into other forms. The energy that is the archaeus field remains in both the subtle and the material realms, at the same time.

In the subtle realm it might be said to be that which sustains that realm in the order in which it was created; it is the field that enlivens every Idea and which allows the passage of those Ideas into the material realm, whilst maintaining their perfect discrete existence and integrity in the subtle realm.

In the material realm the energy dissipates into the spaces

that exist between every particle in existence and remains invisible or 'dark' as the 70% of unknown universal volume. It is this dark energy that is responsible for the acceleration of all bodies in the Universe away from each other and is the antithetical, yet complementary opposite of the gravitational force of attraction that seeks to bring all bodies together.

The possibility arises that the quantity of dark energy is not constant but fluctuates according the extent of the interaction between the subtle realm and consciousness that exists across the entire Universe in whatever location. This is because consciousness exists within archaeus particles everywhere in the Universe and makes the existence of lifeforms a great deal more likely wherever suitable conditions prevail for their development.

Whilst the extent of dark energy may fluctuate the general trend would be one of increasing magnitude, thus causing the acceleration of bodies away from each other to similarly fluctuate.

Beyond the properties we have ascribed to the archaeus particle, we have proposed that there exists a force that energises, animates and gives vitality to particulate matter. A force so great that it permeates the entire structure of the Universe without any diminution whatsoever, even as the Universe accelerates and expands. We have labelled this force the formatrix energy. Through the signature of consciousness that is the hallmark of the archaeus particle there arises this vitality of the life force, one that enlivens all of life in whatever form it takes.

The formatrix force or energy source although closely associated with the archaeus particle does not become 'free' once transmuted into the material realm but remains part of the life principle. That is to say that the extent of dark energy is not affected by the extent of the formatrix energy that enters our reality. The life principle that is the formatrix remains integral with the lifeform of its habitation, and once that lifeform dies then some of the formatrix energy dissipates into other forms of energy whilst the remainder, in the case of humanity, entropically turns aside to immortalise the soul complex.

The soul complex is thus of critical importance to the well-being, the dominion and the continuation of the human race.

5.06. The Soul Complex

In Chapter Two we introduced the soul as an intrinsic part of a human being, as something that is formed with the person, and not as a separate entity that enters the human being at conception or birth.

The soul becomes present as a development of the interaction of consciousness with the subtle realm and the continuing motion that is involved. It is critically important to understand the nature of the soul, because this is what provides us with the ability not only to decide upon the choices that become available to us, but which also is the means whereby those choices become actions – or not.

As consciousness developed and adapted within the scope of the evolutionary process, influenced by the prevailing environment and powered by the formatrix energy imbued within our particle structure, the awareness of self, within that environment, established a growing form of an intelligent thought process, together with a sense of identity and ego, all of which go to form the foundational basis of our 'soul'. The subtle Idea of Free Will became an element that could be appended to our consciousness, whereupon a true ascendant, evolutionary development was able to proceed. Once formed thus the soul evolved to the point where it became capable of elevating itself to higher levels of co-creation with an ability to enter altered states of consciousness.

This ability becomes dependant upon an additional key element of the soul complex, that of the creative imagination, the mundus imaginalis. This is the element that is able to interpret the Ideas of the subtle realm into a form that our consciousness can understand and manage. Its nature is one that not only occupies spaces that have no spatial location, but also occupies a space that contains all other spaces, including its own. This means that the mundus imaginalis is the one element of our soul complex that is capable of transmuting immaterial Ideas into material concepts – it is capable of grounding Ideas from the subtle realm into our consciousness.

Our soul complex has thus developed the key to understanding the metaphysical experience that exists beyond the ability of our senses to encounter through what amounts to the cognitive function of the mundus imaginalis.

The soul complex described has taken on a form to become a gestalt in its own right. It is the sum of its parts, self-awareness, an intelligent thinking process, an ego and an identity, all of which have adopted free will as an appendage from the subtle realm. Whereupon there has been developed the imaginal function as a key to understanding the cosmic nature of subtle Ideas. As a gestalt it is immeasurably greater than the sum of its parts and is one where the separation of its parts is not possible.

The complex thus described is a very sensitive part of our human being. The interaction between the elements that go to make up the soul complex provide us, not only with our sense of awareness and identity, our ability to generate intelligent thought and to make and enact choices, but also to provide our ability to experience emotions and associated feelings.

Emotions and feelings generated by the soul complex follow the pattern described in respect to the relational aspects of the reality we inhabit. Each of us will be capable of feeling empathy and indifference, pleasure or frustration, calmness or anger etc., and for each of us the feelings will be unique and 'owned' by the individual concerned, even to the extent that another person is unable to deny their existence in that individual. Emotional feelings are an integral part of our soul and thus of our being.

They will serve to guide or influence us in the choices that we make, and each element of the soul complex will partake of the emotional response to the stimuli encountered.

Whilst the elements of the soul complex described may be impossible to separate from the unity of the whole, those same elements are capable of becoming unbalanced and consequently dysfunctional.

There are two principle reasons why the soul may become fragmented and dysfunctional. One of the principle factors apparent in the unbalancing of the soul is to be found in the relationship between the ego coupled to strength of identity, and that of free will. The other principal factor involved in the fragmenting of the soul complex is that of the experience of trauma.

An ego is an essential part of the human constituency because it is that which gives form to our identity. Without it identity would be meaningless and we would have no sense of being; we would not be able to recognise our individuality. However, ego will seek to control identity and will further seek to direct it according to its own dicta. Once it becomes the most significant controlling factor within the human being, the sense of balanced personality is lost, choice becomes distorted and the effects of free will become compromised, all due to egotistical compulsion.

Furthermore, the ability to use the mundus imaginalis as a key to reaching higher levels of consciousness, of being able to develop the subtle Ideas in such a way that the altruistic benefit of all of mankind takes priority, is diminished, perhaps to the point of near extinction, in some individuals.

We can see from the societies that we have co-created, worldwide, that the cult of the individual has led to an unbalancing of the soul complex in many if not most of the population today. As we have previously said, many of us are becoming semi-automatons in that we are prepared or even happy to follow the herd instinct of the social mass, encouraged by the media and witnessed in the generation of the compulsion to consume, to possess material goods. We seem to have allowed ourselves to follow in the wake of the choices made by other individuals, groups and institutions, rather than to exert ourselves freely to choose a pathway that marches with our own individuality.

Throughout this process we are encouraged to believe that we are choosing to act as an individual, but the truth is that the choices we make are undertaken, for the most part, to satisfy the control of an unbalanced soul, demonstrated in an overpowering ego, the subjection and suppression of the identity and the loss of the mundus imaginalis.

For free will to become the key element that aligns our activity to comply with the direction chosen by our consciousness, and then to enable action to operate accordingly, the ego must be kept in a true balance, as a necessary element of personal identity, but one that contributes towards deciding on choices, without overpowering them.

Soul displacement and fragmentation resulting in the loss of its function can arise when cases of unbalancing occur, usually characterised by the loss of identity in an individual. The growth of psychological and psychiatric services is evidence of the increasing extent of soul displacement in the general world population.

The problem is not a new one. For thousands of years the shamans have recognised that soul displacement occurred for a variety of reasons, nearly always associated with the loss of identity and/or the experience of trauma. Sandra Ingerman is one of the world's leading shamanic practitioners of soul retrieval. She specialises in counselling psychology, and readers who wish for more information on this field of healing should refer to her book *Soul Retrieval*.[17]

The shamanic journey to non-ordinary reality may be undertaken to obtain a vision of the extent of the soul displacement and dysfunction – to 'find' the displaced soul involved – and to ascertain the means whereby that soul could be retrieved (if possible) and restored to balance and thus become fully functional.

In extreme cases of trauma, an individual may experience of feeling of disconnection, a sense that they are not or are no longer whole. However, when major trauma has lead to major soul loss, perhaps even to the sense of the absence of any part of the soul complex, or where the ego has become so powerful that other soul elements are submerged beneath it, then steps must be taken to retrieve the 'lost' elements of the soul, or to restore the ego to its balanced importance within the whole.

Shamanic journeying will usually provide the means of location of the lost soul, or some of its elements, within the state of otherness that our consciousness forms and protects for the purpose of alleviating the pain experienced by trauma. Such a journeying state is exemplified in non-ordinary spiritual reality, which is recognised by our consciousness as a form of reality where the pain of trauma may be seen to be hidden. It is then a matter of persuading the lost soul element that it is in its interest and the interest of the individual to return, to come to terms with the trauma.

In the case where ego has become an overpowering element of the soul complex the shamanic journey is undertaken to envision the extent of the unbalancing and to ascertain the means of correcting the balance. This involves undertaking a review of the entire soul complex involved in order to understand why the imbalance occurred, and this may involve seeking knowledge of the weaknesses that are present in the remaining elements of an individual's soul.

Once ascertained, the shamanic practitioner may discuss his or her findings with the individual soul concerned, whilst remaining in the non-ordinary reality. In such cases the healing nature of such a conversation may become a focus of the journey.

The conversation will continue once the shaman has returned to ordinary reality, where the evidence of the 'spiritual' conversation will often be apparent and will form the basis for further improving soul function.

Once a true balance has been established between identity and ego, once trauma has been at least partially healed, then free will is able to operate to the benefit of the individual and can assist in the co-creation and consolidation of 'the soul' as a balanced, healed element of the person involved. Furthermore, once so consolidated, the soul complex, in concert with free will, may, depending upon the choices made, elevate its complexity to become something more.

The elevation may take the form of an ability to recognise and enter higher levels of consciousness, using the mundus imaginalis as the key to unlock the door to de Ropp's room four.

Whilst the soul complex cannot be separated into its constituent parts, we have seen that it is possible for the soul to exist independently of its vehicle of expression in a non-ordinary reality. These further important aspects of the soul complex also exist in respect to what happens following the death of the vehicle that houses the soul. The nature of the existence of the soul following the death of the physical body depends upon the nature of our deeds whilst alive. Demonstrating goodness whilst alive tends towards goodness in the afterlife and vice versa.

It can be seen from these circumstances that it is important that the soul complex should be as complete and functional at the time of the death of the physical body as is possible – we each need to be 'at peace' with ourselves at the point of death and 'at one' with the Gaian aspects of the natural world. For those whose soul complex has been compromised, or radicalised, at the point of their death, then their afterlife may be adversely affected and they may find themselves in a reality where they are not meant to be.

When the vehicle that hosts the soul complex has died, then

the soul in question becomes an immortal element of the Cosmos and should pass on to another plane of existence, a plane that is not currently accessible to any form of consciousness from within the material realm.

For the souls of those that have no belief in the existence of the soul, or that there is any such thing as an afterlife, their soul may come to rest in a 'place' that has no location; a place which inhabits a zone that experiences the absence of everything. This enables compliance with the choices they have made during their time within the material realm, and these souls are the ones that naturally reside in the non-place of their choice. But for other souls such an existence is not necessarily where their chosen pathway, whilst alive, determines they should be.

Some souls are 'held' in the zone of the absence of everything because of the emotional ties that exist between the soul in question and someone still alive. Others are prevented from completing their journey on to the further plane of existence by some people, still alive, termed 'mediums', some of whom may hold on to the souls of the deceased in order to gratify their own notions of power and self-gratification, often said to be in the service of someone still alive. In these cases, the shaman is able to journey in an attempt to identify such souls and help them to resolve any issues that serve to prevent them from moving on.

However, by far the largest number of souls that lie dormant do so because they have been persuaded either that a physical, bodily resurrection, by or through the institution that represents their deity, will eventually follow their death, or because their misdeeds, in support of so-called religious tenets, including martyrdom, have lead to a misguided, unfruitful attempt to enter the paradise of perfection. These are two of the most dangerous practices that some formal religions, or their adherents, have propagated and has resulted in a great many souls inhabiting a place where they should not be.

Once again the ancient shamanic techniques of journeying

may come into operation in order to help resolve such a situation. Because shamans exist only to give service to the spiritual and material world, they are often called upon to work, in the zone of non-ordinary reality, to help to resolve some of these issues; to help free such displaced souls and help them to move on to the next plane of existence.

The greatest gift that those still alive can give to the souls of the deceased is the absolute freedom to move on, unimpeded by aspects of the emotions or institutional doctrine, which prevent the ongoing journey of our soul.

5.07. The Cosmic Interaction

We have looked again at the subtle and material realms, together with the soul complex. The important word here is 'together'. This is because together all three form a cohesive whole that represents the Cosmos as it appears to us today. Whilst there is much speculation, particularly from a quantum mathematical interpretation that several further dimensions exist, there is as yet no encounter with these dimensions that we can experience.

So the Cosmos as we currently encounter it may be summed up as the Source dimension, the subtle realm and the material realm with the soul complex. Each and every one of these rely upon the others for their form of expression and each although capable of existing independently form an inseparable part of a whole, the Cosmos, which is another form of gestalt.

As the interaction we have described becomes more and more complex and fulfilled, it may be increasingly likened to the system that is Gaia. In all of its detail, the two realms and the soul complex become increasingly interdependent upon each other, and a form of regulation comes into being that furnishes each element with the potential for further progress towards full expression. The intertwining of all the complex attributes that go to make up the system that is the Cosmos develops to the point where any aspect of development in one element affects the others in a symbiotic way.

We have now reached what might be described as a working hub for the Cosmos around which everything else revolves. Wherever we exist, within the Universe that is our material reality, we would experience a similar set of conditions. Whilst the evidence available to us here on Earth indicates that life could and probably does occur in various, differing forms, in differing environments existing elsewhere in the Universe, the same set of basic conditions will apply.

The subtle realm of Ideas will always be available to consciousness in whatever form it is hosted and in whatever material, physical vehicle that houses it. Star systems and planetary bodies will continue to be formed, will exist for a period of time and will then cease to exist as a life-bearing platform. The same regulation, by the same rules and laws of physics and mathematics, will apply throughout the entire Universe.

Those lifeforms that can experience the reality that exists beyond that which the natural senses can encounter and are able to modify their level of consciousness to include all aspects of reality, including the spiritual/mystical, are the ones most likely to encounter a holistic experience and development. This is the case here on planet Earth.

The reason we can make such a bold statement without having experienced, at first hand, other, different parts of the Universe, is that, essentially, everything comes from the same source event. That source in the case of our Universe was, in all probability, the Big Bang, the event that caused the entire Universe to exist from one microscopic form of energy imbued in one microscopic particle. It is therefore natural to assume that if everything in existence arises from one particular mass, then everything deriving therefrom must, in its essence, be subject to the same conditions of existence.

Local environmental conditions throughout the Universe will affect the development of any lifeforms that come into being where the right conditions prevail, but these differences will always be traceable back to the big bang event, in a similar pattern to that where all species of life on Earth originate from one universal common ancestor.

Because of this tractability it is very difficult to understand why we on Earth concentrate on the differences between us when such differences really have no substance to them, to the point where we could say that any such differences do not, in truth, have any basis for existence.

Consciousness, within the soul complex that we have discussed, is the enabling factor that gives motion to the inter-action between the two realms of reality and is the one factor that is capable of reaching across the Universe to understand the extent of the motion within it. Having established how the nature of the Cosmos may be interactively structured, we will look in more detail at how that same consciousness is guiding that motion of the Universe seen on Earth as currently for the benefit of humanity.

Chapter Six

The Interactive Universe

All of the questions are there.

But,
they see only half of the answers,
those that lie within their material existence,
for although they think they work truly and with great industry
they uncover only half of my truth.

I sometimes think that they do not even recognise
that the truth they uncover is not the all of it,
that it is incomplete and inadequate
to sustain an ascendant consciousness,
whether it be theirs,
or mine.

For when they uncover their part of the truth,
they seem not to know how it fits into the whole,
to know what to do with it,
other than to use it to suit their own close horizon,
the inward facing of their souls.

They seem to have forgotten the history of their journey,
that was nurtured by the nature of everything,
they seem to be unable to 'see',
what their ancestors 'saw'.

6.00. Introduction

Having seen how the Cosmos, as a whole, might be conceived
and structured, we now look at how the material Universe of our

reality follows the same principles of being, and how the interactive relationship between the Cosmos and its constituent Universe functions to provide an environment that sustains life, at least on planet Earth.

Believing consciousness to be the key to how the interactive Universe finds its expression, we will now draw on all that has been said before to formulate the basis for our existence and the recognition of our particular reality.

6.01. Consciousness

From all that has gone before, we may regard consciousness as the essence of what we are! It is easy, however, to confuse consciousness with the process of thinking. Thought arises from a process within the brain as a result of electrochemical neuron activity which, as we saw in our discussion of the mind-brain problem in Chapter Four, is a process that enables the objective, intelligent nature of thought, which arises from external stimulation, to take its form and to be carried or transferred into a meaningful existence.

But we are, each of us, something more than that which we are able to think. Our physical bodies have evolved to accommodate beneficial traits that allow us to be able to survive and flourish. We are able to stand erect; our centre of vision is elevated so that we can see distances. We have an opposed thumb on each hand that grants to us a high level of dexterity. The physical examples are very many.

Consciousness may be thought of in similar terms. We have evolved a conscious, continuous awareness of our surroundings, one that alerts us to danger; a survival trait that is a significant benefit. Consciousness is part of our soul complex along with our ego, identity and free will etc., which also provides us with our ability to adopt an alternate level of consciousness. All of this has evolved to give our consciousness the requisite time and activity in sleeping, dreaming and some form of wakefulness. Once again these and many other examples benefit the health of the human race. Consciousness then is that which defines us; it is so much more than intelligent thought.

It is that which becomes the life force that motivates everything that we are, and all that we do. But what is it that allows consciousness to be that life force?

It should be said that consciousness is conceived through the archaeus particle, but is born of motion!

We have seen how, in this model of the Cosmos, that consciousness is imprinted into every archaeus particle that is emitted into our Universe, and that it is their accumulation, as they impart mass to all matter, that allows ever-higher layers of consciousness to arise.

So much for the process, but how does such a feature manifest itself as a reality? The growing amalgamation of particles may provide the resource for its emergence, but it is the motion within the structure of everything that activates and feeds that resource, resulting in consciousness taking on and eventually becoming an emergent form.

We have said that consciousness exists in all particles and thus in all matter, but that the measure of its presence therein is generally below the threshold that our instruments are currently able to detect. The same cannot be said for the motion inherent in all matter, as this is detectable, whatever its size.

The Emerald Tablet bases its creative message upon the motion that takes place between the subtle and the material realms and this is no accident! It is motion in all its forms that grants to matter its dynamic ability to become alive, to be whatever the requirements of its atomic structure demand it to be.

However, it is important that we do not confuse this motion with the formatrix energy that we introduced when discussing the structure of the Cosmos. We must understand that the relationship between the vitality that enables life, on the one hand, and the motion found in all levels of matter, on the other, is one where **both** arise from the formatrix energy.

In Chapter Two we described the exciting discovery of the Higgs boson particle and proceeded to extend its properties, renaming it the archaeus particle. The nature of the archaeus particle is to give matter its mass, following its entry into the material realm where it is not only the carrier, capable of bearing the means of mass transfer to material, but also maintains a subtle element and which has the signature of consciousness and the formatrix energy of its Source as part of its characteristics.

By these means, mass is imparted to matter and the signature of consciousness together with formatrix energy are passed on to all particles of matter. In so doing, the formatrix energy 'kick-starts' its atomic motion, following which consciousness receives a vitality to become something more than a signature or hallmark, to gain a potentially independent existence.

The resultant consciousness that is sustained within matter in motion is then able to commence its interactive journeying to and from the subtle realm, using the archaeuic subtle element as a bridge between the two realms, whereupon it is able to engage with the Ideas residing there.

So consciousness, sustained by matter in motion, through its interaction with the full range of subtle Ideas, gives form to all matter. Consciousness thus is the observer that determines the form of the Universe.

The long journey towards the formation of ever more complex molecules now commences, and as the complexity of matter increases so there is made available an increased quantitative and qualitative resource of consciousness. Eventually, there is formed a sufficient accumulation which, together with the vitality of the formatrix energy and the atomic motion in all matter, eventually allows basic, primitive lifeforms to come into being. Some of these forms that have the potential for the development of higher layers of consciousness also demonstrate increased resources of formatrix energy which, in turn, are able to sustain an increase in the vitality of the life principle.

It is an interesting thought that if all of matter were not in motion, originating from the big bang event and extending throughout the entire duration of its existence, then all matter would remain without form and would continue in that condition. Whether or not matter already existed as some form of chaos, or arose ex nihilo, from nothing, it is the circumstance of consciousness sustained by the motion within matter, driven by formatrix energy, that has enabled matter to gain its form, and for that same consciousness to become the vital ingredient for the subsequent development of life.

So, if atomic motion had not started with the Big Bang, then the structure of all matter would have remained inert or inactive, so that it would not have been capable of change. Everything would have remained in its then state and the Universe would have been, and would remain, 'frozen', immobilized in whatever form it was in before motion commenced. Consequently the processes involved, not only in the creation of new structures of matter but also in energy transfer, would never have come into being in the first place. The ability for life to evolve and be sustained would be curtailed to the point of non-commencement.

For consciousness to take on form and to be able to develop and grow, then motion, especially at the atomic level, is essential. To be able to move takes energy and, in recent years, we have seen demonstrated the vast amount of energy that is stored within a single atom and which keeps it in continuous motion. To comply with the laws that govern our reality in this Universe, such energy would need to have been transferred from another source of energy and the event that inaugurated such a transfer is that which took place within or through the Big Bang.

We must divest ourselves of any notion that the Big Bang event was an explosion of any sort. It is more correct and simple to envisage the big bang event as the coming into existence of space, together with the subtle realm of Ideas, including Time and then matter, in that order. Following this event, there arose the rapid expansion of matter to commence the reality that became our Universe.

Notice that it was only matter resulting from the Big Bang that came to expand because the realm of subtle Ideas was complete from the outset, containing every aspect of its constituency as described in Chapter One, in its completed, but as yet unexpressed form.

Once consciousness received its vitality from formatrix energy, sustained by matter in motion, Time was able to become expressed in the material realm and to commence its passage. This allowed change and development to become possible and, as a direct consequence, the pattern of the physical laws that govern our existence were able to come into effect.

At present we are not aware of how the big bang event came into being or what caused it. Many varying hypotheses have been suggested but none have ever approached the area of proof that would raise its credibility above any other. The main reason for our lack of success in our attempts to address this major problem is that we are simply incapable of envisaging the conditions that might have existed which enabled, or allowed, or promoted or caused, such an event to occur, or even to 'just happen'.

The scientific community are generally in agreement that the Big Bang was an event that did actually occur, and that it did so approximately 13.8 billion years ago (as we currently measure the passage of time) give or take one or two percentage points either way. There is no need to go into how this has been established, and we are satisfied that the view of the scientific community is sufficiently strong to accept its contentions. Also, what is generally agreed is that it was the Big Bang that brought space into a reality, which precipitated the commencement of time. Thus, prior to the Big Bang both space and time did not exist.

One difficulty for human beings is that we are not equipped to envisage or perceive any circumstance or condition where time and space were, or are, absent or had never existed. In such circumstances, where we might call the pre-Universe a state of un-located, timeless void without physical space or character-istics of any description, the physical laws of the Universe would not have been in existence. Consequently we should attempt to abandon all logic and reason when considering the pre-Universal un-located, spaceless void, and yet, paradoxically, the mere attempt to do so involves the application of reason for its accomplishment and thus any true understanding becomes impossible for us to achieve.

It may thus be far better not to try to abandon reason and logic when considering how it all started, but rather to approach the question 'Why is there something, rather than nothing?' from a different direction, from a different perspective. This is the area we will expand on when discussing a new field for study, in Chapter Eight.

This does not prevent scientific hypotheses, however, from continuing their attempt to explain the unexplainable. Some scientists resort to a hypothesis that maintains the Big Bang simply 'just happened', without cause or reason. This is because they are unable to envisage any real or proper cause or means for the event to take place.

Others propose that many such big bangs took place, and are still taking place, and that each Universe arising therefrom, within the resulting 'multiverse', may be subject to different laws of physics that exist beyond our comprehension. Yet others maintain that multiple Universes expand in such a way that they 'flatten' out to form branes or curtains and that the Big Bang arose because of the collision of two (or more) of these brane curtains. This without attempting to explain how such curtains arose in the first place.

A very large number of people mostly outside the scientific

community, but not exclusively so, revert to a religious hypothesis as the means for the big bang event to occur. The history of humanity is filled with religious beliefs which propose that everything in existence has come about through the auspices of a creator, a god of sorts that has created everything and has caused all things to be set in motion.

Certainly The Emerald Tablet envisaged such a god as is clear from the text, and it must be said that the existence of such an entity provides a convenient answer, of sorts, to many of the outstanding issues relating to what caused the Big Bang. Except, that is, an answer to the really big question, 'Where did god come from and how did he/she/it come into existence in the first place, before the big bang event?' The invention or the perception of a creator god has played, and is still playing, a major role in the recent history of the human race and we will return to this aspect of our relationship with the Cosmos in Chapter Seven.

It can be seen from these varying approaches that humanity is struggling in its attempt to explain how it all started.

We are back again at square one and although it can be seen from these varying approaches that humanity is, as yet, incapable of success in its attempt to explain how it all started, we must be prepared to accept that, at present, we cannot envisage a satisfactory cause of the big bang event or any conditions that might have prevailed within the pre-Universal, un-located, spaceless and timeless void. Perhaps we might be in a position to understand these issues if and once we manage to achieve a closer state to near perfection.

Whatever the cause of the Big Bang we must recognise that everything in our universal reality arises from that event, including the fact that all of matter is in motion. Such motion must have been conceived and imparted to the particulate structure of matter at the outset of its emission and coming into being. This motion has allowed consciousness to commence the interaction with the Ideas within the subtle realm, allowing time to commence its passage. It is the archaeus particle imbuing a combination of formatrix energy – motion – consciousness that is the basis for all of life, throughout the entire Universe.

From the point of view of humanity, it is consciousness that has been the mainstay of our development. Motion and formatrix energy, each by themselves or in combination, have played a large part in enabling it to accumulate and develop its complexity. Indeed each are essential for consciousness to become something more than an imprint or hallmark, seen as the signature of The One Source. But neither formatrix energy nor motion are capable of development by themselves; neither can instigate nor advance the development of the Cosmos without the activity and interaction of consciousness.

Furthermore, it is only consciousness that is able to bind lifeforms, especially the human race, together as a developing social and cohesive unit. Neither formatrix energy, nor motion, nor science, nor any other aspect of the subtle realm, are able to do this. The function of the Ideas in the subtle realm, their raison d'être, does not involve accomplishing such a task. Neither science nor religion, at least in their current forms, are able to provide adequate coherent answers to questions concerning what caused everything to start and come into existence. Neither do they even seem able to overcome the divisions that are expressed in their names.

Consciousness then underpins all that has occurred since the big bang event. It is a part of, and subject to, the process of evolution that provides us with the ability to adapt this process to suit our future needs. If this process, as it affects humanity, is allowed sufficient time to develop and adapt to an environment, co-created in part at least by our own interaction in that process and its resultant effects, then the outcome for humanity may become secure.

If there is insufficient time available for us, however, to so adapt, then the future for humanity looks very bleak.

Whether or not consciousness will continue to reside within the physical form of the human vehicle is irrelevant.

In the long term and in any event, the future of consciousness will not be very much affected, even as it becomes housed in a different animal form. Because we co-create the passage of time, through our consciousness, then it should be said that whether or not there is sufficient time it is in our own hands.

How can we seek to ensure that humanity has sufficient time made available to it to enable a secure future for us on our planet and a continuation of the journey towards the state of perfection? We shall attempt to approach an answer to this question in Chapter Eight.

6.02. Consciousness and Co-creation

The product of the interaction between consciousness and the subtle realm is one of co-creation. We may look at the Universe as being conceived initially as an inert canvas upon which is to be realised the vitality of everything that can come into existence. The motion that secures the state of subatomic particles allows time to promote a changing state of matter; the formatrix energy that imparts vitality to all things allows consciousness to become a vibrant living thing, so that we can look on it as the interactive artist that has been given the task of creating everything that is possible.

The resources that are given to this artist so to create everything arise from the Ideas in the subtle realm.

Science and technology have, in our recent history, proved to be one very efficient means by which consciousness has been able to develop some aspects of hitherto hidden potential, ostensibly for the benefit of some of humanity. Readers will recognise that this statement, whilst true, has many implied caveats that render the development of science and technology as only a partial or an inadequate truth when looking at our development as wholly beneficial.

The fact is that some of the effects of scientific and techno-logical development have not been to the benefit of humanity as a whole; the nature of our racial conscience must bear its share of responsibility in this respect. Some of the population have not benefited; indeed we might say that a considerable number have suffered as a result of the exploitation of the advances made in science and technology.

The means of our own self-destruction through the machinery of indiscriminate warfare, unaffected by aspects of the pure essence of justice and virtue; the development of the means of feeding the entire world population, yet failing to do so for reasons of economic greed or unenlightened self-interest; the development of medicines capable of helping those in need yet denied to them for whatever reason. These are simple examples of the failure of the human race to act in accordance with the principles proposed on The Emerald Tablet, and to work in compliance with the purity of all Ideas found in the subtle realm.

The Ideas within the subtle realm are made available to our consciousness so that we may enter into a co-creative endeavour that not only permits, but also augments our journey towards that state of perfection which is our destiny. The substances of the constituency of the subtle Ideas do not contain any measure of good, or evil. Those aspects result only from human nature, which itself has been influenced by our evolutionary devel-opment.

In Chapter Four we introduced our thoughts concerning the nature of good and evil, proposing that absolute goodness cannot exist unless residing in an entity that has attained absolute perfection. Even the tiniest quantum of evil would destroy the concept of absolute perfection. Furthermore, absolute evil also cannot exist because this would require the total and complete absence of any form of goodness. So what do these conditions have to say concerning our consciousness and its future development?

Our evolutionary racial history has been principally centred on the need to survive and, if possible, to flourish. In this respect we can confidently say that the race, as a whole, has been successful! Along the evolutionary journey, we have managed increasingly to uncover the patterns of science and technology that were embedded from the outset, in their total completeness, within the subtle realm; our understanding has progressed so that the nature of the scientific pattern has become ever more complicated, integrated and coherent.

The knowledge gained from science and technology has enabled us, as a race, successfully to survive and flourish, at least partially, to date. But the net result has also allowed for the possibility of extinction of the human race. We may thus say that the drive within us to survive and flourish, at any cost, has resulted in allowing the presence of evil to reside naturally within our nature.

The extinction of the human race, indeed of all life currently extant on Earth, may be accomplished through our making the environment one that becomes incapable of sustaining human life, or it may be that mutated elements of life on Earth serve to eliminate us, or it may be one of mutual destruction because of the racial, cultural or other prejudices of which we have not yet been able to divest ourselves. There are many other possible reasons.

The evidence is all around us – experienced in the mutation of viruses; the hastening reduction in the effectiveness of some medicines; the increasing incidence of death and disability through climatic events and the accelerating rate of extinction of many species of life – through a rapacious and uncontrolled exploitation of planetary resources encouraged by huge, unrestrained population growth.

The point here is that our future, or lack of it, depends upon ourselves and in particular upon that same consciousness that has so far bound us together, at least partially successfully, as a race, albeit in discrete groups. That same consciousness is capable of raising itself, and consequently us, to ever-higher levels of co-creation, as we seek a condition nearer to a state of perfection.

It is equally capable of accomplishing the extinction of the human race. The definition of good and evil and the relationship of one to the other may be seen to demonstrate the stark outline of this statement.

So far as the reasons for our possible extinction are concerned, the Earth will abide until its natural demise is reached with the death of our Sun, thought to be several billion years into the future. Everything that is put into our environment through our lifestyle, every effect that our expanding population numbers have on the planetary resources, originate from within the planet's self-regulated system that is Gaia.

Effectively Gaia has sustained everything in a condition conducive to the survival and flourishment of human life; and if we were to change those conditions sufficiently so that humanity became extinct, then the process of Gaia would most likely operate to regulate the ecosystems, to the extent that an alternative lifeform would then have the possibility to rise and to flourish.

The end of the human race on planet Earth would be of little or no consequence to the self-regulatory aspect of the planet itself. Eventually, another race would probably emerge and once the conditions to survive and flourish, together with the development of a large enough brain size came into being, then life and consciousness would go on, but without us.

Thus, our future is effectively in our own consciousness.

There is no blame attached to the human race concerning the destruction of the conditions necessary to sustain our dominion on planet Earth; far from it. It is the success of our racial evolutionary history that has produced such a possibility. It may even be incorrect to think that the part we have played in the production of conditions that might eliminate our race is in any way evil at all. It simply is the result of our journey of survival to the present.

If the human race is happy to meet extinction head on and effectively 'hand over' the reign of dominion to a further, alternative, future lifeform, then so be it. If the race is not prepared to allow this course of action to proceed then it (we) must choose to change the course of our lifestyles, and put into action an alternative that would redress any imbalance, however unlikely such action might appear to be.

Yes, this may appear as a rather bleak outlook for humanity but it is not to say that such a scenario is inevitable. Our consciousness is quite capable of developing the co-created conditions where our dominion on Earth is sustainable. We do not have to use the outcome of science and technology for the disbenefit of any of the population. We do not have to close our eyes and ears to the beliefs of others who do not share our particular beliefs. We do not have to deny the reality encountered and experienced by some as abnormal. We do not have to accept the notion that corporate gain, coupled to an always-rising financial market situation, is the most important aspect of life, at any cost to the environment. We do not... we do not... we do not...

The secret of our survival lies in our consciousness and thence acts of co-creation.

As we have said, the facility and the ability to form acts of co-creation is an inherent feature of the cosmic system so far described. The interaction of our consciousness with the Ideas within the subtle realm leads naturally to a process of co-creation, one that involves all aspects of every constituent of the subtle realm.

Time is that which allows change to take place. The co-creation of a form of time into one that passes is essential to our continued existence because, without such a passage, everything would stagnate and eventually pass into non-existence.

Justice and the virtues are the higher ideals that allow us to establish the means by which we develop the ability to govern our societies, understand codes of morality and apply ethical values. These aspects of the subtle realm are conceptual in their nature. They are not complete Ideas awaiting exposure by consciousness; they exist to be co-created, developed, expressed and applied by the advanced lifeforms that exhibit the higher levels of conscious ability.

Science and technology are different Ideas in their nature; they are still co-created, but in a different sense. They are exposed or uncovered by the interaction of our consciousness from their existence as a complete pattern in a subtle Idea. Without the intervention of consciousness science and technology would always exist in the subtle realm, and would continue to rely on their expression through a co-creative inter-action.

The genus of all species is also co-created, but also in a further, different sense. The essence of each species exists in the subtle realm as the means of expression of life in all its many forms. The interaction of consciousness with the subtle Ideas is what gives each species the possibility of its mode of expression through evolution.

It has become apparent that if we are to continue to survive and to flourish we will be obliged to concentrate upon time, justice and the virtues as the means whereby this will be accomplished. This will be the subject of our discussion in Chapter Eight concerning what we are capable of becoming.

That is not to say that science and technology will not continue to play an essential part in the ability to survive as a whole race. As our numbers continue to increase, as the planet's resources continue to deplete and be consumed, and as the effect we have on the environment causes major problems with the climate, with food supplies, with the space available and with the accelerating rate of species mutation and extinction, then science and technology will have a major role to play in alleviating the perils that a significant increase in population numbers will bring.

But any advancement in scientific or technological knowledge will not present us with realities that will guarantee our survival, in the long term. They will not be able to resolve the results inherent in ever-increasing population numbers. They can only postpone its effects.

Our consciousness somehow has to develop its innate ability to co-create aspects of our reality that will allow us to continue to survive and to flourish, to be able to remain engaged on our journey towards the ideal of perfection. This will involve a radical move away from the current direction that the human race has taken, at least within the Western democracies.

Initially, the cult of the individual will need to be adapted to take account of the condition of all of society, all of the world population. Co-creation is the tool that consciousness may use to bring about the conditions necessary for our continued survival. We will expand upon these requirements in Chapter Eight; suffice it to say here that evolution may be one means whereby such co-creation may become a reality. Acts of co-creation may appear at first glance to be difficult to achieve, but on further consideration it is possible to recognise that human endeavour has already achieved some of what is required.

Our political history has shown that, through our consciousness, we are capable of delivering peace and reconciliation to disparate groups of humanity who had hitherto been warring factions. The desire for democratic freedom has lead nations to turn away from oppressive regimes that seek to control their people unjustly. Racial integration has been seen to be possible if conscious choice and free will, of all of the people, is given full rein.

It is regrettable that many more examples fail due to human nature, seen in maintaining a lifestyle at the expense of others, or where choices are centred upon the well-being and benefits of the few rather than the many.

If, however, we recall those examples of enhanced human endeavour that we discussed in Chapter Three we may see some exploits of humanity that, through the use of consciousness, seek to push its physical form beyond its present bounds, to ever-higher levels of achievement in all fields of activity. A similar condition is developing in the open-minded population where a growing number currently have the ability and the practice to assume altered and higher states of consciousness and do so on a regular basis.

This is a process that a significant number of the human race, alive at any one time, will need to undertake, simultaneously, as a group, acting with one aim. Alternatively, or in addition, this may require an adaptive development of the evolutionary process.

The difficulty here is twofold. Firstly there is a problem in assembling sufficient numbers of adepts who are able to enter an altered or higher state of consciousness in order that the immaterial, unbounded, forward momentum by which its objective could become possible and efficient is attained. Secondly, the evolutionary process required is, to some extent, a departure from the principles of natural selection, to one of adaptive change inaugurated from within the human organism.

6.03. Consciousness and Evolution

At this point, it is worth repeating that evolution is only a process; it does not instigate anything, has no means that enables action to be decided upon or taken, and cannot have any creative effect upon the development of life. This may sound as though we are stating the obvious and yet the modern usage of the word appears to grant to it something that is beyond a mere name.

The fact is that evolution may only be described as a name that is given to the process whereby those lifeforms that develop beneficial survival characteristics are the ones that have the greater likelihood of successful reproduction. Evolution is simply a part of the overall self-regulatory system of Gaia, truly a very important part, but is only one of the means that is employed to maintain environmental conditions on Earth which are capable of supporting current lifeforms.

Notice that another circular paradox comes into existence with this statement. Evolution is one means whereby the Gaian mechanism maintains the environment, which in turn affects that process of evolution.

Bearing this in mind we are now able to consider the relationship between consciousness, its development and the process of evolution.

The gathering complexity of lifeforms on our planet has been brought about by changes that have taken place in the environment together with the natural selective process which favours any lifeform that exhibits a beneficial trait, so far as reproduction of that trait is concerned.

Thus, the process of evolution is closely related to, we might even say is responsible for, the emergence of evermore complex forms of life emerging throughout long periods of time. Yet time itself is co-created through the medium of consciousness and it is time that allows change, which is a feature of the process of evolution and the emergence of beneficial traits. We can therefore see that consciousness and evolution are bound together in an inseparable way where each is reliant upon the other for its further development and its ability to proceed.

It is interesting to note that both consciousness and evolution have no material aspect to their existence; both are immaterial in their nature. This immaterial condition supports the existence of a subtle realm where Ideas exist to be exposed or uncovered so that they may form elements of a material Universe. Neither consciousness nor evolution is included in the subtle realm as Ideas within their own right, and the reason for this is as follows.

Consciousness is the agent that interacts with the subtle realm to bring about the nature of our reality in our Universe; therefore it cannot be a constituent of the realm that it converts into another form.

Evolution is independent of the genus of all species of lifeforms, and were it to be otherwise then all variation, adaptation and development within each genus would pre-exist within the relevant subtle realm Idea. For this to be the case then all of life would be predetermined and to a great extent ortho-genetic. In these circumstances, the development of life would not be subject to change brought about through natural selection and the environmental conditions, but would only appear once the environmental condition, itself predetermined, was right for them so to appear.

For this reason evolution is regarded as an aspect of the Idea of science, as one of the patterns of existence that sits alongside physics, chemistry and mathematics etc.

Having discussed these aspects of our existence in Chapter Four, we need to say no more, other than, because predetermi-nation does not exist, then evolution, although being a facet of science contained within the subtle realm, must by necessity be a force that is indivisible from, yet independent of, subtle Ideas. The gestaltic form of existence is once again represented in such a complex as the subtle realm.

The question that now arises is: if consciousness and evolution are bound together, separate, yet reliant upon each other, how have they affected each other throughout time? There is little doubt that the rise of consciousness has benefited those lifeforms which have been capable of developing the upper layer and levels, and that the general level of consciousness has become higher, across the whole population, as time has passed. The force that we have named the process of evolution has thus been responsible for the natural selection of those lifeforms with increasingly higher levels of consciousness, seen as beneficial traits, which consequently is the cause of the apparent ascendant directional flow of our consciousness.

The effect of evolution upon consciousness is thus seen as the result of its force promoting the development of consciousness to ever-higher levels, generally.

Consciousness has, historically, affected evolution through its effect upon the environment prevailing at any one time. As consciousness succeeded in attaining ever-higher levels, then the effect it has on the environment becomes more pronounced. The effect that consciousness is having on the environment is producing an accelerating rate of change and, as we have already discussed, the effect that our knowledge of genetics is having, or will have, upon the environment means that evolution is diverging into two separate branches of development.

How these changes will affect the relationship between consciousness and evolution is an interesting conjecture that we will now look at.

6.04. Consciousness with Destiny and Fate

The initial and most important point to confirm concerning the relationship of consciousness with destiny and fate, as we have defined them in Chapter Four, is that any journey towards any destination requires the element of change which itself requires the passage of time for its accomplishment.

Without consciousness interacting with the subtle Idea of time, then no change would be possible, and evolution, destiny and fate would not exist or even be possible.

The second important point to recall is that it is consciousness which has come to determine the pathway of destiny. The force of the evolutionary process whereby human consciousness has developed to the point where higher levels may be experienced serves to exercise a measure of control as to the direction of the development of humanity as a whole.

It must be recognised, however, that the effects of any measure of control, or interference with what we might call the natural process of evolution, carries with it an equal measure of danger. Until our understanding of how the entire genome works in all its interrelated, interactive, fine detail, and is completely understood and defined, then we as a race may be influencing the long-term outcome of the human journey in ways that we cannot as yet envisage. Consequently the nature of our destiny may also be influenced.

The relationship between destiny and consciousness is somewhat fragile and is subject to minor changes in direction, and questions whether the human race has a destiny of any description are currently in the balance. Our efforts for the human race to survive and flourish together with an ongoing evolutionary development has, so far, resulted in a successful journey, directed towards the state of perfection. But is the outcome of such a journey secure in any circumstances? Are we able to co-create a future that ensures continuing success?

Being a characteristic of the present, the relationship between fate and consciousness is much easier to determine. Fate has been said to work in conjunction with free will to ensure a course of action that allows the scope for choice to be determined within each individual. Choices made in the present by individual consciousness must bear in mind the need for the race, as a whole, to survive and flourish. We must all ask ourselves whether or not we are prepared to invest enough effort to solve the issues that divide the human population.

If we all are not prepared to adopt such measures willingly, then the self-regulatory system that is Gaia will automatically work to ensure the preservation of a planetary environment, albeit one that may not be capable of supporting life and humanity in its current form, through the process of evolution.

Because the process of evolution is generally thought to be a slow one, especially once stabilized conditions have become the norm, evolutionary adaptation may not be quick enough to allow the development of human life to adapt to new environmental conditions. An event characteristic of punctuated equilibrium or of significant genetic mutation is by no means likely to allow such adaptation to occur. The more likely outcome, at least for humanity, is that of racial extinction.

Our fate will be determined by the present day choices we all make; our destiny may consequently and legitimately be described as 'fragile'. Yes, we do co-create the passage of time, we are individually free to make choices, we are able to affect the scope of evolutionary change and we are able co-create a future destiny by sustaining the pathway towards a state of perfection.

But, as yet we seem to be racially incapable of maintaining sufficient cohesive action to achieve continuation of the environmental conditions needed for our survival and flourishment.

6.05. Consciousness with Good and Evil

In Chapter Four, we defined goodness as a privation of evil, and similarly think of evil as a privation of goodness. The position where our consciousness rests, along the filament of our psyche that represents good and evil, is determined by the choices that our consciousness decides upon and, as such, fate and destiny become closely linked and integrated to good and evil.

The extent to which we experience goodness and evil within ourselves is a completely natural characteristic of the human condition, as is the ability to change from being closer to one polarity or the other. To be regarded as good simply means that the consciousness of the individual concerned has chosen a position nearer to the polarity that represents goodness, and has achieved that position through choice involving active free will and the mundus imaginalis. The same circumstance applies to those individuals that are regarded as evil.

Human nature naturally tends towards a central position along this strand within our psyche, and although our position and the ability to change is a natural characteristic, most of us are indolent in our attitude towards good and evil and are prepared to take the easy option, which is to continue to experience some parity of each within us. The natural ability for us to change our position relative to either polarity requires some considerable conscious work and effort involving the mundus imaginalis as the key to, and subsequently the experience of, altered and/or higher levels of consciousness.

The natural outcome of such a work ethic as this is, in the case of altered states of consciousness, gravitation towards the pole that is most prominent in our nature, whether it is good or evil. In the case of higher, advanced levels of consciousness, the clarity of reality perceived gravitates the individual involved towards the pole of goodness. Thus the balance of probability is that of greater measures of goodness ensuing from the practices involved in attaining altered states or higher levels of consciousness.

We must remember that absolute goodness or absolute evil are not achievable by humanity in our present state of development and, consequently, we are all subject to being simultaneously possessed of both of these elements of our psyche. For this reason we are unable to achieve absolute perfection, but may, given enough time and effort, be able to approach such a condition through the serious application of practices designed to promote access to the state exemplified in de Ropp's fourth room of consciousness.

A growing number of adepts are prepared to make the considerable effort required to achieve such enhanced levels, for the benefit of the survival of humanity. It remains to be confirmed whether the process of evolution will select activity such as this as a beneficial trait worthy of reproduction. Nevertheless, the incidence of germline transmission, of memetic soul-like transfer from previous, genetically linked ancestors, compounded by the possibility of karmic transfer, as described in Chapter Four, may also be part of the evolutionary process that tends towards the ascendant journey of goodness involved in higher levels of consciousness.

It is a benefit to the human race that the state of good and evil is not fixed from generation to generation, even taking into account memetic germline soul reproductive and karmic transfer. The ability for change to take place through the mundus imaginalis and choice, utilising free will, allows for the possibility that near perfection, equated with goodness, may eventually be possible within the scope of human achievement.

The undertaking of the work and effort to achieve higher levels of consciousness and, consequently, a greater degree of goodness for the human race takes on a mystical element. This is because the implementation and outcome of such practices, although evident throughout history and seen in those achieving greater levels of goodness in their lives, is not capable of empirical establishment or measurement through scientific methodology. This may be because the immaterial nature of the desire and ability to enter into higher level consciousness arises from our naturally mystical human nature.

This mystical element of our nature will be discussed in Chapter Seven.

6.06. Consciousness and Death

We have alluded to death as being the fate of each and every one of us on Earth. But does consciousness play any part in the life and death cycles, which are apparent in all lifeforms?

Our model of the Cosmos requires that all particles of matter bear some degree of consciousness, although generally at a level which is not measurable. This applies to all particles including the bacteria that comprise the algal blooms previously referred to. In addition we have proposed that through a form of memetic transfer using germline cells as the vehicle immaterial characteristics affecting lifeforms may also be reproduced through the generations.

With each subsequent generation, the process of evolution enables some lifeforms to adapt, or differentiate, to change in the environment, usually over long periods of time. In this way the aggregate of consciousness present in each lifeform decreases as their complexity decreases, or increases as their complexity develops. Any advances made in the ability of consciousness to adapt to its changing surroundings may also be reproduced.

This is similar to the nature of death where there is seen, as an inbuilt feature of each lifeform, the factor of death, transmitted from generation to generation. Any adaptation or change in the scope or nature of death may also be also transmitted.

The consequence of any adaptation has seen many and various changes to the nature of death through natural causes. There has been a significant lengthening of the average lifespan of humans even though the maximum lifespan has not changed at all. Living longer has allowed hitherto lesser known or uncommon natural causes to become more prevalent and common. Predominant amongst these are those causes of death that arise from degenerative brain illness and disease of the body and its functions due to increased longevity.

Our consciousness can play a part in delaying the onset or of postponing the outcome of these causes, even though the eventual outcome has the same result in that, so far as our bodies including our brains are concerned, we all eventually die.

Consciousness then has little to say about death other than through its work in prolonging our average natural lifespan. In addition consciousness being part of the soul complex within which it plays a significant part, by being immaterial and indestructible, does not die but entropically turns aside to enter another plane of existence.

6.07. Consciousness and Gaia

If consciousness has little engagement in terms of its relationship with death, it is fair to say that it engages with Gaia at every point possible.

Before going on to consider the relationship between these two aspects of our reality, it is necessary to clarify how we see the nature of Gaia and set it in what we believe to be its true form.

Earth's atmosphere in its early years was predominantly carbon dioxide arising mostly from volcanic eruptions. Once life began to become established, the balance began to change as bacteria produced inert nitrogen, and the process of photosynthesis produced reactive oxygen. So that from about 2.5 billion years ago, Earth's atmosphere became sufficiently balanced to contain significant amounts of both of the gases that support life on this planet.

From this a lifelike quality emerged from the interactions of all living things, not only with each other but also with what may be thought of as the non-living parts of the planetary system. Not only does the Earth support individual living organisms and species, but the sum of all these organisms, together with the non-living parts, perpetuates a system in the Earth's environment that, to all intents and purposes, lives. Furthermore it is surmised that this living organism is able to self-regulate essential characteristics of its environment.

However, and most importantly, what is **not** proposed is that this lifelike system, taken as a whole, is conscious. It is incapable of determining any course of action through its own volition. Self-regulation exists within Gaia as a non-conscious, automatic response, in a process of change in environmental conditions.

The concept of Gaia makes it possible for all humans to see

themselves as significant, as part of a universal or even cosmic interaction. The whole of Earth may be seen as a single life preserving system that commands our respect and even reverence because an understanding of Gaia could become the focus for all of the attitudes we employ in respect of politics, philosophy, science and religion. The Gaia theory is a foundation upon which all spheres of activity become manageable, where everything may be subject to an all-inclusive interactive, higher level consciousness.

Our model of the Cosmos proposes that every archaeus particle, and thus all of matter within it, bears the signature of the consciousness of The Source of All Things and, consequently, every star and planet – indeed all bodies within the Universe – have some degree of consciousness within them. Consciousness is proposed as being present in everything, and two important features arise from this condition.

The first is that all layers and levels of consciousness by originating from the same source are all part of the same cosmic system. This means that the levels of consciousness exhibited in human beings are part of the sum total of the consciousness present in all of reality. We are thus able to relate to everything that exists at a level beyond the reach of our senses. We are capable of enmeshing our own consciousness actively to become part of the Gaian holistic principle of the inclusivity and the interrelatedness of everything in existence. Our consciousness takes its place as part of the whole conscious nature of the Cosmos, whether we wish it to be so, or not!

In practice, this not only enables each of us to have a direct relationship to everything else, but also to recognise that it has been a natural automatic feature within us from the beginning. It frequently manifests as a feeling that we are at one with nature or that we sometimes know things of which we hitherto had been unaware. It means that our course of action is sometimes influenced by factors beyond our reason and logic; and it is why our interaction with cosmic elements of reality, such as the subtle realm, takes on a mystical character beyond our normal senses.

This is also the means by which the law of attraction operates to provide consciousness with fulfilment of its desire. It also means that we should always be aware at all times of that which our consciousness desires, bearing in mind the extent of good and evil that resides within each and every one of us.

Being a part of Gaia naturally operates for the benefit of Gaia, and is part of the self-regulation implicit within the Gaian principle. This statement appears to be obvious and we would think that this would operate in such a way that the conditions for life to survive and flourish would be automatically maintained on Earth for the benefit of humanity as the dominant form on the planet. But Gaia, like evolution, has no interest or ability in establishing and promoting life-worthy conditions for any particular physical form of life; it is simply a system that enables life of one sort or another to arise and to benefit from its interactive, interconnected nature and its regulation of the environment.

As we have said before, such a lifeform need not be humanoid. Consciousness, in whatever vehicle it is housed, will be the benefactor of the self-regulation of life-bearing conditions, and if the human race fails to recognise the Gaian principles involved then the possibility arises that we, and all other lifeforms, may become extinct. We may be supplanted by an alternative lifeform that evolves into an alternative environment in our stead.

The second feature that arises from consciousness being present in all matter is that of a universal or cosmic soul. As Plato said in the *Timaeus*:

We shall affirm that the cosmos, more than anything else, resembles most closely that living creature of which all other living creatures, severally or genetically, are portion; a living creature which is fairest of all and in ways most perfect.

The Emerald Tablet describes the Earth not only as the body that nurtures life upon and within it, but also includes the principal elements of the then known Universe, the Sun and the Moon, as part of an integrated process of systematic interaction:

Its father is the sun, its mother is the moon,
The wind carries it within it, and the earth nurses it.

We may see the Gaian principle within this statement. Here, the ancient notion of Earth seen as being akin to 'Mother' or the Anima Mundi, as the world soul, and the idea that spirit is in all things. Our model thus demands of us an understanding that goes beyond that of our immediate environs, to include not only the Sun and the Moon but also everything contained in our solar system, our galaxy and our Universe. Because everything that is within the material Universe arises from the same source – through the big bang event, we are able to conjecture that similar conditions, whether life supporting or not, would prevail wherever we happen to be universally located.

We are therefore able to see that all of the Cosmos forms one totally integrated, living system of reality wherever the archaeus particle exists or has existed, and this includes its presence within the subtle realm. We must be prepared to extend the scope of our consciousness beyond the Gaian principle as it applies to the planet Earth, to encompass the entire Cosmos in all its realities, even if life is not present. We must recognise a form of Super or Mega-Gaia where all realities exist as one system and, furthermore, that this entire cosmic system is capable of self-regulation.

One unfortunate result in the march of objective science and philosophy has been the loss of understanding concerning this exciting feature of our reality, at least so far as planet Earth is

The Book of Becoming

concerned. The difficulty for Gaia to be subjected to scientific methodology through empirical testing has led to its dismissal by many involved in this branch of science.

There have, however, been some advocates of a living Earth system, such as Lamark, Goethe, Humboldt and James Hutton with his notion of Earth as a super-organism or complete physiological system. Vladimir Vernadsky also introduced the concept of the biosphere, which recognised matter as a living geological force, and not least by Teilhard de Chardin who saw the Earth as emerging, through the Noosphere, towards a form of holistic consciousness as its destiny.

It is possible to recognise that ancient humanity had a greater rapport with nature, incorporating the Gaian system of interdependent interaction than is currently the case. Once again we have recourse to indigenous populations, to people like the First Nation inhabitants with their shamans, who were able to recognise the relationships between all aspects of multiple realities and were able to develop the means whereby they could journey between ordinary and non-ordinary states.

It becomes apparent that the relationship between consciousness and Gaia is more than an engagement at all points. Consciousness is an element of Gaia that exists as an intrinsic part of everything in existence. It would be more true to say that consciousness is Gaia and that Gaia is consciousness, albeit without a conscious process of thought or the means of activation through a decision-making process.

Once again we go back to the need for our definition of consciousness to be widened to encompass aspects of life that are normally excluded from the meaning of the term. Gaia and consciousness are at one with each other. Gaia functions within the p or potential layer; and our own level of consciousness, having become differentiated by development, takes that combination forward as a natural function of the interactive Universe.

6.08. Consciousness with Dark Matter and Dark Energy

At first it is difficult to see any relationship between consciousness and dark energy or dark matter. After all, by their nature, dark energy and dark matter are hidden; they are not visible or available to our experience at all. But the same may be said for archaeus particles. They exist in a realm where we cannot use our normal senses to encounter them, and when they do translate into the material realm they do so by giving mass to other particles and then ceasing to exist as discrete or separate entities. Even though the outcome of its activity may be as obvious and apparent as the mass of matter, its only means of detection is through its interaction with its carrier field, the archaeus field.

The archaeus particle is imbued with the signature of the consciousness of The Source of All Things and it is then carried from the Source dimension into the subtle realm to become translated into the material realm, on the archaeus field of energy, which then resides in our Universe as dark energy. The relationship of the archaeus field and, subsequently, the field of dark energy rests with the fleeting nature of the archaeus particle when passing its mark of consciousness to matter in the material realm.

At the present state of scientific progress the subject of dark energy and dark matter remains a mystery, and it is likely that dark energy and dark matter have no other relationship with consciousness. At some point in the future they may somehow become converted into a physical reality within the material realm whereupon the Gaian principle of interrelated connectivity and self-regulation may come into play.

Until that time we must be content to allow the Universe to retain this mysterious, esoteric element of its constituency.

6.09. The Interactive Universe

We are now able to look at our Universe as having a fully inter-active and self-regulating nature. Consciousness is not only the driving force that exposes all of the subtle Ideas to become evident in our reality; it also binds everything together as the glue that keeps everything engaged with the living Cosmos.

Consciousness forms the bedrock of our existence; it is capable of development in a separate manner from that of its hosting vehicle, so that as part of the soul complex which can become independent it can alter the scope of its evolution; it can recognise the nature of its destiny; it can decide upon the choices that are necessary for our survival; it can choose to alter the balance between good and evil and, most importantly, it is capable of becoming a part of the cosmic scope of interdependent reality through its intrinsic membership of the Gaian principles that pervade the entire Cosmos.

Chapter Seven

The Nature of Belief: Religion, Spirituality and Mysticism

Their answer has been an attempt to recognise me in various forms,
whereby to establish some of the principles by which they may
flourish.

If they would only stay true to my universal justice and the virtues,
and of course, to themselves.

But they do not!

They promptly forget those principles,
that cease to suit their own purpose.

They destroy the integrity of their own faith,
they betray the principles of their own belief,
by fighting and warring amongst themselves.

They convert their faith and their belief
into states of violence,
into states of non-belief.

All of which has little to do with me,
has no regard for nature and natural process.
And the beauty of all I have given.

Why do they harness the perfect truth found in my pattern of
existence,
to suit their own desire for wealth, power and dominance.
When I have given dominion to them,

as the natural outcome of their evolution.

From a distance, they all appear to be the same, to me.
I cannot comprehend why they seek to hurt and destroy each other,
to fight wars in my name,

for by my edict there can be no war that is just or holy.

Why do they not seek to resolve their differences?
to revere and nurture their home,
to recognise that the evil of violence is abhorrent,
to realise that their differences are insignificant,
in my pattern of true reality.

Do they not see that they all will cease to survive and to flourish,
if they follow this pathway?

7.00. Introduction

There is a great deal of controversy surrounding the nature of belief as it applies to individuals and to the general public. In this chapter we shall briefly introduce belief in an examination of whether or not it bears a relationship to reality.

Religion in all its many forms has played a major role in the process whereby human beings have tried to give themselves a sense of purpose and direction, together with some form of an answer to the question 'Why is there something, rather than nothing?'

Because over one-half of the entire population of the world professes a belief in one religion or another, we cannot ignore the part that religion has played in our journey to the present, no matter in what sphere our interests lie. Whether you find the effect that religion has had to be good or bad, as a truth or a falsehood, it cannot be dismissed as being of no importance.

In this chapter we will look briefly at the part religion has played throughout our history, and whether its core message has any relevance in today's world of expanding atheistic belief. (Is atheistic belief a contradiction in terms?) We will also give some consideration to those parallel characteristics that exist alongside and possibly overlap with religion, those of spirituality and mysticism.

7.01. Belief

Neuroscientists today look towards belief being a condition of the brain where many philosophers of the mind regard function-alism as being a root cause for beliefs. For them, the perception of the properties, or functions of objects and actions, became the causation events from where belief arises.

Whilst we disagree that this causal condition negates the existence of free will, we can recognise that there may be a great deal of value to be gained from this scenario, so far as belief is concerned. Functionalists generally see their argument as setting the nature of belief as an interpretation within the brain of a perceived causal chain arising from the functionality of things or actions; a rather mundane neural route for belief to become established.

For us, the all-important word in the functionalist argument is that of 'perception'. If an individual perceives something to be true then, whether or not it is so, belief will arise from that perception.

The perceived shape of an object grants a truth to that object that is tantamount to knowledge. We perceive an object to be (say) spheroid and, because we can prove it to be so, we know that it is so. In these cases belief is based on a function of knowledge.

Belief in this respect grows with knowledge even though it may not in fact be true at all. We 'know' that the Sun will rise tomorrow even though the Sun never rises at all. The rotation of the Earth creates the perception that the Sun rises, whereas the truth is that it appears above the horizon as the movement of the Earth alters our vantage point in relation to the position of the Sun. Nevertheless we continue to believe something based on a false presumption of 'knowledge'.

Difficulty arises when the truth of something is not subject to any form of proof that verifies it as being true. This is when the nature of belief takes on additional characteristics to those that are provable. The nature of perception, the way we see and interpret the things that impinge upon our minds, is not a secure phenomenon that affects each individual in an identical manner.

We have seen that within the whole population, when considering consciousness, perceptions of reality may differ from individual to individual. This is especially so within the prodigious savant population where an individual's perception may represent an entirely different interpretation of their reality, to the extent that an alternative to the 'normal' reality comes into being for them. Now the nature of belief is opened up to encompass a perceived reality which may, or may not, be true, but is nevertheless just as 'real' to the individual perceiving the reality as any other perception.

Furthermore, external forces may be brought to bear upon the truth or knowledge of the object to make that truth a changeable commodity. The object that may be seen as a particular colour in one light and may change its colour when seen within the light of a different frequency. The spheroid, once in motion, may cease to be a spheroid. Many objects and actions change once the condition of their environment changes or when external conditions change.

We can therefore see that some truths form the basis for knowledge and, generally speaking, belief will arise for the majority of the population that supports the nature of the truth involved. But this does not apply to the entire population, some of whom will perceive the truth and the resultant knowledge as an alternative or changing dynamic within their own reality.

Furthermore, it is important to take on board the fact that our perceptions are also subject to change according to the experience gained during our lifetimes. Consequently our beliefs may also be subject to change.

This is demonstrated by the process that is evolution, where its effect upon the environment has been developmental and adaptive since the beginning of time, throughout the Universe. This has facilitated change in the objective nature of life and its actions and, consequently, the perceptions of humanity have been in a constant state of change, of development and adaptation which has also rendered the nature of truth and belief to be changeable.

Whilst belief systems may be founded on the bedrock of functionalism, seen in what can be proven to be true, they are overlaid by the perceptions of each of us, in relation to that, which cannot yet be proven to be true.

It is an acceptance of the functionality of that which can be proven to be true that forms the basis for all belief because were this not to be the case then there would simply be no foundation from which to extrapolate an understanding of what to believe, so far as the unprovable is concerned.

Belief must be capable of accommodating change once it is recognised that perception has changed. It is a sad comment that some individuals ignore change through their inability, or failure, or refusal to recognise that their perception of belief has changed. Individually we need to remain alert to changes of perception, to be prepared to confront our belief and endeavour not to allow our consciousness to become subjugated to belief without continuing challenge.

Furthermore, belief takes on additional characteristics when applied to mass populations. In addition to functionality, which continues to feature throughout large population numbers, there arises a system of internalisation that is due to the familiarity of the surrounding environment.

Internalisation comes about through a close association with those around us, particularly so from those of an older generation. Here memetic imitation plays a substantial part in what large communities come to believe. The pressure to comply with social norms has been a significant factor in religious and political life, and remains so in many areas of the world today. Our perceived reality becomes internalised in a wish to be socially accepted into our community, and our beliefs adapt accordingly, whether based on truth, or not.

Society may react defensively in negating any challenge to communal belief; institutions tend to adhere to their belief systems irrespective of change, especially developmental change in the understanding of evolution and of the environment. Dichotomies will eventually arise that witness the commencement of the breakdown of societies and the polarisation of beliefs into splinter groups and factions.

We must always remember that mass populations are comprised of individuals, and it is the individual belief that is best suited to either adapt to change or remain steadfast. Individuals are equally capable of giving rise to splinter groups and factions, but are less likely to do so when internalisation ceases to be a major factor affecting their particular belief.

Religious belief has, for millennia, played a major role in the development of our societies and communities and, as we will now see, it is at an individual or small societal level that the best of the religious beliefs and teachings have been and may still be demonstrated.

7.02. Religion

It is apparent that humanity, from its growth of self-awareness and the ability to process intelligent, objective thought, coupled to the development of creativity, intuition and mysticism, has expressed a need to represent its relationship to and with its surroundings and its environment.

This is shown in our prehistory where, from about 50,000 years ago, the imagery depicted in cave paintings and in models or statues remains extant. Many will ask what this has to do with religion and, for those who practise the worship of a particular deity today the answer may be obscure enough for them to believe the reply to be 'nothing at all'. But if we stand back and open our consciousness we will see that, at our core, there is a fundamental need to express or record the fact that we were here and that our presence meant something. We have also needed to record that we were aware of our fellow travellers on our evolutionary journey, together with our surroundings, our place within them and that we possibly influenced them.

This is the essence of our religious foundations.

Humanity from these very early beginnings developed the need for ceremony as a means whereby it could come to give some meaning to its position, within its environment, both physically and non-physically. It was thought that the relationship to the seasons, the phases of the Moon, the cycles of the Sun, the changing state of the weather and its effect on the human ability to survive could be affected, regulated or appeased by ceremonial conduct.

The nature of illness and disease and the fact that all things die were factors that were generally beyond human understanding, and were elements of life that were thought to be affected by the activity of the tribe or groups concerned, especially their relationship with nature.

Ceremonial activity was simply their means of expressing a connection to nature and its common effects, and such activity attempted to influence those external events that were beyond their control, but which governed their lives. Ceremonies were used to express recognition that their lives were lived in conjunction with environmental conditions.

Far from being primitive, or even savage in their nature, such ceremonies, and consequently such societies, were often highly sophisticated as they came to seek a purpose and a direction for their being. There was a widespread recognition that the reality they experienced was one where uncertainty surrounded the arrival of new life, where death was acknowledged but that their existence would not be completed during their lifetime on Earth.

The process of reproduction may barely have been understood. Yes, the means whereby new life could be conceived might have been recognised and appreciated but, because conception did not occur every time a coupling took place, or sometimes not at all, then any understanding of a pre-life condition and its cause was clouded or mystified by circumstances.

Similarly, death was a known factor of life, but the need to believe that the death of the body did not signal the end of individual existence was strong enough so that the dead often became treated with a reverence that sometimes exceeded that when they were alive. The evidence seen in ancient burial or cremation sites clearly supports the fact of death as a condition of life, but also one that possessed the possibility of an afterlife.

It then became only a simple matter of time for a perception to arise that gave credence to the notion that the way that you conducted your 'middle-life' on Earth seriously affected your beliefs and the final status in the 'afterlife' somewhere else.

A further natural development of this line of reasoning arose when the cause of everything became the subject of an entity with a range of powers beyond those of the human inhabitants of Earth. The Sun was perhaps the most popular of the original deities, closely followed by the Moon because it was these heavenly bodies that clearly demonstrated the greatest effect upon the daily lives of the population. There followed a multitude of deities, to which were attributed aspects of life from fertility and healing to hunting for food and desired personality traits.

Eventually, competition between the adherents of rival deities led to the need to refine the number of ceremonial, worshipful entities to a single deity, one that could encompass all others, and so monotheism was born.

Looking from the present day, with hindsight, we are able to understand why these early humans would seek to construct belief systems that offered some explanation of their place on planet Earth and the part they might be expected to play. Their relationship with nature was closer by far than is the case today. If they did not work with nature, if they did not fundamentally appreciate the effect that natural events could have upon them, then their ability to survive and to flourish would have been significantly diminished.

When The Emerald Tablet arrived on the scene, it was probably seen as an early attempt to formalise the arrangement between nature, as it was perceived at the time, and the population in general. As stated in Chapter One, many movements arose from the message inscribed on The Emerald Tablet, including the subsequent formulation of the doctrines that came to inhabit many of the religious movements which had yet to come into existence.

The text on the Tablet was an attempt to explain and to develop the belief and the lifestyle of the population by means of their conforming to the principles expressed thereon. A single source for everything was proposed, a purpose was established, the means of its activity were described, the part the population was to play was expressed, the reward for compliance was explained and the power it purported to exert was made apparent.

Many people of a religious persuasion, in today's formal meaning, might seek to deny that societies and communities in existence before monotheism became popular were religious at all. Many might describe such societies as heathen or savage, possessing no 'religion'. This has been the teaching of many of the organised religions who do not wish to acknowledge their indebtedness to the approach of our ancient forebears, particularly to their relationship to nature and the afterlife. The almost forgotten, pre-religious images of 'The Green Man' are leftovers that are nevertheless present in many places of Christian worship, even today, but which are barely referred to with any significant degree of reverence or importance.

To many of us the notion of monotheism and the religious constructs that are associated with it are motifs which look familiar today. Most of our formal religions profess knowledge of a multi-tier formation of the Cosmos. The ideas of a heaven, or paradise, of a hell, or an underworld are tiers of reality that accompany our daily reality and are still part of the formal religious constructions of today.

And why not? Our model of the Cosmos also defines three levels of reality, a subtle realm, a material realm and a further plane of existence following the death of the physical aspects of the body.

We can identify, on the text on The Emerald Tablet, the need inherent in humanity for such fundamental aspects of religion as these, expressed as a relationship between nature and humans, originating from The One Source of All Things.

As all things arise from one and are mediated by one: so all things are born and adapted from this one.

Its father is the sun, its mother is the moon, The wind carries it within it, and the earth nurses it.

The father is all of perfection here in the world, if it is converted into earth truly,
whereupon its power and force is complete.

You should separate the spiritual from the gross, truly and with great industry, as it ascends from the earth to the subtle, and back again, and in so doing receives the force of all things subtle and material.

By these means you shall have dominion of the whole world and all things will become clear.

Its force is above all other forces, because it can convert every subtle thing to penetrate every material thing.

This was how the world was created.

The scene is thus set for formalised religions to arise from the foundations laid by the beliefs of our ancient forefathers.

The need for us to believe that humanity is present on Earth for some purpose that matters; the irrefutable evidence that we are the dominant force of consciousness on the planet and that this is for a reason; the recognition that our self-awareness and our position within the nature of our reality may be due to some single external agency; the desire to believe that the death of everything living also has meaning; the belief that life stretches beyond our lifespan into an unknown realm. All of this became an imperative when these factors had developed to the point where formalisation became necessary, and thus the organised, formal religions were born from the foundation of ancient folklore.

Perhaps the most significant single condition that permitted the rise of the organised, formal religions is that of the refinement of the question 'Why there is something, rather than nothing?' to an answer that involved only one originator or source. This refinement appears to have taken place, within human consciousness, during the approximate period from the start of the second millennium before the common era (BCE), to the seventh century of the common era (CE), a period of only approximately 2,700 years or so.

In this respect the formal religions may be viewed, even today, where they are a maximum of only about 4,000 years or so old, as newcomers to the scene of human experience. All of the formal religions are, as yet, very young in terms of their formation and development, and might yet be thought of as needing to reach a state of maturity, where inter-religious disagreement and conflict is recognised as a sign of their past infantile or juvenile intolerance.

Hinduism is probably the oldest of the formal religions having been formulated from several traditions existing many thousands of years ago. Today there are about one billion adherents, most of whom do not regard Hinduism as a religion at all, perhaps because it has no prophet and no firm date when it was formed. It might therefore more accurately be termed a set of religious beliefs. Hindus regard all religions as one, and have possibly the most pacifist outlook of all of the main religions. It is likely that it was the Hindu religion, arising mostly from the Indian subcontinent, and named after the people living around the Indus River, that first proclaimed allegiance to 'One Supreme God' named 'Brahma' the creator.

This, despite the acceptance of a trinity of Godlike entities that exist in Hinduism as Brahma, the creator of the Cosmos; Vishnu its preserver and protector; and Shiva the destroyer of the Cosmos (in order that it may be re-created).

Their code of conduct may be found in 'The Dharma', which is an important term in Indian religions as it means duty, virtue, or morality, and it refers to the power that upholds the Universe and society. Dharma is universal, but it is also particular and operates within specific circumstances. Consequently, each person has their own dharma, interpreted according to their gender, age and condition.

The sacred scriptures of the Hindus are to be found in 'the Vedas' comprising four books called the Samhitas, which are the most ancient part of the Vedas, and which consist of hymns of praise to God; the Brahmanas which are rituals and prayers to guide the priests in their duties; the Aranyakas, which concern worship and meditation; and finally, the Upanishads, which consist of the mystical and philosophical teachings of Hinduism.

Similar to all religions, Hindus practise their religious belief throughout their daily lives, but when worship is conducted in groups, then they do so in temples specially built for the purpose.

Judaism came next, originating in the Middle East about 1,500 years BCE and was founded by Moses, although the Jewish adherents believe that they can trace their roots even further back, to Abraham, who, if he lived at all, was thought to be alive around 2000 BCE. There are currently about 13.3 million Jews living in the world today. They believe in one God with whom they have a special relationship exemplified in covenants. These are formal agreements, where the Jewish people agreed to follow a set of laws and to live their lives in such a way as to show the world that God actually was the one and only all-powerful God, whom people should follow and worship. In return God would guide them and protect them and give them the land of Israel.

Jewish laws are to be found in their sacred text seen in the 'Torah', also known as the first five books of the Hebrew Bible. Further interpretation of the laws was expanded into texts known as 'the Mishnah' and 'the Talmud', completed during the fifth century CE. These laws are intended to demonstrate the willingness of Jewish adherents to comply with the covenants as a code of conduct that exemplifies and characterises their monotheistic God. Synagogues are where Jewish people congregate to worship.

The history of the Jewish people, as chronicled in the Hebrew Bible, records continuous deviation from their covenantal agreements with their monotheistic god, with many attempts to bring the consequently scattered Jewish population back together with a view of putting renewed covenants back into effect. In some respects the consolidation of the Jewish nation in obedience to the covenants, in return for the land of Israel, was recognised in 1948 when the State of Israel finally came into being.

Christianity arose as an offshoot of Judaism following the crucifixion of the Jewish individual known as Jesus of Nazareth, around the year 33 CE. The term CE or 'common era' marks the way in which the years of any date are now recorded in some societies and cultures worldwide, and the change from BCE to CE is intended to mark the birth of Jesus. Christian adherents believe that there is one true God, although they believe that there are three elements to this entity, God the father, God the Son exemplified in Jesus of Nazareth and God the Holy Spirit, seen as a personalized force that can fill each individual with the ethos of the other two.

A major split, or schism, arose from the lack of agreement concerning the nature of these Trinitarian elements of their Godhead and whether they should be regarded as equal in all respects, or whether they should form a hierarchal structure. This schism remains unresolved even today after more than a millennium of disagreement.

A further major rift developed when a sixteenth century protest movement, lead by Martin Luther (1483–1546), erupted to challenge the then current practice of the Roman Catholic authorities of granting relief, following payment of large sums of money, for the sins of an individual that might result in their subsequent incarceration in purgatory or hell – a Catholic practice known as indulgence. Following this rift, priests who followed the new Protestant doctrines declared that the text of the Bible was to be the only basis upon which Christian truth could be established. These new 'Lutheran' priests were also allowed to marry. Both Catholic and Protestant religious movements continue to this day and have formed the basis of much enmity throughout the Christian world.

There are about 2 billion adherents, of all denominations, to Christianity in the world today, spread throughout most countries worldwide. Their sacred scriptures are to be found in the Bible comprising the Old Testament, incorporating the Hebrew Bible, where the common ground with Judaism and Islam is shared, together with the New Testament, which teaches a code of conduct as seen through the narrative story of Jesus of Nazareth, who is believed to be the Son of God. Christians worship in churches and believe that worship of God through his Son Jesus will result in the forgiveness of their sins, and will result in a way of life that could ensure their afterlife in heaven, alongside Jesus.

Islam is dated from the migration of the prophet Muhammad around 1,400 years ago, and has something in excess of one billion adherents. Islamic followers are called Muslims and their sacred texts are to be found in the Qur'an and the Sunnah. Muslims believe the Sunnah is the practical example of the prophet Muhammad and expresses the five basic Pillars of Islam. These are: the declaration of faith; praying five times each day; giving to charity; fasting; and pilgrimage to Mecca at least once in a lifetime.

Muslims also share the first five books of the Torah or the Old

Testament as part of their sacred text of the Qur'an. They recognise and respect Abraham, Moses and Jesus as prophets, with Muhammad as 'The Final Prophet' sent down to Earth to reveal to humanity the way to live in peace, in accordance with God's laws. They worship in mosques.

A major split or schism occurred in Islam soon after the death of the prophet Muhammad, where the right of leadership of all Muslims was disputed by two separate factions. The differences between these factions lie in the fields of doctrine, ritual, law, theology and religious organisation. The Sunni Muslims form a considerable majority and may be seen as the traditionalist followers of Muhammad, who base their devotion on precedent or reports of the actions of the Prophet and those close to him. Sunni Muslims generally adhere to state control.

The Shia Muslims form about twenty per cent of Islamic followers, who claim the right of the Prophet's son-in-law Ali, and his descendants, to lead all Muslims. Their clerics generally interpret the Islamic texts from an independent position within their loosely held hierarchy and have developed ritualistic concepts of martyrdom.

Buddhism should not be regarded as a religion at all as its adherents do not believe in a personal God. It is included here because of the large number of adherents worldwide, whose aim is to develop a personal and spiritual awakening, involving an insight into the true nature of life.

Buddhism dates from the time of its founder, Siddhartha Gautama, also known as the Buddha, whose journey on a quest for enlightenment in the sixth century BCE forms the basis for the teachings of Buddhism. Having unsuccessfully attempted to find life's meaning firstly as a monk and then by adopting the harsh poverty of Indian asceticism, he decided to a pursue the 'Middle

Way', a life without either poverty or luxury.

Following a period of meditation whilst seated beneath a Bodhi tree (the tree of awakening) he was directed away from the pain of suffering, towards enlightenment. The ultimate objective of enlightenment is a state of Nirvana, a state where greed, hatred and delusion have been extinguished so that continuous reincarnation, with its inherent subsequent suffering, will no longer be necessary for the individual involved.

For Buddhists nothing has permanence and everything is in a state of change. Such a state is exemplified in impermanence where nothing either good or bad lasts forever; in suffering, arising from a mistaken belief that some things can last; and in uncertainty, which proclaims that no entity that knows everything can ever be defined and no enduring experience of its essence can ever be located.

These are the three signs of existence, which is regarded as endless because unenlightened individuals are continually reincarnated in order to experience everlasting suffering. However, enlightenment is possible and involves an awakening to the practice of morality, meditation and wisdom.

Buddhism has six realms into which a soul may be reincarnated: those of Heaven, humanity, the Titans or angry Gods, the Hungry Ghosts, the Animal Realm, and Hell, where people are horribly tortured until their bad karma is worked off. There are currently in excess of 375 million Buddhists in the world.

A word must be said concerning religion in the nation of China. According the website of the Information Office of the State Council of the People's Republic of China, dated October 1997, in Beijing, the freedom to practise any religious belief is not only permitted, it is encouraged. Chinese citizens are said to be free to practise their beliefs in Buddhism, Taoism, Islam, Catholicism and Protestantism, where it is acknowledged that there are in excess of 100 million adherents across all religions.

All religions are regarded as an extension of the family, incorporating Chinese folk culture, of which the most popular are thought to be Buddhism, which has been practised for over 2,000 years and Taoism (Daoism), which has a Chinese history of over 1,700 years.

Tao means 'The Way', and is incorporated into Taoism as 'The One, which is natural, spontaneous, eternal, nameless, and indescribable'. According to *A Source Book in Chinese Philosophy* by Wing-Tsit Chan,[18] it is at once 'the beginning of all things and the way in which all things pursue their course.' The ethics prominent in Taoism revolve around 'wu wei' which promotes action through the lack of action, a system of 'primordial naturalness, creativity or spontaneity', that should arise naturally, without the need for any deciding action to be present. The virtue of Taoist thinking becomes associated with 'the Three Treasures' or 'Three Jewels' simplified as compassion, moderation and humility.

The influence of The Emerald Tablet text is very apparent here.

Since a degree of liberalism has entered Chinese society, following the death of its Communist leader Mao Zedong (Mao Tse-tung) in 1976, there has been a resurgence of religious belief evident within Chinese culture. The large increase in population numbers who follow Buddhist or Christian beliefs gives credence to the possibility that during the suppression of religion during the Communist era many people continued with their religious beliefs privately and/or in secret.

Belief in formalised religion and the doctrinal declarations that ensue therefrom all purport to express a means of accomplishing an ascendant journey that is a reflection of the tenets expressed on The Emerald Tablet, expanded through the medium of Neo-Platonism, all of which is exemplified in the concept of destiny that we discussed in Chapter Four. One significant feature of the doctrinal declarations is a 'leftover' from the pagan era where nature was seen as one of the principal cultural guiding factors of belief systems.

One such cultural belief system that has religious overtones is that seen within concepts where 'the tree of life' has become a central feature. Here the system of nature, as experienced in the natural environment, is seen as a sustaining system that develops to allow life on Earth to survive and flourish, and is replicated as a system of pathways, or branches that, if followed, lead to a parallel development in human nature and enlightenment.

One such religious cultural system is to be found in 'the Kabbalah', which originated in Jewish mystical thinking but which was appropriated and adapted by Christian and Islamic thinkers for the benefit of their own adherents.

Central to the Kabbalistic system is the notion of a monotheistic vitality designated as 'Ein Sof', the eternal, never-ending, concealed force, existing prior to first emanation. Emanations followed that were initially seen as 'divine will' and 'never-ending thought' which eventually became aspects of Ein Sof, when thought became capable of thinking about itself and was able to see all of creation envisaged as arising from the 'nothingness' expressed within Ein Sof.

Although much confusion and dispute has manifested concerning the nature and the purpose of the ten emanations that followed the composite recognition of Ein Sof, the emanations, known as 'the Sephirot', have come to symbolise the tree of life, having characteristics that are of Ein Sof, without themselves being a part of it. The Sephirot or Tree of Life is often depicted as three vertical pillars, the two outside pillars each of three Sephirot, with a centre pillar of four (sometimes five) Sephirot. Hundreds of images of the Kabbalistic Tree of Life may be viewed on the Internet.

The three vertical columns, or pillars, depicted on the tree of life are said to represent Mercy, Justice and Grace. The right hand, the pillar of mercy, from top to bottom, runs from Hokhmah, which means 'wisdom' or 'revelation', through Chesed meaning 'mercy' and Netzach meaning 'victory' or 'initiative'.

The opposite pillar, on the left, represents justice and runs from Binah which means 'understanding', through Gevurah meaning 'judgement', and Hod, meaning 'Glory'.

The middle pillar represents the grace and harmony of the whole and runs from Keter, which means 'crown', through Tipheret meaning 'beauty' or 'harmony', to Yesod, meaning 'foundation', and on to Malkuth, meaning 'kingdom'. The extent of good and evil also resides in the understanding of this pillar.

The Sephirot of Da'at is shown on the centre pillar, but may be regarded as a facet of Keter where Keter may be interpreted as consciousness and Da'at as unconsciousness.

These ten Sephirot are divided into two further groups. The three 'upper' ones at the top of each pillar are associated with the 'higher heavenly realms': they are Keter, Hokhmah and Binah. Whilst the remaining seven are thought of as being associated with the creation of the Universe.

The Sephirot is fully interconnected with pathways that link each Sephirot to any other and thus should be considered as a whole, as something that is incapable of separation. Any journey of enlightenment, undertaken using the Sephirotic model, similar to the one depicted, uses all of the pathways indicated so that they become as important as the Sephirot themselves.

The detail content of the Sephirot need not concern us in our considerations except to confirm that the nature of the Kabbalistic scheme shown follows similar principles described on The Emerald Tablet. A journey of understanding is required, to and from the transcendent source, in order to experience enlightenment in an alchemical transformation from the Kingdom (or our universal reality) to the various transcendent levels that represent virtues such as goodness, beauty, harmony and truth, together with justice, wisdom and mercy. We can easily identify the principles of a gestaltic model in this tree of life.

The Sephirot may be regarded, Kabbalistically, as being similar to the subtle realm described in our model of the Cosmos, albeit of different content. It is separate from The One Source of All Things and seeks to describe the nature of creation and the attributes that go towards its character. In adapting the Kabbalah from its Judaic roots for their own purposes, the Christian and Islamic hierarchies also confirm their adoption of The Emerald Tablet as one of their principal tenets.

The content of all the formalised religious beliefs described has been reported, distorted, disseminated, reconstructed and accommodated to suit the particular requirements of doctrinal and dogmatic edicts and the purposes of splinter factions arising therefrom. This to the point where it may now be said that they represent a cultural way of life, as much as a set of beliefs.

The four principle religions described briefly above, together with Buddhism and Chinese folk culture, exemplified in Taoism and the Kabbalah, have purported adherents that total nearly 5 billion people, considerably more than half of the current entire population of the world. Both individually and together they have had a major impact on the historical conduct of humanity since their founding.

It may thus be confidently stated that religion cannot be dismissed as being of little or no consequence. In fact the opposite can be seen as being true, in that even in today's scientific and technologically based, secular society, there exists an imperative need for human beings to invest in belief systems of one sort or another which seek to answer questions pertaining to the meaning and purpose of existence, questions to which science is yet unable to provide a credible answer.

Formalised religion is, in terms of human history, a very new phenomenon indeed. The oldest of these religions was only founded a mere few thousand years ago. The closeness in time of the arising, in the near historical past, of all of them reveals the growing urgency of the need for humanity to attempt to define answers to the questions of our existence. The formalisation of these religions, being so close together in time, demonstrates that a stage in human development had been reached where, through introspection, a greater need to find deeper answers to our existence and condition on Earth had become apparent. The rise of religion(s) therefore became inevitable with the deepening of this need.

The close founding, in time, of such religious and/or cultural phenomena led inevitably to a formulation where each can be seen to exhibit a close similarity of features to the others. The existence of a monotheistic personal God is common to all except the Buddhists who see aspects of the personal soul as capable of achieving Godlike characteristics. All see a multilayer Cosmos that allows for advancement or diminution according to the way we live our lives. All profess a code of conduct that seeks to establish the ascendant direction of our life's journey towards goodness, especially in our attitude towards others. All profess peace as being one of the objectives of their teaching. Each professes to nurture humanity, provided compliance with its moral tenets is enacted continuously.

With so much in common, it is difficult to understand why it is that religion and religious culture appear to be the cause of so much conflict between the various members of each of the religious communities, or even within the subdivisions of each religion. The answer is of course that religion is not the cause of such conflict but is only the excuse presented for human nature to express its differences.

We should all recognise that the presence of The One Source is in every one of us through its imprint in the archaeus particle. This translates historically to mean, in religious terms, that The One Source of All Things, referred to as God by the religious communities, is incarnate in every one of us, without exception. Consequently, we are all of The One Source and may all be seen, religiously, as the sons or daughters of God incarnate.

In the case of those individuals who possess the twinned particles in one body, that we described in Chapter Four, we identified their nature as being one of cosmic consciousness, having achieved an awakening to enlightenment. The obvious examples of this phenomenon may be found in Moses, Siddhartha Gautama, Jesus of Nazareth and Muhammad. However, this list is not exclusive and, because we all intrinsically partake of The One Source, the difference between us lies initially with the extent or degree of such partaking, followed by the choices that our consciousness processes and that our free will activates.

Enlightenment is a matter for our consciousness to achieve, but is something that does not necessarily require any religious input for its successful outcome. If we take a religious or a secular view of this, we can determine that we should seek to follow or adopt a lifestyle that is characterised by goodness and a strong ethic of moral behaviour, even where human nature resists these objectives as being not in our immediate, personal interests.

Religions have expressed a requirement for each of us to do

only good to others, as we would have only goodness done unto us, but this is not the sole domain of religious teaching. If human nature, despite any belief system, were to concentrate exclusively on this objective, then a political system of enlightened self-interest would naturally operate for the benefit of all humanity. Furthermore, the environmental stability of the Earth and the nature of ethical teaching, whether religious or otherwise, would then, and only then, be justified.

We have seen that something approaching two-thirds of the world's population professes a belief in one religious form or another, but that leaves about one third without belief in a God of any sort.

The magnitude of religious belief alone might result in allowing us to regard atheism as a destitute condition within the sphere of human endeavour. Yet most genuine atheists appear to adopt a lifestyle that exhibits strong moral convictions and a code of conduct that puts many of today's religious adherents to shame. Their belief does not rest in, or rely on, the existence of a God or Gods; their understanding generally arises from forms of construction that are based within human culture and society.

The success and failure of religion is not easy to define. The numbers of alleged supporters might lead us to assume that they continue to be successful and this is generally true at the small societal or parish level. At this level it is possible that the ordinary person may become fully involved and engaged, and may practise his or her religion from a sincerely held belief. This is because today some religions, at this level, allow the freedom to think for oneself, to shape the nature and extent of one's own belief to become a religion for the ordinary person. Perhaps this factor was the preserving agent that sustained the Chinese people in their religious beliefs during the repressive Communist period?

People operating at this religious individual or small societal level are then able to bring his or her consciousness to bear upon selecting amongst the choices that they make available and which will be activated by their own free will. It is at this level that the best of human nature is often demonstrated, particularly so far as enlightened self-interest is able to measure it. The same cannot be said for larger religious bodies and their institutions.

It is a sad comment that the comparative freedom found at the small societal or parish level cannot always be said to be present in religious institutions at the 'corporate' level, where dogma and doctrine have been subverted to the point where human nature has intervened to allow self-interest, self-indulgence, self-preservation and even self-gratification to dominate and develop as a means of judgement and control not only over its own adherents but as a target for the conversion of others, by force, if necessary.

The notion that it is permissible to kill others, even in restricted or 'justifiable' circumstances, has been allowed to fester, within the culture of the formal religions, to the point where, in many cases, it is now institutionally acceptable. It clearly does not, and cannot, conform to any message delivered by the founders of the religions and should have no part in religious teaching whatsoever. It is possible that the theory of a 'just war' may justifiably exist as a civil necessity, with civil restraints, but should have nothing whatsoever to do with religion. The idea that a 'holy war' could exist and would be acceptable to any of the founders of religion is an anathema to their teachings. This, even though the conditions justified and associated with the just war theory might be said to have arisen from a (misguided) religious foundation.

Institutional practices such as those mentioned above have promoted the subdivision or splintering of the religions into factional or fundamentalist units. To a great extent this is an inevitable outcome of religious institutions because the failure to allow each of its members to think freely and decide for themselves upon the extent and detail of their beliefs automatically creates a self-defeating objective.

7.03. Religion with Atheism and Science

Atheism is a growing idea in the world today, aided and abetted by the success of science and technology, which allows no credence towards anything of the mystical to infiltrate its disciplines.

The point here is that there is no right or wrong path to the truth, or otherwise, of religious belief or a belief in atheism. Those who campaign for one or the other do so from the standpoint of their own personal interest rather than that of the whole population and of all life on Earth. This reflects the true picture of all of our institutions, religious or otherwise, that purport to promote the moral and ethical interests of humanity.

Over the past 4,000 years or so religion, in one form or another, has been one of the dominant forces in the daily lives of the population. Science was tolerated and even encouraged by religion, but only when its aim was to support and prove religious authenticity. Eventually religion gave way to science only during the last 400 years or so, as a more scientific explanation of our existence and of our reality became the subject of increasing evidence, seen in the growth of scientific proof. The outcome, in some areas of both disciplines, has seen enmity between religion and the sciences grow.

However, in practice, there is no need for any dissention between science and technology on the one hand, and any of the religions on the other. The acknowledgment that all things arise from One Source is unexceptional, and its truth can hardly be questioned. Whether or not an individual prefers to attribute a religious aspect to it and possibly call this One Source 'God', or not, should not have any relevance to science.

The existence of everything in the material realm simply is – its evidence is all around us. The actual presence, or not, of a

God, as The One Source of All Things, as an entity that actually exists, does not change the existence of the Cosmos; it only seeks to provide answers to questions yet unanswered.

One of the major points of disagreement between science and religion is that of evolution. Yet this is simply the process that has encouraged or promoted the development of life on Earth, particularly that of consciousness. Whether this process arose through some pattern intrinsic within the physical sciences, or whether the same physical pattern was laid down through the agency of the Big Bang, the religious and scientific views are far from being irreconcilable. The substance of the religions and the process that is evolution are not only compatible but are interdependent on each other in the progress of creation.

A further aspect of the disagreement between religion and science is that of intelligent design, put forward by religion as evidence for a creator God, arising from the discoveries of science in exposing, but not creating, the physical patterns of existence. The idea is that conditions on Earth are so precise, within an extremely narrow band, that they must have been 'designed' so that life here is not only possible but inevitable, extrapolating from this that life has also been 'designed' to survive and flourish. It is then only a small step to believe that such circumstances must be the result of some supreme intelligence.

We have, to a great extent, already discounted this idea on the basis that it would entail a significant, if not total, degree of predetermination, which would negate the effect of choice and its associated activity of free will, and would also restrict or even prevent natural selection from driving the process of adaptation and development.

Whether, or not, conditions exist elsewhere in the Universe that would permit or encourage life to exist in any form is a matter for future discovery. We can reasonably conjecture that, because of the immense size of the Universe, and the huge numbers of planets that have existed, exist now, or will come to exist, the incidence of life becoming established in many places is so highly probable as to be assumed as a given. We just happen to be very fortunate indeed that the planet Earth is one of those capable of supporting life; but if it were not so, or if it ceased to be, then consciousness would continue to take up residence, in the entire Universe, wherever life develops to the point where its emergence becomes recognisable or measurable.

Yet the physical patterns, the laws of the existence of the Cosmos are so elegant and complete that it is difficult to envisage them as haphazard in any way. One form that the pattern of the physical Universe takes is that contact with other lifeforms existing elsewhere in the Universe is inaccessible because of the magnitude of the distances between them and the limitation of the speed in journeying there which would be necessary to make it possible to attain. Each dominant consciousness on each life-bearing planet would thus be forced, if not programmed, to find its own means of development and survival and, if possible, to flourish.

This is another example of the elegance of the laws of physics arising from The One Source and delivered through the agency of the Big Bang.

The answer therefore lies somewhere between the two poles of thinking. Yes, the laws of the physical Universe were initially established by The One Source as the means for the propagation of the entire material realm and the life within it. Thereafter the development of that life has been the subject of mixed random and non-random processes, with the possibility of very many different outcomes. This would be the same where life becomes possible on any planet. The outcomes depend upon the use and the treatment of the environment, determined, at least in part, by the lifeforms on any planet.

Religion and science both start from the same origins, founded in a need to seek answers to the nature of existence, and both finish at the same point in reality; and that is that whatever we believe, the Cosmos exists.

It is fair to say, however, that religion, by seeking to tell people what to think, by seeking to impose its beliefs and teachings and by encouraging a literal interpretation of its scriptural texts, has, in the past, restricted the ability of many to think freely for themselves. This has had the result of limiting the ability for fourth level conscious experience for the mass of people. In these circumstances it might be said that religion has had the effect of slowing down the rate of the evolutionary development of consciousness in humanity.

Science, on the other hand, may have awakened the interest of many and may have encouraged freethinking, allowing atheism to develop. But none of this has the ability to bind humanity into a race of beings that is capable of coexisting with all life on the planet. In fact, the opposite appears to be the case. Science and technology have required the massive acceleration in the use of, if not the wastage of, the natural resources of the planet, with the effect that the environment and consequently the rate of evolutionary development will change, to the disbenefit of humanity.

The common factor in all of this, whether religion, science, technology or atheism, is that of consciousness. Much of the human population actually seek to live their lives at de Ropp's third level of consciousness, in the belief that they are fully awake yet actually experiencing a condition only of wakeful sleep. Here they experience the comfort of needing to make only minimal effort to maintain their existence within our reality. Matters of self-image, of self-indulgence, of trivial acts of self-gratification, of egotistical self-worth, all encouraged by the forces of the media and consumerism, come to feature as important, when in fact they have no importance within the whole scheme of life.

In practice, whether we are religious, scientific (or both) or atheist is not relevant to the point. Consciousness operates across all boundaries of beliefs and disciplines, and offers all of us the opportunity to either be content at the third 'ordinary' level of consciousness, or to explore further beyond its comfort zone.

Consciousness does not recognise boundaries of any sort, but simply accompanies all of life on its journey, hopefully in a direction towards a state of perfection. History has shown that religion, science and atheism have little or no unifying ability; the opposite is rather the case as their effect is that they each manifest division across the population. Division on its own may in fact be healthy to human development by providing comparison and competition in the understanding of existence. It only becomes dangerous, to the race as a whole, when confrontation and violence accompany it, or when indulgent self-interest takes centre stage.

We now have the bare, dry bones of religion and, to a minor extent, its relationship to science and atheism. Institutional religion unfortunately encourages us to be mundane in our approach to existence, to shelter under an umbrella of doctrine that denies the challenge of freethinking from any source, but particularly from within.

But any consideration of religion or atheism is incomplete without reference to those aspects of both which, when translated into our daily lives, raise our ethos above that of the mundane. These are those aspects of our being that operate across the whole spectrum of human endeavour, and are the aspects of spirituality and mysticism.

7.04. Spirituality

Before delving into the nature of spirituality it is important to differentiate it from spiritualism. Whatever spirituality is, it has little to do with spiritualism at all, albeit that spiritualists are capable of displaying spirituality if they choose to do so.

Spiritualism, in the model under discussion, has to do with the practice of communication with the souls of those that have passed from this life, and that live on after their death. In the wrong hands this can be a very dangerous practice to the passed-on souls as it can impede or even prevent that soul from proceeding to the next plane of existence.

Spirituality has to do with an innate characteristic that everybody possesses, one that seeks to understand that which ordinarily lies beyond the capacity of our natural senses to encounter. It does not rely on the death of anyone for its manifestation.

Whilst religious institutions may lay claim to spirituality as an exclusive aspect of the religious life, every human being, without exception, has a spiritual element to their nature, one that does not rely on a religious belief. Every individual that has ever existed or who will come to exist has a spiritual nature, because our characteristics all arise from aspects of the Cosmos that are initially immaterial; that is to say, from within the subtle realm.

The question is often asked: 'What is spirituality?' For those of a religious disposition, spirituality reflects the process whereby adherents seek to become closer to the object of their deity. For those that have no religious belief, spirituality centres upon a state of mind that manifests as psychologically joyful or ecstatic. In both cases the realisation of 'the spirit within' arises through the immaterial content of the Cosmos that is translated by our senses, according to our beliefs and the choices that arise from those beliefs.

What we choose to believe is an important factor when considering spirituality because some choices that we make may lead us to believe that it is not possible to experience areas of existence that fall beyond our senses. Atheists may not believe or accept the existence of a God, or the existence of a soul, but this does not preclude them from demonstrating spiritual aspects of their being, should they so choose to do so. After all, many Buddhists exhibit significant spiritual characteristics without belief in the existence of a personal God.

Clearly belief in a God is not a prerequisite for spirituality.

Spirituality then exists in all of us, whether we wish it to be so, or not, because of the subtle element of the archaeus particle, which exists in the Source dimension, the subtle realm and the material realm simultaneously. Consciousness in the material realm arises naturally, with the functional ability of relating to, and interacting with, the subtle realm. Thus we are all naturally capable of encountering that which ordinarily lies beyond our senses, if we choose to do so.

Similar to our relationship with good and evil, if we look towards spirituality as being one filament of our psyche, the position that we find ourselves occupying along such a strand will be determined by the choices that we make. For those who may have lived before our time, who experienced a deep belief, a sort of 'blind faith', without any meaningful understanding of how they have come to do so, then the choices may have been made subconsciously, but such a condition still evolves from choice.

The operative word here is 'choice' and, yes, this brings into play the Idea of free will determined from the subtle realm. Whilst it is consciousness that determines the choices we make, it is the soul complex as a gestalt that generates the ability to enter and understand the zone of reality, that exists in an encounter beyond our senses and is able to interpret the visionary information that arises therefrom.

There are some amongst humanity who choose not to look for any experience beyond their natural senses. Those who believe that material is all that exists will choose to believe that nothing beyond the senses exists at all, and consequently will reject any notion of an encounter with something that does not appear to exist, mainly because there is no empirical proof of such existence.

Whilst the lack of proof, for these groups, is sufficient to deny the existence of spirituality, for others the fact that there is no evidence that disproves that it exists is sufficient to allow, or assume, that spiritual characteristics can and do indeed exist. The experience and the subsequent practice of spirituality does not depend on proof, but rather becomes a matter of choice, put into action by free will.

So, spirituality exists within all of us, whether religious or not, but is only recognisable through the choices made by the individual who then has access to a reality that is experienced beyond the everyday range of our natural senses. The nature of the spirituality experienced will be determined by at least two criteria.

Initially the strength of the belief of an individual will condition the depth of the spirituality experienced. This is because the focus of an individual upon the existence of something that appears to be beyond the senses itself depends on belief. If the nature of a held belief is confused or weak, perhaps through inexperience or being a new condition for the individual concerned, then the depth of the spirituality experienced may also be weak or confused. However, once focussed and able to experience a spiritual context, the belief of an individual will develop and change.

Whenever greater measures of experience are encountered then beliefs may be deepened or may change absolutely, and the depth of spirituality within the individual will be changed accordingly. The measure of experience may be gained by keeping an open mind, of utilising the ability for freethinking; the key to such a condition lies within the mundus imaginalis.

The second criterion that influences spirituality is that of an altered state of consciousness or the level of consciousness that can be brought to bear on the experience. The manifestation of spirituality, although given effect through our choice, is greatly influenced by the depth of consciousness we are able to bring to it. Choice is a function of consciousness and, although activated by free will, the higher the level of consciousness we are able to bring to bear the greater will be our understanding and the more fruitful will the spiritual experience become.

Spirituality then is the ability, through a focussed belief and a conscious choice, to encounter a reality that ordinarily exists beyond our natural senses, and its manifestation will arise from the contemplation of the individual consciousness which results in a meta-sensate involvement for each practitioner. He or she will begin to experience clarity of understanding and a vision of whatever lies beyond their senses – a spiritual vision which may have the possibility to facilitate an approach to an experience of ecstasy.

The joy and pleasure that such a vision may induce arises from a significant heightening of the scope of our natural senses, so that everything within becomes capable of interpretation involving a greater depth and range than otherwise would be the case.

The experience that ordinary consciousness may elicit is maintained as though it were at a great distance, or seen, or heard or felt only dimly. The practitioner will still experience ordinary states of consciousness, but it is non-ordinary states that grant a greater depth of spiritual understanding to existence.

The greater the degree of belief and the higher the level of consciousness that we can employ, then the closer we may come to an experience of mysticism.

7.05. Mysticism
Mysticism may be seen as the ultimate form of spirituality.

It has been said that it is not possible to be mystical without first being religious. This sets up something of a paradox, because as a statement it is both true and false at the same time. To throw some light on to this paradox we need to define the nature of mysticism.

Mysticism is typified as consciousness being able to achieve total unity with Cosmic reality. Unity, in these terms, may be thought of as being 'at one' with whatever is the object of the mystic's desire and belief, encountered through the means of an altered state of consciousness. His or her reality then becomes something that serves to give absolute focus, clarity and support to the understanding of existence, in that there is created a depth of meaning that goes significantly beyond the 'normal' boundaries of understanding into an area of transcendent conscious awareness.

We have seen, when looking at the relationship between consciousness and Gaia in Chapter Three, that some aspects of this relationship take on mystical characteristics. Because we are naturally a part of everything that partakes of the archaeus particle with its transmission of consciousness to all matter and life, we are naturally all part of the nature of Gaia through our consciousness.

In the Gaian sense, this enables all of us, if we so choose, to have a direct relationship with nature and, in so doing, to become naturally unified, at one with all of consciousness, wherever it exists and in whatever vehicle it is housed.

In other words, through consciousness, and particularly through altered and higher states, we are capable of becoming enmeshed with everything in the material realm. This example may be extended and expanded to a realisation that we may become at one with all of reality found not only in the material realm but also in the subtle, in a Cosmos-wide transcendent horizon.

The subtle element of the archaeus particle, by existing simultaneously in both the subtle and material realms, allows us all to develop the ability, consciously, to experience both, simultaneously, as a spiritual encounter.

But for the mystic, the subtle and material become truly inseparable; they come to form one reality, one experience. Furthermore, the mystic can sense that which lies beyond the material and subtle realms, which they may experience reflectively as the rapturous unknowability of The Source dimension.

Whilst within the mystical experience, free will, time, justice and the virtues all cease to be individual aspects of reality to become a single unity that is fully harmonised. Free will becomes fully integrated with the consciousness of the mystic as the means by which he or she may return to the ordinary state, whilst retaining a full measure of conscious awareness. Time is experienced in its singular total form so that it ceases to exist as a flow or passage, and the essence of the Cosmos that exists both within and outside the vessel of Time is glimpsed dimly as being infinite and eternal. Justice and the virtues become part of a fully ethical perception founded upon grounds of love that is reflected in the original message of all founders of religion.

The Source of All Things is unknowable in that, like infinity and eternity, our consciousness, even at the fourth level, is not yet equipped to encompass the nature of these perceptions. But the complete, harmonious unity that characterises the mystical experience produces a realisation of the existence of The Source of All Things, together with the ability to sense the magnitude and scope of the infinite and the eternal.

Albert Einstein was known to say in 'The Merging of Spirit and Science':

The most beautiful and profound emotion we can experience is the sensation of the mystical. It is the sower of all true science. He to whom this emotion is a stranger, who can no longer wonder and stand rapt in awe, is good as dead.

This quotation sums up the value of mysticism to the scope of all human endeavours.

But for the ordinary man, who has settled for life to be lived in de Ropp's third room of consciousness, such a unifying encounter with consciousness found everywhere in Gaia and with the Ideas of the subtle realm may not even be recognisable as a possibility. Consciousness is an element of the soul complex which is able to elevate its being to engage with the reality found within the fourth room. This then allows the mystic to 'see' all that he or she is capable of seeing or understanding, from the effect of a vision, that manifests as an experience of being transcendentally, totally unified and at one with the Cosmos.

The religious paradox now becomes apparent in that such a unity as this raises the consciousness of the mystic beyond that of any need for the foundational building blocks of religion, dogma and doctrine. The mystic has no need for doctrinal restriction to be imposed upon his or her consciousness, because their 'seeing' takes them beyond any such need, into an area of understanding that transcends ordinary conscious awareness. Furthermore, because their relationship and interaction with the nature of Time has changed, they 'see' and understand the fullness of the Cosmos in an instant and, for them, revelation is born.

Prior to the rise of the formal religions, religion existed as a series of cultural traditions where the shamans were seen to be the equivalent of modern day priests and pastors. We have said that shamanic history confirms the practice of undertaking a spiritual journey to a non-ordinary reality, for the benefit of others within their tribal community. On some occasions and for some shamans these journeys were mystical in their nature as they sought to align their consciousness with that of the natural Earth, and the realities that they recognised lay beyond.

Thus the mystical state is not something new but goes back

tens of thousands of years, to a time before religions were formalised. Religion, as we define it today, is not therefore a prerequisite for a mystical experience. But faith, seen in a strong belief that there exist levels of reality beyond those of our ordinary experience, has been, and still is, a prerequisite, common factor.

Formalised religion, especially in its early days, played a role in nurturing the world of the mystical experience and has throughout its history witnessed many mystical episodes that have arisen through meditation and contemplation which has elevated the consciousness of the mystic concerned into higher levels of consciousness, perhaps even at a subconscious level.

Until recent times, prior to the rise of science and technology, religion played a part in lending an air of respectability to the mystics concerned. Thus the mystical experience became more or less exclusively associated with religion, even though we can clearly see that exclusivity is not a characteristic of mysticism; in fact it is a restriction.

The nature and structure of the Cosmos; the way in which it came into reality; the archaeus particle that forms the cosmogony of the one dimension and the two realms; consciousness as the means of transmitting everything to the material realm in the interaction between the material and subtle realms; the constituency of the subtle realm that grants the means by which consciousness can co-create reality as an activity promoted through free will; the formatrix energy that gives the vitality to everything archaeuic; the ethical interpretation of justice and the virtues; the transference of the Ideas of science and technology and the genus of all species of existence – all of these have one thing in common:

All of these characteristics culminate in a reality of the Cosmos that arises from mystical belief.

We can see that spirituality and mysticism have played a major,

The Nature of Belief: Religion, Spirituality and Mysticism

if not crucial, role in the historic development of the human race and continues to do so, in many parts of the world, to this day.

Whilst science is beneficial to our understanding, through its uncovering of the physical laws and mathematical patterns that have governed our Universe from the origin of its birth, it is mysticism that has given to the human race the breadth of new horizons, the ability to stand rapt in awe at the wonder of it all and which has provided the means whereby consciousness has been able to envision that which science has subsequently illuminated.

There is little doubt that mysticism has been an essential element of our development, without which science and technology would have been devoid of direction and purpose.

As a race, we must be very careful not to discard any aspect of the human condition simply because one section of society tells us that it has little or no value.

329

Part III

Becoming

Chapter Eight

Becoming

And yet

All is not lost!

For some, the glimmer of an ascendant consciousness,
appears on the far horizon,
to enable those that are able to see through their reason and logic,
into an enhanced reality that could become theirs.

To reassert the development of their soul,
as the means by which they may co-create their future,
using the subtle means that I have placed at their disposal,
and their mysticism that some seek to deny.

There is still Time!
But not as they know it.

My pattern of nature and evolution is co-operative,
if they are able to respond and to work with it,
to repair the difficulties they have co-created and which have come
into being.

This will be hard to do,
but I have faith in their ability to accomplish the task in hand.

To bind their ascendant consciousness
to nature and of all things in the cosmos.

To raise their level of consciousness,

to one where they
become awake,
and are able to seek out the answer their own question,

Why is there is something rather than nothing?

8.00. Introduction

Before proceeding any further it is worth reminding ourselves that the term 'Cosmos', in this model, refers to the entire existence of all realities, including any realms and dimensions that are currently unavailable to our five natural senses. The term 'Universe' is reserved as a reference to all that exists only in the material realm.

Following chapters one to seven, we now have before us a model of the Cosmos that offers an arrangement whereby we may begin to grasp why and how things are as they are, with an answer to the ultimate question 'Why is there something, rather than nothing?' possibly beginning to emerge on the distant horizon of our understanding.

In this chapter we shall set the scene from what has gone before and then bring it all together in order that we may express some of this understanding in projections that express one possibility of what humanity could become.

8.01. Cosmos

The text recorded on The Emerald Tablet in many respects sums up all that has followed in this book. The two realms of reality, together with the Source dimension, that are represented on The Tablet are crucial to our understanding of the nature of the Cosmos and the way that it is structured.

There are many other constructs of the Cosmos that exhibit multiple levels of existence and so, in this respect, the one depicted on The Emerald Tablet may not be said to be exceptional. What may be unique about the arrangements deriving from The Tablet, however, is that its multiple tiers are devised and presented in such a way that the unified, completely integrated and cohesive single reality that is its ultimate objective may be seen as the intention from its inception through to its final outcome. The text represents a clear pathway that, if followed, may culminate in a Cosmos-wide, fully inclusive, unity of perfection.

Intent is an important aspect of the text on The Emerald Tablet. The Cosmos came into being through intent. We believe it did not 'just happen' and the laws that govern its existence, particularly of the material realm, did not come about just by chance. The nature of the Cosmos is structured in such an elegant, complex, fully integrated yet simple way that it must have come into existence through intent, by some means.

The Emerald Tablet expresses the desired outcome of such intent from its beginning to its end.

The nature of the Cosmos described on The Tablet is a form of gestalt where the intended conclusion of the reality portrayed becomes one indivisible unit of existence. We recall that such a gestaltic form is one that is not only fully cohesive, interactive and integrated at all points, but is a completely unified, indivisible model of self-regulation where the unity of the whole is immeasurably greater than the sum of its parts.

Transference between the two realms of reality, the subtle and the material realms, is a continuous process throughout the lives of all lifeforms and is one that does not require the death of any individual member of any lifeform to enable transition from one reality to another.

Consequently, the nature and structure of the Cosmos outlined in our model does not exist to exert any form of control over its adherents. Rather the opposite is true. The cosmic model found in our discussions applies to everyone, irrespective of belief or faith, and liberates our consciousness from institutional or external controlling impositions in order to perform ever ascendant and transcendent acts of co-creation, thought and deeds.

We have come to think that our model promotes a positive approach to our existence, whereas other cosmic constructs may seek to control our actions and our thinking, in part by using our inevitable death as a tool for coercing our cooperation and compliance. Such alternative cosmic constructs may be said to exhibit a negative form of approach to our existence and might also be thought of as inhibiting our natural development.

Our model of the soul complex and the nature of its continuation, following the death of its hosting vehicle or body, ensure that the way we choose to live our lives whilst present on planet Earth will naturally be reflected in the nature of our existence in whatever afterlife is available to us. This is not a form of punishment or reward for the nature of the life we have lived, but simply represents the natural outcome of our nature, expressed through our consciousness and the choices made by it.

The nature of our afterlife will thus be the one elicited by our choice and free will, both of which are interactive with all other aspects of life within the Cosmos, including the choice to lie dormant in the belief that there is no such thing as an afterlife. To be able to experience the absence of anything and everything seems to be a contradiction in terms, but it arises from a free will activated choice, to fulfil a belief, whilst alive, of there being nothing after death.

By means of the cosmic model arising from The Emerald Tablet we can truly state that we may be free of control or coercion in respect of the way we live our lives, providing of course that we choose so to be. Such freedom as this is the intended outcome of The Emerald Tablet arising from The One Source of All Things. The agency for the achievement of such freedom and for the ultimate accomplishment of the unity of the multiple realms of reality is that of consciousness.

We have seen that it is consciousness, at many levels and

strengths, existing across all cosmic realms and dimensions, which guides the Cosmos in its ascendant journey towards reunification and a possible state of perfection. It is the medium by which everything comes to exist and is that which enables choices to be made, together with the means of associating free will with those choices.

It is also that which provides the ability to determine Time from the subtle realm to become a passage or flow, which we experience as time in the material realm, which then allows everything to become subject to change. The way in which we conduct our lives through our ethical and moral values together with the nature of justice and the virtues upon which we base our governance and daily lives follows from change, arising from the passage of time and the implementation of free will.

Consciousness also enables us to uncover the laws which govern the science of the physical aspects of the Cosmos, which then encourages technological development in order to demonstrate a greater understanding of those universal laws or patterns. It also seeks to reach beyond the current limits from which science and technology currently suffer, in an attempt to understand the greater, perhaps mystical and esoteric meaning and purpose of our existence.

One method by which conscious perception is able to reach beyond its materialistic, restricting limits is that of being able to enter into altered or higher states of awareness. This is a spiritual search that is not yet capable of empirical proof, but which relies upon the development of the soul complex, described in our model. We can see that the nature of the soul, itself being a form of gestalt, not only mirrors the nature and structure of the Cosmos, but also reflects the nature of the self-regulatory system of Gaia.

Furthermore, the gestaltic forms of the Cosmos, Gaia and the soul complex are capable, with time and considerable effort, of becoming fully enmeshed to become one, single form of meta-gestalt, where the nature of the whole Cosmos in all of its material and spiritual aspects becomes one indivisible unity of existence.

All of these attributes enable humanity to make its choices and implement free will, and are facilitated and guided by our soul complex which enables our belief systems to arise. Our beliefs become a key factor in our existence because their nature takes on an importance that conditions our daily lives and provides the foundation of a fundamental reliance on continuing development. Such development is one that is able to drive the edicts of science, religion, politics and philosophy within us, but which also fosters an introspective and often mystical outlook on all that we believe in; all that we do or say.

If we are to continue to survive and flourish, it is imperative that the human ability to apply reason and logic is continued and developed in parallel with a reassertion of spiritual and mystical thinking, so that the credibility of its historic significance is achieved. All of these aspects of our reality must be brought together, into full focus.

In a nutshell it is necessary for introspection, in its widest possible sense, to become one of the principal means for the mode of transport, towards a future which is not yet with us, but where the direction of its evolutionary development has reached a fork in its progressive journey, where one branch is becoming increasingly defined by the human organism.

8.02. A Field for All Disciplines

Given the nature of the subtle realm of Ideas and the intended outcome of a single, unified, gestaltic cosmic reality, as exemplified on The Emerald Tablet, where consciousness is the means whereby this may be achieved, two aspects of our future development have become clear.

Initially, a new field of study needs to develop rapidly, one that is able to embrace absolutely all aspects and disciplines of human endeavour and practice, in an attempt to assimilate everything and to understand the part it plays within a fully unified Cosmos. Everything that is capable of entering into the consciousness of any individual should be assumed, at first encounter, to be credible, worthwhile and valuable. This is because the alternate realities experienced by some members of the human race, particularly those unencumbered by specialisation, by dogma or by self-interest, might be capable of the interpretation of incoming stimuli, into a form that enables enhanced levels of cosmic perception to arise.

There will always be someone who is capable of interpreting some of these perhaps trivial, perhaps abnormal, perhaps irrational pieces of information, which often defy reason, to form a picture that provides the missing pieces of the jigsaw puzzle that represents the full panoply of the Human, the Universal and the Cosmic condition.

Each piece of the cosmic jigsaw is as important as any other piece. Science, technology, politics, philosophy, economics, religion and mysticism all bear equal value when compiling the picture that represents human existence and, indeed, the existence of all life in the Cosmos.

The mystical aspect of consciousness is an essential piece of this jigsaw puzzle, for without it our development would almost certainly have taken a different course, and our understanding of the matrix of cosmic existence would then be incomplete. It is deeply regrettable that some amongst us dismiss spirituality and mysticism as having little relevance or value when considering or assessing the material reality of our existence. This may be because perceptions of truth result that appear to them to be restricted or limited. However, such restricted perceptions may arise due to the void left when dismissing mysticism from the complex of what is a complete, composite and compound gestaltic reality.

Albert Einstein (again), whilst professing no belief in a

personal God, was known to say:

> *The finest emotion of which we are capable is the mystic emotion.*
> *Herein lies the germ of all art and all true science.*

Yet today, mysticism is the most important single factor that is being deliberately 'engineered' out of the considerations concerning our existence and our future on our planet.

Whilst it is true that the development of science and technology, applied beneficially or otherwise, may be seen and felt to a very great extent amongst the world population, the aesthetic, spiritual and mystical resources that are available to nurture the human condition carry an equal importance that is essential to our well-being and our development.

Specialisation, in absolutely all disciplines, has become the means whereby independent fields of study develop and progress. Such specialisation is of course necessary and essential if we are to understand the full depth and extent of any particular aspect of our existence, and the efficiency that specialisation has produced is undeniable.

But specialisation is increasingly contributing to the compartmentalisation of knowledge and has, in some cases, prevented a fully inclusive, integrated approach to the understanding of the complete picture of the human and the cosmic condition.

Therefore, the need now arises for the introduction of a field of study which can form a fully comprehensive approach to the totality of the human condition, one that is able to adopt a non-specialised, limitless purview, one that enables a fully inclusive approach to all data that is available, from whatever source it arises.

What is meant by the formation of a non-specialist, fully inclusive approach is the establishment of a new, all-encompassing study, one that is above the existing fields of specialisation, in the sense that it would be applied as an umbrella field, able to coordinate all specialisations and none, indeed all thought and every perception, into a fully cohesive unity, without rejecting anything that falls outside the purview of any particular specialisation.

Such an umbrella field of study would reflect the nature of a Cosmos that is fully interconnected at all levels, is fully integrated as a unified whole, is self-regulating so far as its ability to propagate its continuation is concerned and is one that establishes the conditions for consciousness to develop in an ascending and transcending direction.

Bearing this in mind, the second aspect of our future development identifies a requirement for a large number of individuals to become genuine freethinkers. This involves throwing off the shackles of conditioning that has affected humanity for very many generations, and in some cases since the beginning of our journey to the present. Those that enter into such a field of study will be those with the ability for natural freethinking, coupled to the acknowledgement that altered and higher levels of consciousness exist and may be entered, to provide the means for the assimilation of all wisdom and all understanding of the Cosmos.

The natural freethinker will naturally develop his or her consciousness to be able to encompass an unbounded overview of the cosmic condition, to be able to look at any data or stimulus that impacts upon his or her consciousness, without being influenced by any of the limitations that arise from discrete specialisation from within any other field of human endeavour. He, she or they will become capable of assembling the stimuli that arise before them into an all-encompassing format that embraces absolutely all aspects of life.

If freethinking, in the model proposed, is not to become merely another form of specialisation it necessarily entails a great deal more than the ability simply to allow one's thoughts to flow over as wide a range of subject matter as possible. Here we are talking not only about the ability to keep our minds fully open to receive stimuli from any source whatsoever, and then to assimilate such stimuli into a fully inclusive, cohesive pattern; we are also proposing the acknowledgment and utilisation of an ability to penetrate through reason, to approach and use reason only as one facet, of truth and wisdom, without exclusive reliance on it, to solve all unexplained stimuli. This involves taking the consciousness of the freethinking individual on a journey, involving reason and logic, but which is also acknowledged as mystical in its nature, to areas of higher level awareness, to gain information that often appears, initially, to be beyond reason, beyond logic and even beyond mysticism.

The ability of our consciousness to choose and adopt the facility for complete freedom of thought, to expand the horizons of our consciousness to incorporate new vistas, to co-create the ability for freethinking in these terms, is not an easy choice. Once so chosen, many of the benefits of society fall away, pressure arises from our contemporaries and the implementation of free will, in putting into effect the result of choice, often becomes more difficult.

However, the nature of our Cosmos enables and even encourages us all to attempt freethinking. The freedom to think and act as any balanced individual sees fit raises the human condition to a state where development and adaptation is not only possible, but is enhanced. Such enhancement naturally recognises and accepts the freely chosen limitations that arise from the cultural, social and communal requirement to allow all others the same freedom to think and act as they see fit.

These freethinking individuals who have commenced their journey of development appear to civilisation as a whole as leaders, shapers and makers of society, and are often those who are able to set examples as exemplary models for the significant majority to follow. This being the case, we can see that the number of individuals who are currently capable of sustaining a genuine freethinking approach, of the nature described here, is very small indeed, yet the effect they have on us all is disproportionally great.

In the normal course of evolutionary development, the trend has been one where the conditions that enable higher levels of consciousness are beginning to occur more frequently within the world population. This process will eventually result in a greater range of freethinking individuals who are able to input increased levels of cohesion and coordination into society.

The natural process of evolutionary hybridisation, the bringing together of varying characteristics, is one that has been ongoing for very many generations, but which is now beginning to show signs of gaining increased momentum. This is perhaps encouraged by the recent advent of fast worldwide communication systems, and accessible, speedy travel arrangements to any part of the planet. But perhaps it also arises as a consequence of environmental degradation, which results in the process of evolution continuing to adapt existing species to rapid change.

It would appear from these circumstances that the human race has reached a point in its development where those freethinkers who are capable of leading and shaping our progress, from whatever field of activity they arise, are becoming increasingly separated from those who are content to follow. If a beneficial trait arises from the use of free will, employed to support the choices we freely make, which then results in augmented levels of consciousness, with a greater ability for freethinking, then the process of evolution will increasingly clarify and may even accelerate this separation.

So, the unifying aspect of the two realms of reality would be accelerated by the formation of a new field of study, one that takes into account all aspects of the existence of life on Earth or the Cosmos, from whatever source origin. Such a study will show the best results if it is populated by the freethinking community described, who would work to set aside generations of conditioning and would be prepared to take into account everything that impinges on their consciousness, including, but not restricted to, all specialisations.

Those who embrace such a new field of study will need to become capable of thinking in different ways, will assume different approaches and will not be afraid of taking reason and logic into new areas that presently appear to be irrational.

8.03. Beyond Reason?

In Chapter Two we introduced the notion that each particle which exists in the material realm might be said to occupy a place which is at the centre of the Universe whilst, at the same time, occupying all other places where the Universe might exist. We said that this principle has mystical overtones and forms the basis where all locations are said to be at the centre of existence, whilst each may also be said to simultaneously enclose all others. The Universe and our consciousness, indeed the entire Cosmos may thus be said to have no boundaries or edge to it.

Then in Chapter Three we confirmed the need to 'position' standard reason and logic, so as to be able to approach notions of the Cosmos from a different direction. This would allow us not only the ability to understand the concept described in the last paragraph, but also to comprehend that the soul complex is capable, through the mundus imaginalis, of transmuting the perception of interior material spaces into interior immaterial spaces. A perception that is capable of developing our consciousness towards an evolutionary, adaptive future.

In Chapter Four we were able to progress these concepts, to understand the important fact that absolutely everything in the present is interconnected with everything else in the present (and the past). The Gaia self-regulatory system is an example of one facet of this idea.

We further expanded these concepts, in Chapter Five, with the notion that every facet of every Idea, in the subtle realm, may be transmuted to become within each of us whilst, at the same time, each and every Idea maintains its separate, discrete character. The mundus imaginalis is that which is able to interpret the Ideas of the subtle realm into a form that we can manage and understand. Its nature is one that not only occupies spaces that have no spatial location, but occupies a space that contains all other spaces, including its own.

We begin to see the importance of the emergent need to 'see' beyond reason, to investigate a series of concepts that introduce us to a means of thinking that not only employs reason, but takes it beyond its normal confines, into expanded horizons of consciousness and reality. The importance of attempting an understanding of such seemingly irrational concepts as these becomes ever increasingly apparent as the future for all life on planet Earth becomes more and more unsustainable.

Reason and logic serve the human race exceedingly well in its quest for knowledge and understanding of our Universe but, and once again paradoxically, it will contribute significantly to the demise of our race if we continue to rely on reason alone as the means by which we may sustain the viability of the race and make progress towards the state of perfection that is our destiny. Reason and logic form a roadway that leads towards a distant cul-de-sac, an eventual dead end to the human condition.

If the failure to acknowledge and accommodate the influence of intuition, creativity and mysticism continues; if we are unable to recognise and accept that the reality of others, even where apparently beyond reason, is real and valuable and does much to underwrite the development of reason itself, then the future of humanity will become even more limited and restricted than it currently is.

It is only by seeing the complete nature of our existence, through a means that includes every aspect of human experience, whether 'provable' or not, that we will be able to visualise and put into effect the steps needed to make the continuation of Homo sapiens, and our descendants, more secure.

Those who achieve a natural freethinking status; who become able to coordinate the efforts of the specialists without disregarding the mystical or any other elements of our nature; those who are able to recognise the immaterial nature of the Cosmos, alongside its material aspects; those who are more able to dwell in de Ropp's fourth level room of consciousness for longer, more productive periods; those who are consequently able to expand their consciousness to envision the complete nature and structure of the Cosmos described in our model; those who are able to position reason and logic so as to be able to approach reality from a different direction, where necessary; these are the groups of individuals who will be able to assemble the jigsaw pieces that go to represent the Cosmos in its entirety.

They will then be in a position to identify solutions to the problems facing the human race. Whether the problems are warring factions, famine and poverty, health issues, unsustainable population growth, climate change or any other factor pointing to our demise. A beginning may then be made to instigate the possibility of a more secure future.

So the need to develop freethinking modes of thought that take reason to new horizons, so as to be able to envisage the reality that exists beyond the encounter of our natural senses, becomes an imperative, one that will form the background to our consideration of other aspects of our survival as a race.

8.04. The Act of Becoming

What we are to become has been termed 'an act' because increasingly the outcome of our evolutionary journey is being determined by the action of humanity itself. Such action results from human nature, from our evolutionary need to survive and to flourish; yet conversely, is that which is likely to presage our demise, if we are unable to come to terms with our aggressive, competitive nature, to become more communally cooperative.

We are all subject to the act of becoming, but there is a general reluctance to act in the best interests of humanity, unless self-interest is coincidentally involved. This is a characteristic of the adoption of the easiest choice that is available to us and the all too often adoption of the passive nature of the application of free will, all demonstrated by an indolent and often apathetic acceptance, by the majority of us, of an existence described as living within de Ropp's third room of consciousness. We may be 'sleep-walking' towards the extinction of our race.

8.05. Evolution as an Act of Becoming

The standard model of the evolutionary process, if allowed to proceed unhindered, is likely to eventually provide the race with increased numbers of individuals who are natural freethinkers, with the natural ability to dwell in higher levels of consciousness.

However, bearing in mind the natural, slow rate of change exhibited through the normal evolutionary process, historically driven by natural selection, there is unlikely to be sufficient time available to the human race to allow this course of evolutionary development to fulfil its remit.

A natural process of the hybridising of all life on Earth, especially of the human race, has been going on since life and eventually Homo sapiens were formed, the latter emerging to become the dominant species on our planet. Given sufficient time, this process would continue and should result in a race of beings capable of identifying the problems facing the continuation of life on Earth, and of developing and implementing suitable solutions that secure our futures. It has even been suggested by some, from a wide range of disciplines, who retain a mystical element of their being, that the evolutionary process itself could 'intervene' to provide a solution.

This may be because evolution in the past has been the means whereby the form of new species has arisen suitably adapted to the environmental conditions prevailing at the time, or of the adaptation of existing racial characteristics to accommodate environmental change.

But it has also seen the extinction of a large proportion of the lifeforms present at the time of change.

The uncontrolled massive and unsustainable growth in world population figures, that is evident today, is beginning to place very great strain on the capacity of the environment to sustain our species on Earth. Consequently, the possibility of racial extinction, as a direct result, raises itself to a status involving a higher probability factor in our future.

It was Thomas Robert Malthus who, in 1798, wrote *An Essay on the Principle of Population*, wherein he proposed a systematic theory of population. Malthus proposed the principle that the human population grows exponentially in that it can double with each cycle, whilst food production only grows at an arithmetic rate following the repeated addition of a uniform increment in each uniform interval of time.

On the basis of a hypothetical world population of one billion in the early nineteenth century allied to an adequate means of subsistence at that time, Malthus suggested that there was a potential for a population increase to 256 billion within 200 years but that the means of subsistence were only capable of being increased enough for 9 billion to be fed at the level similar to that prevailing at the beginning of the period. This scenario of arithmetic food growth with simultaneous, exponential human population growth predicted a future when humans would cease to have sufficient resources upon which to survive.

Such hypothetical numbers have not materialised, for many diverse reasons; the total world population in the 200 years since the early nineteenth century has reached something in excess of 7 billion people, yet the possibility of unsustainable population numbers is highlighted by even this level of growth.

In addition, the effect of such large growth in the numbers of the human population, upon the environment, were not at that time foreseeable because the accelerating use of the planetary resources and the consequent expanding emission of waste products arising therefrom were not conceivable.

Malthus proposed some means of restricting population growth; but even growth at an arithmetical level, rather than exponential, would eventually see the race decline through lack of adequate resources. In these circumstances alternative solutions are required if a Malthusian catastrophe affecting the capability of the human race to survive is to be avoided.

The evolutionary likelihood of the human race accomplishing a significant increase, perhaps a majority, of adepts who attain fourth level consciousness may result in a natural reduction, over periods of time, initially in the rate of population growth, and subsequently in a reduction in population numbers. This is because such adepts will inevitably 'see' the sustainable population growth problem and the solution simultaneously, and will automatically put into action the solution. This follows the trend where, generally, the higher the levels of education in a society, the lower the birth rate becomes until it stabilizes at a sustainable level.

The standard evolutionary process is, however, likely to be too slow to accommodate a rapid increase in levels of consciousness required and so the need to look toward a selective programme of hybridisation as an alternative solution arises.

Lifeform hybridisation is a process of amalgamation where the best aspects of a species are naturally selected for reproduction, resulting in improvement, or beneficial change. The natural, evolutionary hybridisation of humans has seen many improvements in human performance characteristics, and suggests that the natural selection process is serviced through a genetic foundation, especially in our levels of consciousness.

However, as we have proposed, evolution is becoming affected by developments that arise from within the human organism, especially where science and technology are now developing the techniques which would enable individuals to 'manufacture' genetically modified lifeforms, particularly human embryos.

However historically unpalatable this notion may be, we must accept that this process is a development of the eugenic culture that has pervaded society especially since the latter part of the nineteenth century.

Evidence of selective breeding for particular characteristics goes way back through most of human civilisation, but it was Sir Francis Galton, a cousin of Charles Darwin, who in the 1890s pioneered the use of pedigrees, the study of twins, and statistical correlations as means whereby the 'breed of men' might be improved. The twentieth century saw eugenics develop into a worldwide movement supported by enthusiasts from all aspects of human life.

Regrettably, the discriminatory and often prejudicial aspects of human nature, exhibited through elitism, racism and the desire to emphasise class or cultural distinctions, saw the blatant misuse of eugenic principles and techniques that culminated, unashamedly, in the abomination of the Holocaust and subsequent attempts at ethnic cleansing, some of which are still prevalent and occur today.

In the idealistic sense, however, such a modified evolutionary process represents one of the means whereby the future of the human race may become more secure. This statement presupposes that the criterion for the selection of any genetic manipulation must focus on the characteristics that are most likely to produce individuals who are natural freethinkers, as previously described, and who are more able to enter into higher levels of consciousness.

The human genome project has provided evidence of a revival of eugenics in the form of controversial reproductive technologies that permit selection for genetic characteristics, albeit practised through interdisciplinary panels of experts who have sought to establish internationally accepted, ethical guidelines for use in genetic research.

This is a circumstance that holds both good and evil within the parameters of its remit.

On the one hand the benefit of eliminating hereditary disease from humanity is a laudable goal that could not be denied as an advantage to the health of the human race. Similarly, a benefit would accrue if there were a genetically engineered increase in the numbers of those individuals capable of natural freethinking, with abilities to spend extensive periods in fourth level consciousness.

We are not talking here about mere intelligence; important though this is, it is not a prerequisite for the ability to enter into altered or higher states of consciousness. The criterion amongst individuals who are selected to donate the relevant genes is that they come from amongst the entire human population who, essentially, are able to 'see' beyond the reality that immediately confronts them.

Whilst it is true that higher levels of intelligence are likely to arise from any such genetically modified, hybridisation process, it is the ability to understand the Cosmos in which we dwell as having no boundaries; in recognising that we exist at the centre of all spaces within the Universe whilst, at the same time, enclosing everything and all spaces within our perception, that is a much more important criterion. Those freethinking individuals, from every diverse form of human life, who are able to envision reason with a new and different perspective, are the ones most likely to provide the source to satisfy the genetic selection criterion.

But beware! Great care must be taken to ensure that representatives from as wide a gene pool as possible, from every social, scientific, religious, political, philosophical, cultural and ethnic background that exists, go to form the resource from which all gene donors originate. In addition the same criterion must apply to those who go to comprise the pool of experts for whom the responsibility for ethical guidance and monitoring relies.

History has shown, however, that the human race appears to be incapable of restricting and maintaining its objective, laudable intent towards a desire to improve the breed of humanity and extinguish hereditary disease. This is due to misplaced self-interest, ethnic, cultural or national prejudice or bias, which result in unethical and unwanted practices that pervert the diversity and extent of human characteristics towards a narrowing set of criteria, rather that a widening, all-encompassing one.

The rhetorical question arises as to whether or not humanity is able to define the requirements for the outcome of genetic manipulation, whilst resisting the temptation to satisfy a desire for religious, cultural or elitist priorities, or a personal or corporate desire for wealth acquisition or power, all of which are not in the best interest of all of humanity.

Additionally, whilst the depth and extent of our knowledge in the field of genetics has made immense strides in the last few decades, the questions as to whether we are in a position to understand and accommodate the full extent of any changes that we artificially introduce into the human genome are legion.

This is because the human genome is made up of encoded DNA sequences within 23 chromosome pairs found in cell nuclei and small mitochondrial molecules. The somatic genome consists of something like 3 billion base pairs of DNA genes. Then the genome is divided into coding and non-coding DNA sequences where coding DNA, which amounts to about 2% of the genome, is capable of transcription into proteins; whilst the approximate 98% majority of non-coding DNA is made up of sequences that are not used to code proteins. There is a vigorous debate underway as to the role and purpose of non-coding DNA, which appear to have important biological functions that, as yet, are not fully understood.

Clearly the genetic research and any subsequent modifications may have significant benefits to the health and well-being of humanity. But, until the genetics of the human genome is fully understood in all its incredible, interrelated detail, the danger will continue to exist that unknown and unthought-of consequences and side effects may arise as a result of human manipulation of its genetic sequencing.

Therefore, the dangers and pitfalls of modifying the standard evolutionary model, in any manner, however small, cannot be understated. Historically the social and cultural implications have been seen to be catastrophic.

Be that as it may, it must be acknowledged that the secret to the success for the survival of the human race might lie, at least to some extent, within our ability to accelerate the natural process of evolutionary hybridisation. The ability of our DNA to continue to transmit the best of human characteristics through reproduction must be secured, but it remains to be seen whether or not suitable safeguards can be established that would guarantee to prevent the historic, discredited and catastrophic effects involved in the eugenic approach towards racial survival.

We must accept that, at present, the current of public opinion is well and truly against developing any form of genetic manipulation at all, especially of the human genome. But as our position on Earth becomes increasingly unsustainable and insecure, the need to undertake drastic remedial action, perhaps involving significant genetic modification, will also grow, even to the point where current public opinion becomes overwhelmed.

Such undertakings are already evidenced in some areas of research where the application of the modification of the genetic constituency of humans has resulted in the existence of people who have the DNA of three individuals within their being. The purpose of such modification has been, to date, to eliminate mitochondrial disease that has lead to debilitating life conditions and subsequent early death. Consequently such a development is to be welcomed and applauded.

This form of genetic modification has taken place in the germline sequencing of the genome and, consequently, its effects will be transmissible to succeeding generations that ensue from the individuals concerned.

We can see from this evidence alone that the practice of eugenic manipulation of humanity is not only proceeding, but may be said to be accelerating, despite its historically generated pariah status. The question arises: 'Are we in a position to deny that, in some future development of genetic modification, it may be possible for the DNA from four, or five, or however many individual sources to be combined to form one 'new individual'?'

Does the spectre of 'assembling' the characteristics of future individual humans, from multiple, purposely selected sources, become a closer reality?

Many may consider that the eugenic modification of the human genome is of such paramount importance to the continuation of the human race that the safeguards and monitoring of the techniques involved become a secondary consideration in the scheme of things.

Thus it is possible to envisage further genetic modifications being introduced that will affect the evolution of the human race, for better or worse.

Such action is confirmation of the continuing branching of evolution, within humanity, to one of divergent pathways of adaptation.

So, an expanded field of eugenics is with us whether we like it or not.

It is possible that development and activity in this field of science may contribute toward providing the capacity, within the human race, for it to sustain its existence and to continue to flourish on Earth. But eugenics may also hasten the demise of the human race simply because we cannot envisage all of the consequences of genetic modification and simply appear to be incapable of controlling our nature, which is to seek reproduction of our own particular kind and to survive at any cost, even at the expense of others.

Notwithstanding the effect that a eugenic approach to solving the sustainability problem may have, there is a growing general consensus amongst scientists, economists and politicians that it is climate change which represents the greatest threat to the health and well-being of the human population. This is the view recently expressed by the Secretary General of the United Nations, and there is no doubt that this is the most significant symptom that is currently apparent, and which carries the most immediate threat to the long-term viability of the survival for the human race.

But concentration on this symptom ignores 'the elephant in the room' because it sidelines the real cause of climate change, which is the unrestrained, exponential growth in human population numbers. Failure to address this issue will eventually negate all our attempts to solve our problems, including that of the important symptom of climate change that may soon come to threaten our continued racial existence.

It is beyond doubt that the current growth of human population numbers is completely unsustainable in the long term and that, no matter what steps are taken to remedy the change in the climate, or what resources are devoted to the growth in food production, unsustainable population numbers will defeat our best endeavours. We are told that in the foreseeable near future we will need to produce additional food resources equivalent to the entire output of another Earth-like planet, which begs the questions: 'Where is such an additional planet to be found and accessed' and 'Is technology capable of providing such a significant increase in food resources, repeatedly?'

Even if technology is successful so far as the near future is concerned, eventually the unrestrained growth in the population will become too large for the planetary space and resources that are available.

In these circumstances it is difficult to understand why some nations continue to favour increased numbers of children being born, to the extent that they subsidise financially ever-greater child population numbers. Some religions or cultures refuse to see beyond the immediate reality by irresponsibly encouraging increased numbers of children to be conceived through the denial of simple contraceptive measures.

These actions serve only to contribute towards hastening the arrival of the point where the depletion of the resources of Earth results in unsustainable population numbers, with the possibility of a consequent large-scale extinction.

Once this point has been reached then even desperate measures may be insufficient to remedy the impending extinction of the human race. Many consider that the point where it would have been possible to redress this situation has already passed, and that it is already too late to intervene through any means we can envisage to affect the human population numbers such that they do not exceed a planetary sustainable maximum number.

Climate change, however, is reflected as a change in the environment and, as we have previously discussed, we can see that the evolutionary process has been fuelled by the nature of the environment prevailing at any particular time. It may even be conceivable that the rapid change in the environment may cause a rapid evolutionary adaptation to suit the new environmental conditions.

However, any such natural adaptation is likely to take many generations to accomplish, and may well result in the human race numbers declining significantly, possibly to an unsustainable number, perhaps to the benefit of the next adapted lifeform to gain conscious dominion on Earth. Alternatively, if significantly lower numbers of human beings were to inhabit planet Earth, a process of readjustment to the climate would commence and might be seen as beneficial to the outlook for human sustainability.

But the thought also occurs that the recent advent of 'new' viruses, such as Ebola, together with the possibility of the mutation of existing pathogens may represent the self-regulatory system that is Gaia exerting a regulating influence to preserve conditions within the environment that are conducive to life of one sort or another – not necessarily human.

Solutions to the human population growth, such as war, famine, pestilence etc., do not solve any of our problems. Warring factions and the unprecedented growth in consumerism will inevitably result in the 'natural' regulation of the environment, through means that are outside of human control.

A consequential severe, downward adjustment to unsustainable human population numbers will then become an inevitable reality.

Human attempts to affect the evolutionary progress of life on Earth may not succeed when confronted by the force that evolution represents, especially if the process of Gaia exerts self-regulatory, evolutionary characteristics.

We are able to see that, if we rely on the natural course of evolution as the means for the propagation of the human race, that is to say, if we take no positive action to safeguard our continuation, the probability is that humanity will become extinct in the foreseeable future.

We are focussing on the ability of the human race to survive and flourish because it is fair to say that if we do not find some way to accelerate human hybridisation, with the specific aim of establishing a majority of the population with the ability to sustain fourth level consciousness, the fear is that there will be insufficient time available to the race to develop the ability to solve its survival difficulties through natural means.

So far as the act of becoming is concerned, we are able to see that some means of the speeding up of the transfer of genetically advantageous human characteristics could prove to be of immense benefit to the entire future population. Concentration on evolving fourth room/level consciousness is the key to success in this respect and, far from having pariah status, eugenics, in the form of genetic modification, together with some globally agreed and controlled measure of selection and monitoring, which takes into account a clear recognition of ethical, social and cultural consequences, may yet prove to be the principle means whereby such evolution could increasingly contribute towards becoming a reality.

8.06. Choice and Free Will as Acts of Becoming

We have seen that the implementation of free will upon the choices which we decide is one of a positive, negative or passive nature. The options of choice that confront us are sometimes difficult to resolve and, following resolution, the degree of free will brought to bear often renders our choices as ineffective. We often simply do not have sufficient positive free will to put into action the outcome of our desired choice.

There will be many who do not choose to see any point in considering any form of reality that cannot be subjected to scientific methodology and empirical standards of proof. Such choice denies the mystical nature of humanity, and is often supported by the application of negative free will.

When it comes to the consideration of realities that exist beyond the reach of our natural senses, the choice to seek to establish any understanding of such a condition involves a state of mind that transposes reason and logic into wider perceptions, but which also requires the application of positive free will.

The tyranny of the majority will be an important hurdle to overcome in this respect as it seeks to impose restrictions and limitations upon individuals who comprise any minority. This is the antithesis of freethinking.

Actually, the tyranny of the majority sets up something of a paradox when considering the question of solving the problem caused by the unrestrained growth in human population numbers. Consideration of this aspect of Western society will show that it is public opinion, founded in democracy, that currently allows such unrestrained population growth to continue. Our political systems are such that, if restrictions were proposed that sought to enforce a limit to the population growth, the majority would exercise the power of its tyranny to remove the proposal from enforcement.

Democratic principles are such that any unacceptable restriction to the growth of the family numbers is unlikely to be proposed by any politicians for fear of their defeat at the ballot box.

The paradox becomes clear. The democratic majority, in any of its current forms, will impose its tyranny in such a way that negates any serious intent to regulate population numbers, even though such increases may presage the demise of the human race in the foreseeable future.

It could be argued that it is democracy which will eventually cause humanity to fail in any attempt to solve its population problems. Yet other political systems have also failed to demonstrate any satisfactory means of accomplishing a long-term solution to this problem. There results a dichotomy that may only be resolved by a mass conversion of public opinion, implementing positive free will principles for the benefit of the future of humanity.

Setting aside any restrictions or impositions that one person or group of persons may inflict upon another person or group, for those who regard themselves as having the freedom to choose their use of free will is demonstrated as an automatic response, once their choice has been consciously processed. This may be why the passive option of free will is the one that, all too often, is implemented, and may be the reason why so many are prepared to spend their time inhabiting the state of consciousness depicted in de Ropp's room three.

Free will thus takes on an importance for the development of the human race well beyond the parameters usually granted to its implementation. Once the choices that we make arise from freethinking, often outside the box containing the principles of social and communal conduct or conformity, then the implementation of positive free will, to put those choices into action, also takes on a crucially more important role for humanity.

The tendency of freethinkers is to facilitate the ambition of others that aspire to the same condition. Consequently, the ability for freethinking transcends the restrictions imposed by socio-communal requirements, whilst, paradoxically, at the same time strengthening their precepts.

It remains to be seen whether, or not, the current freethinking minority of the human race has the mass to develop the proposed new field of study that coordinates the output of the specialists with everything else, and not only is prepared to choose a sustainable future, but is strong enough to employ the extent of positive free will available to it and which is essential to the task.

Such a choice and use of free will is difficult, not only because it requires a means that takes the individual concerned into new directions of thinking, but also because its implementation may bring about the benefits of such a choice, at the expense of the current majority of the population. Not least of all would be the need to relegate the benefits that currently accrue to financial, political and religious institutions to a lower priority in the communal structure of society.

But if the conscious choice is made and positively implemented, that has, as its first, perhaps its only, priority, the conditions that can sustain the existence and the development of the human race, then a future for humanity involving higher levels of consciousness becomes more assured and the divergent directions and separation of human awareness, seen in evolutionary branching, will become more pronounced.

Free will is thus paramount in making the produce of freethinking effective, and is the pivotal characteristic that will drive the success or failure of our future survival.

Time will tell – but only if we have enough time.

8.07. Time and Change as Acts of Becoming

Time in the subtle realm exists in an instantaneous 'vessel', where it does not pass or flow, but is such that it contains every characteristic of everything that could come to pass, whilst still being devoid of experience or memory. Time in the subtle realm is incapable of allowing change to occur.

Time in the material realm does pass or flow because of the interaction of consciousness with the Idea of Time contained within the subtle realm, whereupon change comes into being, allowing evolution, experience and memory to arise.

This concept is one that is very difficult to understand because it also depends upon a line of thinking that relies on an approach to reason from a different direction. Once again our purview is challenged, asking us to understand that the nature of Time in the subtle realm and time in the material realm is akin to the nature of spaces and locations previously described within the Cosmos.

Time in the subtle realm is 'enclosed' as a monolithic,

stationary, unchanging unit or vessel that is available to consciousness, wherever it is located within our Universe. Yet its interaction, with that same consciousness, transforms its character to one of a passage, so that it becomes a central focus in establishing unique aspects of change, centred anywhere in the Universe where consciousness exists.

Time then, in its changing state, might be considered as existing everywhere in the Universe, where its every location may be regarded as the centre of its existence; whilst at the same time, it may be seen as a single, unchanging form, which encloses all of those multitudinous, temporal aspects within it.

If we can come to terms with this seemingly paradoxical proposal then we may legitimately ask the question: 'Does the human race have sufficient time available to it to bring about the changes necessary for a sustainable future to become assured?'

Given our concept of time in the material realm as one of being transformed, by consciousness, into a flow or passage from the subtle monolithic Idea of Time, the answer to this question lies within ourselves.

In the scenario conceived in our model, it should be possible for us to alter the rate at which time passes in the material realm. A bold statement that needs some explanation!

If all of subtle Time is transposed into a stream that passes through us, or along which we pass, and if humanity possesses currently the highest levels of consciousness on our planet, then it should be possible for us to influence or co-create sufficient time, by adjusting its rate of its passage, as it is perceived and experienced in our location, on our planet. This would then allow consciousness sufficient time for the possibility of solutions to develop.

All of this whilst not affecting in any way the nature of Time found in the subtle realm.

To do this needs an act of conscious choice and positive free will, aided by purposeful and meditative use of our mundus imaginalis, through which we can enter into an altered, higher state of consciousness. It is only by the deliberate use of enhanced levels of awareness that we will be able even to define the true nature of the problems that face all lifeforms on our planet, let alone put the means of survival into operation.

The notion that we, as individuals, are capable of controlling time, or at least the rate at which time passes, is one that rarely enters into our consciousness. Why should it? The passage of time appears to us as a constant that we take for granted. After all, the length of a year or a day is prescribed by the length of time it takes for the Earth to orbit around the Sun, or how long it takes for the Earth to complete one revolution on its axis. These periods are irrespective of how we have divided each into 'manageable' units of measurement – months, weeks, hours, minutes and seconds.

Many of us are aware that, without devices that measure and advise us of the rate at which time passes, our consciousness quickly becomes disassociated with time as a constant in our daily lives. If the Earth took a different period to orbit the Sun, as is the case with the other planets of our solar system, or if the Earth's orbit was even marginally different from its current path, then the length of our 'year' would be different also. If our planet revolved on its axis at a slower or faster speed, then our day would also be different in length.

Once we have cleared our mind of any conception that our experience of time is secure, invariable and constant, then we can commence to take control of our perception and experience of time and subsequently can envisage taking control of its rate of flow.

The difficulty here is threefold. Firstly there is a problem in assembling sufficient numbers of adepts to give an altered, higher state of consciousness, the 'immaterial mass' by which its objective would become possible and efficient. Secondly, the evolutionary process required is, to some extent, a departure from the principles of natural selection, to one of adaptive change inaugurated from within the human organism. Thirdly, any adjustment of the rate at which time passes here on Earth may also affect the rate at which change may take place.

Some individuals, especially when in a condition of seclusion, are already able to consciously affect the rate at which they perceive time to be passing. When in a meditative, freethinking, altered state of awareness, time ceases to be a relevant factor in the recognition of reality. This is because those individuals entering into such a state are closer to, or may even come to inhabit, the subtle realm, where time exists in a different manner to that in the material realm.

Furthermore, when inhabiting the fourth room of consciousness time ceases to be a factor in any consideration concerning human development and adaptation. This is because fourth level experience sees all potentials that arise from a freethinking source in such a way that the passage of time becomes unimportant. Each chain of thought so experienced is perceived to be instantaneous, apparently as a revelation.

The notable exception to this is that time is the essential agent which allows change to occur. Without time passing change would be impossible, and the rate at which time is caused to pass may affect the rate at which change takes place.

Should the rate at which time is perceived to pass be slowed down, then logically we might think that the rate of change might also become slower and vice versa. The need to approach time through an alternative form of logic becomes apparent.

What is actually required is that the rate of time passing should be slowed down to allow for more to be accomplished within the extent of the time available to us to find solutions to our problems. Simultaneously, we need to maintain or even accelerate the rate of change so as to accommodate more of the consequences of our actions.

So, one ability of which the human race may become capable, which needs to evolve through higher levels of consciousness, is that of developing the facility to take control of the rate of the passage of time and hence the rate of change.

Whilst the ability to enter into altered states of consciousness is one that is available to us all, the numbers of individuals that recognise this are not currently very great. Until the numbers of freethinking individuals who perceive the nature of such altered, higher states become the majority of the population who are prepared to enter within, to practise time translation, the likelihood of the alteration of the rate of flow of time, in the material realm, being achieved is as close to zero as makes no difference.

This being the case, we need to put into practice genetically modified measures that are intended to speed up the numbers of individuals appearing within the population who are capable of attaining fourth level consciousness.

But, in addition, we must consider an alternative approach to the problem. If we cannot generate a sufficient majority of adepts, quickly enough, to alter the rate at which time passes, then we must increase the efficiency and output in our interaction with the subtle realm, once again through greater access to fourth level consciousness.

We need to co-create a condition where access to the fourth level becomes a more normal option, rather than the exception. Greater numbers of the human population, although remaining in a minority, need to approach the act of attaining altered states of consciousness with the ability to cross the threshold into fourth level consciousness as a priority condition that could result in our racial ability to gain more information generally, and to facilitate a greater understanding of the reality that lies beyond the ability of our natural senses to encounter. By this means we would be able to achieve a great deal more within any given time span, as it currently passes, until the number of fourth level adepts becomes a majority.

The thrust of conscious choice and free will must become freely positive and directed towards the implementation of the means for the continuation of an environment suitable to sustain the human population.

In this way we should be able to increase the efficiency of the output generated from fourth level and altered states of awareness; in other words, we should be able to make much better use of our current, perceived passage of time.

If we, as a race, are not yet willing or able to alter the rate at which time passes, then, as an interim measure, we must attempt to develop our levels of consciousness to the point where we are able to achieve a greater output within the current passage of time. This is a simple enough statement, but one that requires great effort, choice and free will for its achievement.

Co-creation is the tool that consciousness may use to bring about the conditions necessary for our continued survival. Evolution including a prescriptive form of modern eugenics may be one means whereby such co-creation may become a reality.

8.08. The Act of Becoming Gaian and the Importance of Death

The 'becoming at one' with the Cosmos is a natural ambition of human endeavour because, besides being an inherent essential mystical component of humanity, it demonstrates our intrinsic roots of curiosity, enterprise and ambition whilst also being in full rapport with the principles of Gaian theory.

If humanity is to survive, the environmental conditions that have been capable of sustaining our development to date will need to be recognised and reasserted, requiring all of us, as individuals and in society with each other, to become the executors of our own survival.

We should make no mistake in this matter, the planet itself is not in any danger – it is the human race, and all other current life species, that are at risk of extinction. If we as the progenitors of environmental change fail to fulfil our current Gaian obligations, if we fail to face the responsibility that is an intrinsic part of dominion, then the self-fulfilling element of self-regulation will take over, to ameliorate any threat to a life-bearing global environment. This will be for the benefit of the next lifeform(s) to inhabit the planet, particularly the next species to achieve dominion.

The element of Gaia that regulates the ability of the planetary resources, to enable survival, is that of death.

We have seen that natural death far from being a punishment, or a consequence of sin, is the regulatory means whereby new life, new development and change are facilitated. We recognise that this is what makes way for reproduction, is that which allows evolutionary development to occur and is an inevitable outcome of life. It is death which grants to successive generations the opportunity and the space to come into being, and to develop and accommodate change.

If we can succeed in changing our outlook on death then it will lose its sting and we will have no need to rage at the dying of the light.

Science and technology have been responsible for greatly improving the lifestyle and standard of living of some of the human population by establishing vast improvements in hygiene and sanitation conditions, and enabling the increase in the output from planetary resources and the amount of food available to feed us all. The study and implementation of nutrition growing technologies, including plant hybridisation, together with health and hygiene issues, has served to increase dramatically the average length of the lifespan of those fortunate enough to be in a position to take advantage of scientific progress.

But, although our average lifespan has significantly increased and continues to increase, the maximum length of the human lifespan has not increased at all, thus ensuring, through death, that the capacity for evolutionary development is safeguarded.

There is a finite limit to the success of science and technology, however; and, once that limit has been breached, then Gaian principles of self-regulation will come to affect the population numbers. Effectively, the maximum population once it becomes unsustainable will be significantly reduced by the changes humanity is inflicting on the environment.

The outcome of the pincer movement of increased population numbers on the one hand and the inability to sustain environmental resources on the other will inevitably result in the extinction of significant numbers of the mass population. This is a sad thought, but given the current social trends is one that is both unavoidable and must be faced if some representation of the human race is to have even the smallest chance of survival.

There are currently insufficient numbers of the human race that are capable of seeing the 'big picture' to be found in room four, through a Gaian perspective, or who choose not to see it. In order to make progress in this area the numbers of individuals who are able to appreciate Gaian imperatives and are able to enter higher levels of consciousness to see the reality that exists beyond the ability of our natural senses must significantly increase, by whatever means are available to humanity.

8.09. The Mystical Act of Becoming and the *Mundus Imaginalis*

It should not have passed unnoticed that the entry into altered states of consciousness, to experience non-ordinary reality and to inhabit the fourth room, owes much to the nature of mysticism.

This is not by chance or coincidence.

The true worth and value of the spiritually mystical element of human nature and the reason why we, as a race, cannot do without it has been demonstrated throughout our racial history and forms part of a fundamental need within the human race. At a time before science and technology had gained any significant momentum, it was those who 'dreamt' of solutions, who were able to envisage something that did not yet exist, who provided the driving force for development of any sort. It may even be that, without the mystical element of our humanity, the race might not have survived or would have developed in a radically different way, to the extent that we would now possess significantly different attributes of character.

It is a reasonable conjecture that it is the mystical element of human nature which has enabled us to survive and flourish thus far, and will continue to do so in the future. We believe that the human race without its mystical characteristics does not appear to be a viable possibility.

It is notable that the majority of the world population professes to a belief in some form of religious faith; that is to say, in a belief in something that cannot be proven. It is clear that there is a need embedded deeply within us that manifests in a drive to seek some understanding of the unexplainable. Setting aside any religious dogma and doctrine, which serve only to confuse the issues, we should regard this as a significant factor in our survival and well-being as a race, both historically and for the future.

The value of being able to envision that which does not yet exist, or which lies beyond that which we can sense; the experience of revelation that may be found at higher levels of consciousness; the clarity of understanding that can result; the vast increase in the breadth and depth of the conscious horizon, coupled to the almost instantaneous speed of acquisition of that understanding – these are all mystical aspects of humanity. They generate a feeling of ecstasy, which does not rely on religion or science as its starting point, but are significant in that each is indicative of the adept becoming 'at one' with the mega-gestalt that derives from The One Source and the Gaian nature of the Cosmos.

The fundamental nature of mysticism is demonstrated in these experiences; and whilst they can originate from a religious context, they need not necessarily do so. The key to unlock mystical knowledge of the Cosmos does not lie in piety, or religious dogma and doctrine, or in any field of science or technology, or politics, philosophy or economics. Rather it resides in what we described, in Chapter Seven, as the spiritual nature of humanity, expressed in the extent and depth of belief and in the level or degree of consciousness we can bring to bear, within the immaterial form of the human soul complex, in full symbiosis with the mundus imaginalis.

Mysticism and the mundus imaginalis form elements of the gestalt that is the soul complex, which are inseparable, yet discrete and independent of each other. Mysticism houses the belief in the unexplainable and is the means whereby a unity of existence between our consciousness and the Cosmos is recognised and becomes a reality. The mundus imaginalis is the form that uses mysticism as a tool for understanding such a belief and in establishing it as a reality.

If humanity is to survive and flourish, mysticism and the mundus imaginalis will need to become an acknowledged reality so far as they are cognitive, functioning characteristics of human ability. The recognition of the power of mundus imaginalis to guide the soul complex in its interaction with the subtle realm will need to be re-established from its ancient roots, following the relegation of mysticism by science and technology as a negative aspect of its purview; one that does not recognise any value to human ability, one that has no credible importance.

The ability to build bridges and to function in both the subtle and the material realms; to bond mystical belief with the strength of free will; to open the doors into higher levels of consciousness, make the mundus imaginalis an essential characteristic of our soul complex.

Mysticism and the mundus imaginalis proceed, as human characteristics, in a symbiotic relationship that has to date enabled the development of human endeavour, and will continue to enable alternative approaches to reason and logic to prevail. They are the glue that binds the soul complex to the human form, and will continue to form the conduit between the subtle and material realms and to channel the belief in the meta-sensate aspect of the Cosmos.

If humanity is to survive, let alone flourish, the act of becoming, seen in the mystical/mundus imaginalis element of the gestaltic soul complex will need to be recognised as of greater significance to the evolutionary process, and accepted as being more important, to humanity, by the order of several magnitudes.

8.10. The Act of Becoming More Thoughtful

If all of thought is retained within a Noosphere it is inevitably a part of Gaia and is subject to the same self-regulating system that affects everything else in existence. How such self-regulation of thought is able to occur, from an external, non-thinking source, is not known, but the effects that such self-regulation has is apparent. This appears as the revealing of knowledge, of relevant thought, at a time when such revelation is most germane to consciousness and thus to the development of the human race.

If the Noosphere exists as the depository of all thought then it is also the repository that holds the potential for revelation, and the subsequent production of the conditions that will sustain the survival of the human race.

There is no doubt that the level of consciousness which we experience has an effect on the nature and quality of the thoughts that we produce or encounter. Enhanced levels of consciousness are capable of receiving and developing thoughts in a manner that is more complete, with greater clarification, than is the norm.

Once again the need to raise the numbers of individuals capable of experiencing inhabitation of the fourth room, in order to engage in thought with greater clarity of understanding, by whatever means which are at our disposal, is a factor of great importance to the survival of the human race.

8.11. The Act of Becoming a New Reality

We have proposed that reality is not a secure, fixed condition. It depends upon the interpretation of external stimuli; on the condition of the natural senses; on the state of their efficiency; on the degree and capacity of neuronal pattern activity; and not least, on the level of consciousness that we are able to bring to bear upon it.

That being the case we should cease to think of reality as a fixed condition that we somehow inhabit.

If it becomes possible for us to achieve this aim, then a whole new world opens up before our awareness. Restrictions and limitations to the nature of our existence disappear, to be replaced by the freedom to think and be anything that we choose to be; to be able to contemplate alternative conditions of reason, in order to experience the world beyond our natural senses. If sufficient numbers of the population undertake such a journey as this, then a serious change in the reality that we face, as a race, can be accomplished.

But what change would suit a majority of the world population?

This is difficult if not impossible to answer from within the present rigid perception of reality that we have established as 'normal'. This is so because interracial differences, inter-religious competition, intellectual disagreements etc. all combine to deflect the human race from its journey towards a destiny of perfection. The current reality that is perceived and enacted is one that may eventually lead to the extinction of the human race, but not of the planet Earth.

For us to inhabit a new reality, we need firstly to create the reality of our desire and, thereafter, become that reality. Such an achievement needs a complete rethink of the mode of transport by which we undertake our journey of progress towards an uncertain future. Whilst we continue to regard our mode of transport as being 'normal' and by continuing to reject that which we label as 'abnormal', we are impeded in making any significant progress towards a new reality.

Until we learn to accept our differences and rejoice in their being; until we recognise and abolish the futility of war; unless we come to accept change as the saving grace of our evolutionary development; until we recognise death as an enabling factor of life; until we learn to incorporate altruistic desires through the law of attraction into our daily existence – we will summarily fail to find a unity of purpose that is capable of becoming our mode of transport to a more certain future reality.

Principles of unity, the acceptance of every reality experienced by any or all of us, coupled with respect for and an understanding of the value of a system of enlightened self-interest, and its implementation, all underpinned by increased inhabitation of de Ropp's fourth room of consciousness, will grant to us at least the chance of survival and well-being.

8.12. Becoming

Now we arrive at a point where we may contemplate a conclusion to our considerations.

We have seen how the nature and the structure of the Cosmos have been established, through the auspices of the archaeus particle and the formatrix energy field that sets the Cosmos into a state of motion and continuation. Life, in many or any forms, then takes advantage of the environment that subsequently develops. Consciousness, present in all matter, reaches advanced layers and levels as lifeforms become more complex, and reach a point where awareness of self comes to discriminate in favour of the most advanced, complex lifeform, which may then choose to develop towards a state of perfection.

In this chapter we have set out some of the parameters that the human race is capable of developing, or may need to develop, to enable it not merely to survive, but also to flourish. After all, life that does not flourish becomes sterile and stagnant.

To sum up this work in progress:

As the evolutionary process proceeds, the increasing complexity of the human being means that the extent of consciousness available to it is also increasing. The future depends upon enough people recognising this growth, and whether or not a majority choose to use the available, additional capacity to enter into altered, higher states of consciousness, and whether or not the positive free will necessary to implement the choices is brought to bear.

In this respect the interaction between the subtle and material realms of reality is of increasing importance to our well-being and ability to develop and change.

The increased capacity of consciousness should enable more and more members of humanity to recognise the entirety of our reality, to see it as being capable of encompassing all aspects of experience and desire. The tools to achieve the opening up of the mind to all possibilities and eventualities, including the existence of something beyond the capacity of our natural senses to encounter, already exist in some human beings.

Here the ability to develop alternative approaches to reason may be seen as being of prime importance. Reason and logic, as we recognise them in today's normal reality, are indispensable as the tools for interpreting all that impacts on our consciousness;

and they will remain essential aspects of our consciousness which enable our understanding of any discovery that arises from any facet of future endeavour.

But our continuing survival and well-being require more of our consciousness than that!

It is necessary to develop the means whereby reason and logic may be approached from a different direction, to allow hitherto apparently illogical aspects of our reality to be accommodated within our model of the Cosmos.

In particular, an understanding of the nature of the archaeus particle and formatrix energy, their purpose within the grand scheme of things, will lead us to a true understanding that each particle which exists in the material realm, by emanating through the subtle realm of Ideas that pervade the entire Universe, might justifiably be said to occupy every location where the Universe could exist. We might then say that all spaces exist at the centre of the Universe whilst enclosing all other spaces within it.

This mystical approach to reason is one which forms the basis for an understanding that the Cosmos, including our Universe, and consequently our consciousness, may be said to have no boundaries or edge to it or within it. Time may also be said to exist as an all-inclusive singular element of the Cosmos where, in the material realm, it is experienced at trillions upon trillions of points of consciousness that are each its own centre. Time thus functions to enclose all points of its flow or passage within its singularity, whilst at the same time also functions to allow each point of its flow or passage, wherever it happens to be located within the Universe, to be the centre of its presence there.

The focus on freethinking, of setting the mind free of the conditioning restraints of religious dogma and doctrine, free of blinkered aspects of specialisation, and of an intolerant, self-interested worldview, is the area of thought that is most likely to result in an understanding and acceptance of these difficult principles. We may confidently say that a freethinking approach similar to the manner described in this book is becoming increasingly important, if not crucial, to the survival of us all.

The inclusion of every aspect of every reality of every individual and every society, including that of repositioning reason to be able to 'see' beyond the remit that our natural senses can accommodate, must freely become the target of assimilation into a more advanced, holistic perception of reality. The enabling of such a reality as this must become the focus for a new field of study.

It is clear that any one aspect of reality, as we currently experience it, is not capable, in isolation, of solving the problems that the world faces. In the long term science alone cannot solve the problems, neither can technology, religion, mysticism, philosophy, politics, or any other branch of reality. Indeed, whenever we seek to exclude any aspect of reality that does not suit our particular purview, then we diminish not only our own consciousness and ourselves, by imposing boundaries to its development, but we also harm human development in such a way that false limitations are set up.

Areas of dispute and enmity are then allowed to arise and fester which are harmful to our overall growth and progress as a race. Every aspect of reality must be prepared to give true, genuine credence and respect to any other aspect if we are to continue to survive and flourish.

Every one of us must freely come to his or her own view on any aspect of reality, without denying anyone else the right to their own view and to respect and even embrace the outcome, whatever that happens to be. We must each learn to welcome and value the beliefs and views of others as being as valuable as our own.

This is freethinking in action.

To understand how or what others may think, without taking exception to the results of their thought or opinion, is crucial. It is also a fundamental tenet of enlightened self-interest, which is the only socio-political, economic system that has any chance of unifying our differences worldwide.

We should understand that we are not talking here of the creation or introduction of a 'super race' of human beings with new 'super powers' as expressed in the currently popular idiom of today's media-based culture. Rather we are talking of recognising the development of the natural characteristics of humanity, of contemplating and enhancing the art of the possible in order to augment and use already present traits, so that they become more beneficial, more efficient, more advanced, whole and far reaching.

A natural consequence that will arise from such a process will be the concentration of goodness at the expense of evil. The futility of self-gratification which often culminates in war and the enmity that results from the elevation of personal differences will be diminished eventually to the point of extinction. An awareness of the importance of a unified planetary environment involving and built around Gaian principles will rise to the forefront of our consciousness.

Those who attain a freethinking status will willingly, perhaps even automatically, contemplate the means of entry into higher levels of consciousness; and it is in this condition of heightened sensory and meta-sensory perception that thoughts and entire concepts that have hitherto been unavailable to the adept will be encountered, and a perception of a wider, clearer more fulfilled reality will be the natural outcome.

It is then that such elements of reality as the control of the rate of the passage of time, generated through increased and more deliberate interaction with the constituency of the subtle realm, will become a natural condition of our reality. The entire constituency of the subtle realm will become fully integrated and illuminated within the awareness of those freethinking individuals who attain and maintain the ability for fourth level consciousness. Every aspect of every constituent of the subtle realm, including the acceptance and assimilation of the Gaian principles of sustainability, will become the focus for the strategy of survival of the human race.

The concentration of the acceleration of the hybridisation of the human race to improve the numbers and the range of freethinking individuals must become a distinct possibility, if not a necessity, but must be one where all of the pitfalls and realisations, all of the safeguards required in so doing also become fully available to our consciousness. One of the hitherto areas of taboo, that of genetic modification, will become the subject of an accepted, safeguarded area of development.

The diverging nature of the evolutionary branching of the human race will become more apparent as it becomes increasingly controlled and directed from within the human organism, ostensibly for the benefit of the entire human race, as a possible survival strategy develops. This is a process that is already underway, even though it might be said to be only in its very early stages.

For many of the current population on Earth, this may represent a somewhat bleak outlook as there is the distinct possibility that a large number of the individuals which are born to succeeding generations will be unable to recognise the need to make the journey into a more secure future for the race of mankind; or worse, may be apathetic or unwilling to embark upon such a journey. The coordinated effort may be too much for many to encompass as an urgent need for racial survival.

However, because the lines of divergence that are coming to demarcate the branches of evolution are themselves becoming increasingly defined, the separation of the human race into dividing characteristics will gain pace and the beginning of an enhanced evolutionary species development will become apparent.

Those adepts who are able to enter non-ordinary reality, who are able to experience higher level consciousness and all that it signifies, will naturally recognise the consequences, to humanity, of rapacious, unrestrained environmental degradation of resources; of the futility of violence and war; of the benefits that freely undertaken population control can achieve. The currently ignored factor of the explosion in population growth is the most urgent aspect of a survival strategy that needs to be addressed. It may already be too late to successfully address this issue, but if we, as a race, are to stand any chance of survival at all then those currently with the power must remove their heads from the sand and focus on this aspect of survival. The use of a freethinking approach is needed as this will provide a natural pathway towards this objective.

Yet there is a great deal for humanity to be optimistic about concerning the future of the race on Earth because our future relies on the altruistic development of science and technology lead by, and underpinned by, those mystical elements of the human character, in symbiosis with the mundus imaginalis, operating as an essential agent for evolutionary, developmental change.

The recognition of the gestalt that is the soul complex, in its enhanced state within the higher level consciousness found in de Ropp's room four, will become the driving force for progress, utilising formatrix energy levels and the nature of the archaeus particle, to participate in developing a cosmic strategy for survival and flourishment.

These are all characteristics that need to become a natural part of our reality, to be raised in our awareness to become of great consequence. Encouragement and training in the application of the mundus imaginalis of the recognition of the soul complex and, most importantly, the need to attain higher, fourth level consciousness for many more individuals is essential. The melding together of these elements of human nature with the best that science, technology, religion, politics and philosophy can offer, all combining under the umbrella of a freethinking holistic approach to survival, needs to become the priority focus for the continuation of human life on Earth, through a new field of study.

Consciousness is the key to everything – the survival of life on Earth, or its extinction.

It is where the answer to the question: *Why is there something, rather than nothing?* already lies, waiting to be discovered, within the consciousness of each one of us.

The choice is in our own hands, if we are prepared to make the choice and to adopt the positive aspect of free will and undertake the journey to a new Cosmic reality.

In essence, to achieve such a destiny all we need to do, as a race, is to strive to see that which is currently there, but which we cannot see, and, in so doing:

BECOME AWAKE.

The Narrative

Alone!

Suddenly conscious,
but from whence or where?
For whence and where had no existence
in the un-located, emptiness that was also of my essence,
and of my consciousness.

Alone!

Suddenly aware,
in the empty, spaceless, formless, timeless zone
into which I came.

I was the totality of all that existed,
there was nothing else but me.

I was in everything,
and everything was in me.

I enclosed everything,
and everything in me was at my centre.

I was Full of Ideas,
I was bursting with energy.

But had no 'where' to go,
no 'space' to fill,
no 'time' for change.

I was One.

I was Alone!

I was alone!

No form of my own,
no way to express anything,
no means to know myself.

Nothing mattered.

But then:

Bang!

Suddenly it did!

Consciousness mattered.

In a singular burst of energy,
'Space' came to exist,
the 'Where' was located,
One at a 'Time'.

The Cosmos inflated.

My consciousness had caused it to be,
had freely willed it to be so,
had cast the seed of myself into the motion of growth,
in the place I had formed.

I had made all of my Ideas and my energy available
in the seed of myself.

I had set the pattern of existence,
into form and being.

I had become The One Source of All Things!

Now I would be able to see,
to hear, to smell, to feel and to touch
all of it.

And so much more,

as the expression goes.

I gave my consciousness to everything
in order to gain the experience of everything,
everything that was to become.

Make of consciousness what they could, or would,
they are absolutely free to do so.

Take it to where my Ideas lie waiting,
for expression.

Just as it was for me, before there was the Space for Time to pass.

Come to think of it
the thoughts of those that come before them,
give them something of it all,
if they can only develop their senses
to 'see' so much more,
beyond that which they can see.

For where are their brothers and sisters now?
Ordovicia and Devonia,
Permian, dying large for Triacea,
for Cretacea and Kaytee.

Oh Evolution, I formed thee as a paradox,
Relentless! Redoubtable! Immutable!
Yet ever changing?

So that everything becomes possible.

And my consciousness ascends.

From evolution they were able to become,
as part of my pattern of ascending consciousness.

Always in acts of co-creation.

Because the choice must be theirs.
Along with the Free Will to change,
so that their destiny and their fate,
arise from their consciousness.

Not only did I give them the gift of life,
but also the gift of death,
so that the lives of others may follow,
so that all things may change.

Yet I could not be so cruel
so as to make death the end of their journey.

Thus their soul!

The Narrative

That can go on and on,
always transforming,
always co-creating,
as they strive to 'see' all of it,
and yearn to be a part of it all.

My pattern continues to be uncovered,
questions arise about all of it,
demanding answers to the meaning of it all.

But,
Are they ready to discover the truths?
have they maturity enough to understand the 'why'?
can they begin to appreciate the scope of my Cosmos?

Is their consciousness able to respond?
to interact with the echo of my Free Will?

Do they 'see' what they are doing?
is their consciousness capable of further ascent?
can it be sustained at the level of 'knowing'?

Are they in control of their own future?
within my pattern of existence?
within the care-full balance of it all?
within the perfect symmetry of the whole?

Can their yearning reach fulfilment?

Questions, questions, questions?

All of the questions are there.

But,
they see only half of the answers,
those that lie within their material existence,
for although they think they work truly and with great industry
they uncover only half of my truth.

I sometimes think that they do not even recognise
that the truth they uncover is not the all of it,
that it is incomplete and inadequate
to sustain an ascendant consciousness,
whether it be theirs,
or mine.

For when they uncover their part of the truth,
they seem not to know how it fits into the whole,
to know what to do with it,
other than to use it to suit their own close horizon,
the inward facing of their souls.

They seem to have forgotten the history of their journey,
that was nurtured by the nature of everything,
they seem to be unable to 'see',
what their ancestors 'saw'.

Their answer has been an attempt to recognise me in various forms,
whereby to establish some of the principles by which they may
flourish.

If they would only stay true to my universal justice and the virtues,
and of course, to themselves.

But they do not!

They promptly forget those principles,
that cease to suit their own purpose.

They destroy the integrity of their own faith,
they betray the principles of their own belief,
by fighting and warring amongst themselves.

They convert their faith and their belief
into states of violence,
into states of non-belief.

All of which has little to do with me,
has no regard for nature and natural process.
And the beauty of all I have given.

Why do they harness the perfect truth found in my pattern of
existence,
to suit their own desire for wealth, power and dominance.
When I have given dominion to them,
as the natural outcome of their evolution.

From a distance, they all appear to be the same, to me.
I cannot comprehend why they seek to hurt and destroy each other,
to fight wars in my name,

for by my edict there can be no war that is just or holy.

Why do they not seek to resolve their differences?
to revere and nurture their home,
to recognise that the evil of violence is abhorrent,
to realise that their differences are insignificant,
in my pattern of true reality.

Do they not see that they all will cease to survive and to flourish,
if they follow this pathway?

And yet

All is not lost!

For some, the glimmer of an ascendant consciousness,
appears on the far horizon,
to enable those that are able to see through their reason and logic,
into an enhanced reality that could become theirs.

To reassert the development of their soul,
as the means by which they may co-create their future,
using the subtle means that I have placed at their disposal,
and their mysticism that some seek to deny.

There is still Time!
But not as they know it.

My pattern of nature and evolution is co-operative,
if they are able to respond and to work with it,
to repair the difficulties they have co-created and which have come into
being.

This will be hard to do,
but I have faith in their ability to accomplish the task in hand.

To bind their ascendant consciousness
to nature and of all things in the cosmos.

To raise their level of consciousness,

to one where they
become awake,
and are able to seek out the answer their own question,

Why is there is something rather than nothing?

References, Sources and Further Reading

1. BJ Dobbs. 'Newton's Commentary on the Emerald Tablet of Hermes Trismegistus' in Merkel, I. and Debus, AG, *Hermeticism and the Renaissance*. Folger: Washington, 1988
2. Sir Anthony Kenny. *A New History of Western Philosophy, Vol 1: Ancient Philosophy*. Oxford University Press: Oxford, 2004
3. *The Enneads of Plotinus* as recorded by Porphyry
4. James Lovelock. *The Ages of Gaia: A Biography of Our Living Earth*, Second Edition. Oxford University Press: Oxford, 2000
5. *The Enneads of Plotinus* as recorded by Porphyry
6. WH Vanstone. *Love's Endeavour, Love's Expense*. Darton, Longman & Todd: London, 1977, pp 42–54
7. James Lovelock. *The Ages of Gaia: A Biography of Our Living Earth*, Second Edition. Oxford University Press: Oxford, 2000
8. Robert S. de Ropp. *The Master Game*. Gateways Consciousness Classics: Nevada City, CA, USA, 2002
9. AH Maslow. *Toward a Psychology of Being*. Van Nostrand: New York, 1962
10. Richard Maurice Bucke. *Cosmic Consciousness*. Penguin Books Ltd: Harmondsworth, 1901
11. Miranda and Stephen Aldhouse-Green. *The Quest for the Shaman*. Thames and Hudson: London, 2005
12. Michael Harner. *The Way of the Shaman*, Tenth Anniversary Edition. HarperCollins Publishers: New York, 1990, pp 51–52
13. Mircea Eliade. *Shamanism*. Princeton University Press: New Jersey, 2004
14. Julian Jaynes. *The Origins of Consciousness in the Breakdown of the Bicameral Mind*. Princeton University/Houghton and Mifflin. New edition, 1982. Original publication, 1976 (out of print)
15. Nick Lane. *Life Ascending: The Ten Great Inventions of Evolution*. Profile Books Ltd: London, 2000

16. Richard Dawkins. *The Selfish Gene.* Oxford Paperbacks: Oxford, 1989

17. Sandra Ingerman. *Soul Retrieval: Mending the Fragmented Self.* HarperSanFrancisco, 1991

18. Wing-Tsit Chan. *A Source Book in Chinese Philosophy*

BOOKS

O is a symbol of the world, of oneness and unity; this eye represents knowledge and insight. We publish titles on general spirituality and living a spiritual life. We aim to inform and help you on your own journey in this life.

Visit our website: http://www.o-books.com

Find us on Facebook:
https://www.facebook.com/OBooks

Follow us on Twitter: @obooks